THE PALM AT THE END OF THE MIND

THE PALM AT THE END OF THE MIND

Relatedness, Religiosity, and the Real

MICHAEL JACKSON

Duke University Press

Durham and London   2009

All rights reserved
Printed in the United States of America
on acid-free paper ♾
Designed by C. H. Westmoreland
Typeset in Monotype Bembo
by Tseng Information Systems, Inc.
Library of Congress Cataloging-in-Publication data
appear on the last printed page of this book.

CONTENTS

PREFACE

In the early 1980s, a religion reporter for the *New York Times* took a year's leave from journalism and enrolled in several courses at the Harvard Divinity School. What began as an academic interest in comparative religion became a spiritual journey in the course of which Ari Goldman reappraised his faith as an Orthodox Jew and explored the meaning of religion in radically different traditions and communities throughout the world. Twenty years on, Goldman's account of his sabbatical year, *The Search for God at Harvard*, is still selling well, at least in Cambridge, Massachusetts, and when I read this book in the summer of 2005, not long after taking up a teaching appointment at the Harvard Divinity School, I toyed with the possibility of writing something along the same lines. As an anthropologist, I was intrigued by whether something one might call "religious experience" could be identified in all cultures and all people (including skeptics like myself), and what meaning could be ascribed the term "religion" when the people with whom I had sojourned as an ethnographer in West Africa and Aboriginal Australia had no equivalent concept in their languages. Mindful of Talal Asad's argument that Euro-American notions of religion tend to be uncritically grounded in post–Enlightenment, Judeo-Christian thought, and that "religious experience" can never be reduced to institutionalized "religious belief,"[1] I decided to turn my attention to those critical situations

---

1. Talal Asad, *Genealogies of Religion: Discipline and Reasons of Power in Christianity and Islam* (Baltimore: Johns Hopkins University Press, 1993), chap. 1. Jacques Derrida also cautions against a "globalatinized," Greco-Roman bias in our thinking about religion. Jacques Derrida, "Faith and Knowledge: The Two Sources of 'Religion' at the Limits of Reason Alone," in *Religion*, ed. Jacques Derrida and Gianni Vattimo (Stanford, Calif.: Stanford University Press, 1998), 4, 30. It should also be noted that current notions of religion and of religions as do-

in life where we come up against the limits of language, the limits of our strength, the limits of our knowledge, yet are sometimes thrown open to new ways of understanding our being-in-the-world, new ways of connecting with others. Whether such border situations are quintessentially "religious," "spiritual," "historical," "social," or "biographical" may be beside the point,[2] for though such terms help us describe the conditions of the possibility of our experience or help us retrospectively explain our experience to ourselves and to others, the meaning of all human experience remains ambiguous, containing within it both the seeds of its own comprehensibility *and* nuances and shadings that go beyond what can be comprehensively thought or said. To capture this sense of experience as occurring on the threshold between what can and cannot be entirely grasped—intellectually, linguistically, or practically—I use the image of the penumbral (from the Latin *paene*, almost + *umbra*, shadow) with its connotations of a phenomenologically indeterminate zone "between regions of complete shadow and complete illumination," "an area in which something exists to a lesser or uncertain degree," and "an outlying or peripheral region."[3] I also take

---

mains of intelligible truth(s), rather than faith and passion, are largely products of eighteenth-century Enlightenment rationality. Wilfred Cantwell Smith, *The Meaning and End of Religion* (New York: Harper and Row, 1978), 37–50.

2. Jaspers contrasts *Grenzsituationen* with *Altagssituationen* (everyday situations). While we are able to "gain an overview" of our everyday situations and get beyond them, limit situations "possess finality"; "they are like a wall against which we butt, against which we founder." Karl Jaspers, *Philosophie*, vol. 2: *Existenzerhellung* (Berlin: Springer Verlag, 1932), 178–79. For an account of *Grenzsituationen* in English, see *Karl Jaspers: Basic Philosophical Writings*, ed. and trans. Edith Ehrlich, Leonard H. Ehrlich, and George B. Pepper (New York: Humanity Books, 2000), 97. Though Adorno treats the term "frontier-situations" as part of a jargon of authenticity—on a par with "being-in-the-world," "individual existence," and "heroic endurance"—a way of "usurping religious-authoritarian pathos without the least religious content," I see it as a way of escaping from the two dominant discourses of our time, the first that reduces all meaning to political economy, the second to religious belief or doctrine. In my view, it is precisely this tendency to politicize or intellectualize religious experience that the existential concept of *situation* helps us to overcome. Theodor Adorno, *Minima Moralia: Reflections from Damaged Life*, trans. E. F. N. Jephcott (London: Verso, 1978), 152.

3. From the "penumbra" entry in *The American Heritage Dictionary of the English Language*, 4th ed. (Boston: Houghton Mifflin, 2000).

my cues from Wallace Stevens's late poem "Of Mere Being," where "the palm at the end of the mind" stands "beyond thought," on "the edge of space," while a gold-feathered bird sings in the palm, "without human meaning, without human feeling, a foreign song."

Border situations not only imply a radical break from the known; they presage new possibilities of relatedness that often transcend specifically interpersonal ties. Lost souls variously hit the bottle, do drugs, distract themselves in work, appeal to God, or seek out some wilderness, real or symbolic, where they may take refuge and regroup. I refuse to pathologize any of these transmutations, or interpret connectedness with nature, the cosmos, the divine, or an imagined community as escapes from social reality, mere opiates, illusions, or defenses. That people throughout the world speak of abstract and far-reaching relationships in terms of kinship—using the terms "brother" and "sister," "father" and "mother" to connote ethnic and religious identifications, or imagining political leaders, ancestors, and Gods as parental imagoes—does not mean that kinship is the sole source of our experiences of kindness. And the human capacity for forming bonds knows no bounds, encompassing other persons, objects, animals, abstract ideas, ideologies, possessions, and even the earth or cosmos.[4]

This broad field of connectedness is my point of departure for exploring fields of experience that overflow and confound the words with which we conventionally describe the world, and for describing the subtle ways in which one human life shades into another, and the shallows of the familiar shelve into unfathomable depths. But in moving from a consideration of the way fate unfolds through genealogical time, to the mystery of elective affinities, and to the interplay of opposing notions of value, I waive the conventions of lineal argument and

---

4. One sees this vividly in initiation ritual, where neophytes die to their childhoods and are reborn as members of a moral community with allegiances to ancestral values. The classical Hindu "stages of life" from student, householder, hermit to world renouncer succinctly summarize this movement from personal to transpersonal connectedness, with the *sannyasi* (renunciant) sloughing off earthly attachments in order to achieve union (*yoga*) of self (*atman*) and cosmos (*Brahman*). And the same dialectic, in which relative attachments are eclipsed by absolute bonds, is spelled out in Luke 14:26 where Jesus says, "If any man comes to me, and hate not his father, and mother, and wife, and children, and brethren, and sisters, yea, and his own life also, he cannot be my disciple."

the search for firm or final conclusions, embracing Wittgenstein's view that to say something is often less interesting than to disclose connections,[5] not only because statements can never convey everything that is existentially and most immediately the case but because our most illuminating glimpses into the nature of things emerge in the shifting spaces *between* statements, descriptions, and persons, and in the course of events. Hence perspicacious presentations, juxtapositions, analogies, poetic images, epiphanies, and anecdotes may best do justice to the ephemeral and transitive character of experience and carry us into those penumbral regions where the unnamable begins or, as Wallace Stevens puts it, "The search for reality is as momentous as the search for God."[6]

5. See Ray Monk, *Ludwig Wittgenstein: The Duty of Genius* (New York: Free Press, 1990), 302–3.

6. "An Ordinary Evening in New Haven," in *Collected Poems* (London: Faber and Faber, 1955), 481.

1. ANCESTRAL ROOTS

The Real

I am listening to Osvaldo Golijov's *Ayre* on my car stereo. Along Concord Avenue, the rising sun is like a gobbet of molten glass burning through the wintering trees. As I park my car in Cambridge, Sephardic street cries and a poem in Arabic are still echoing in my head. It is only a short walk from the parking garage to my office at the Center for the Study of World Religions. Before settling to work, I gaze at the reproduction of one of Paul Cézanne's paintings of Montagne Sainte-Victoire that I have pinned to my wall. I can hear the wind soughing in the pines and smell sage and thyme. I check my e-mails. My daughter Heidi has sent me a sonogram of her baby at thirteen weeks. She also tells me about an Aboriginal painter whose works I should see. On Google I track down images of Paddy Kuwumji Jawaiyi's emu dreamings from the East Kimberleys. I am moved by something I cannot name. What do these things have in common? This strange musical work by a Jewish composer, born in Argentina but now living in the United States. This French painter who returned time and time again to the landscapes of his natal Provence. This fetal image of my first grandchild. This Aboriginal painter whose elemental canvases take my breath away. What moves me to think that these are all of a piece? Is it that they carry me to somewhere I have never been before, or somewhere I once knew and have forgotten? Harbingers of the new, they are nonetheless reminders of something very old. I have a sense of being grounded in something I can only call "the real" that connects my life to the life of the earth itself, its generations succeeding one another over time, its multiple geographies and cultures. Is this what the Greeks called *apo-kalypto*, the sudden disclosure of the ordinarily hidden relationship between ourselves and that which came before us, that will follow us, and that lies beyond our ken?

Only Connect

That I have become so preoccupied by connectedness and transmigration may have something to do with the vicissitudes of leaving Europe and resettling in the United States as a "resident alien." Perhaps it is because I have uprooted myself so many times in the course of my life that I am skeptical about identity and definition, preferring to explore transitive or transitory phenomena, including the fields of relationship within which our sense of self emerges and is transfigured — fields that extend far further in time and space than many of us are prepared to acknowledge. If I repudiate a priori distinctions between *types* of connectedness — familial, affinal, economic, religious, political, etc. — it is because, for me, the most intriguing thing about human relationships is that they include relations not only with other persons but with abstract ideas, imaginary beings, and inert objects. Moreover, they are in constant flux. Much as we try to name, contain, and control our interactions with the world around us, the interplay between self and other has a life of its own. It is this intersubjective life, rather than any one life, that I feel compelled to explore.

Nowadays, the word "connection" is practically synonymous with networking, and we often think of sociality in corporate or technological terms. But there are limits to what we can accomplish with the digital gadgetry with which we currently chat, communicate, and go about our business. In London, my friend Sewa Koroma struggles to resolve a political crisis in his natal chiefdom in Sierra Leone, making calls on his cell phone, urging friends and kinsmen to do his bidding, but exasperated that he must live in England to earn money when he is needed back home. On the T from Boston to Harvard Square I read a Corporate Networking Collaborative advertisement: "We help you make those right connections by pointing you to the right event. Networking is about building connections, and the best ones are made in person." The ad reminded me of Sewa's dilemma and sharpened my sense of the difficulty we have in reconciling the familiar, face-to-face worlds of which we have direct experience with the far-reaching and remote worlds that also determine our fate. There was another advertisement on the T that also caught my eye—a dating service, promising romantic connections. That dating agencies have failed to come up with any scientific system for matchmaking also brought home to me the gap between what can and cannot be achieved by reason or will. Was I old-fashioned in thinking that we set too much store by the idea that our lives can be consciously pro-grammed, that we are losing the knack of letting go, allowing nature to take its course, accepting that connections are often made, insights given, and life most fully realized when we open ourselves up to that which lies beyond our knowledge and control? In his ethnographic study of networking in contemporary Japan, Brian Moeran notes that people are "always looking for suitable excuses or justifications for being together." Although age, place of origin, kinship, and education are, as elsewhere in the world, the usual ways of establishing common ground, people occasionally come up against limits, and it is here that mystery begins.

When all else fails, there is always the fallback position of "fate" (*go-en*). A man may pore over a visitor's name card, examining the fine print, asking questions about the other's past and present life, searching for a connection. How long has he been in his company? So he must have graduated from university in such-and-such a year (indicating a possible age connection)? And where did he go to university? Does that mean he is from such-and-such region of Japan? Perhaps he knows so-and-so in such-and-such a company who also went to the same university and is from that part of the country? And so on, and so forth.

This kind of inquiry borders on the hopeless when conducted of a for-eigner in Japan. Once age has been found wanting as a method of bond-ing, there is little likelihood of the foreigner being able to satisfy other criteria like kinship, geographical origin, or university. A potential line of help exists if the foreigner is married to a Japanese, because questions can then circle around the spouse. But generally the only way in which the informal relationship can be formally sanctioned is when, having socialized with the foreigner sufficiently to be able to judge whether he or she wishes to continue the connection or not, the Japanese can exclaim with unconcealed pleasure, "It's fate that's brought us together, isn't it?"

The Japanese word for fate (*en*), a little like the Greek *moira* (thread), literally means "connection."[1]

In these fragmentary and inconclusive sallies, I suppose I was trying to fathom the kinds of connections, so crucial to our well-being, that refuse cognitive closure or codification—the bonds of close friendship, for instance, of parenthood, of elective affinity, and of love. The sense of inevitability and fate that the Greeks captured in the image of a thread spun at a person's birth, binding him or her forever, or that Norse and Anglo-Saxon traditions depicted as a web or weave, hanging over every man, whether on the battlefield or in the "fetters" and "bonds" of pain, love, and death. And then there was the question that crops up in both Norse and Vedic texts, as to what powers, human or divine, can loosen the knots that hold us or magically tie up the forces that constrict our freedom.

95 Irving Street

Whenever I feel the need to stretch my legs and clear my head, I go for a walk through the streets behind the Center where I work, often passing 95 Irving Street, where William James lived between 1889 and 1910 and wrote his most enduring work. There is a commemorative plaque on the stone-gray picket fence, and the house, still a private home, has been well maintained. Sometimes my passing contact with this house brings to mind a passage in James's writing that resonates with my own work in progress and helps me clarify what I am struggling to say.

One cold March morning, for instance, I was passing the house just as a City of Cambridge Recycling Collection truck was moving laboriously down the street, as if to remind me that I was simply putting back into circulation ideas that James had set down one hundred years ago. "Reality, life, experience, concreteness, immediacy, use what word you will, exceeds our logic, overflows and surrounds it," James declared in a lecture given in Oxford in the spring of 1908, adding that by reality he meant "where things happen."[2]

1. Brian Moeran, *The Business of Ethnography: Strategic Exchanges, People and Organizations* (Oxford: Berg, 2005), 108.
2. William James, *A Pluralistic Universe* (Cambridge, Mass.: Harvard University Press, 1977), 96–97.

One can, I think, readily understand why James's notion of radical empiricism, with its emphasis on relations as well as relata—flights and perchings, rivers and embankments, verbs and substantives, conjunctions and disjunctions—proved so difficult to spell out and so irksome to many of his readers, for who in his right mind would identify reality with things that cannot be readily grasped or systematically named, with phenomena outside the reach of reason? Yet James insisted: "Our fields of experience have no more definite boundaries than have our fields of view. Both are fringed forever by a *more* that continuously develops, and that continuously supercedes them as life proceeds. The relations, generally speaking, are as real here as the terms are."[3] Nor is it the world that lies about us that is refractory to comprehension and control; it is also the world within. "Whatever it may be on the *farther* side, the 'more' with which in religious experience we feel ourselves connected is on the *hither* side the subconscious continuation of our conscious life."[4]

There is probably no human being who has not been intrigued and troubled by the mysterious relationship between his or her own immediate world—a world of direct experience—and all that lies beyond it. It is never simply a matter of acknowledging or naming this extramundane dimension of our existence; it is most vitally a question of our

3. William James, *Essays in Radical Empiricism* (Cambridge, Mass.: Harvard University Press, 1976), 35. I have discussed at length elsewhere the ways in which James's relational view of reality anticipates D. W. Winnicott's work on "transitional phenomena," replacing notions of ontologically discrete domains like self and other, object and subject, inner and outer, with the image of "transitional" or "potential" space as an indeterminate zone where various ways of behaving, thinking, speaking, and feeling are called forth from a common pool, combining and permuting in ever-changing ways, depending on who is interacting and what is at stake. See D. W. Winnicott, *Playing and Reality* (Harmondsworth: Penguin, 1974); Michael Jackson, *Existential Anthropology: Events, Exigencies and Effects* (Oxford: Berghahn, 2005). Also, directly relevant to this theorizing is Hannah Arendt's concept of the "subjective in-between." *The Human Condition* (Chicago: University of Chicago Press, 1958), 182–84.

4. William James, *The Varieties of Religious Experience: A Study in Human Nature* (New York: Signet, 1958), 386. There are, of course, profound similarities between James's notion of "the more" and Jaspers's notion of "the Encompassing" (*das Umgreifende*). Karl Jaspers, *Reason and Existenz*, trans. William Earle (Milwaukee: Marquette University Press, 1997).

relationship with it—how we reckon with it, draw on it, and control it. Of this liminal zone,[5] John Dewey observed:

> The visible is set in the invisible; and in the end what is unseen decides what happens in the seen; the tangible rests precariously upon the untouched and ungrasped. The contrast and the potential maladjustment of the immediate, the conspicuous and focal phase of things, with those indirect and hidden factors which determine the origin and career of what is present, are indestructible features of any and every experience.[6]

Although we often assume that reason enables us to grasp the unseen intellectually, if not actually, Dewey declares that this invocation of scientific rationality is as much a "magical safeguard against the uncertain character of the world" as the so-called mumbo-jumbo and superstition we attribute to premodern peoples.

Dewey's remarks echo certain passages in William James's *The Varieties of Religious Experience* where he too speaks of the ways in which our private and mundane lives are embedded in wider fields of being from

---

5. My project may be seen as a *phenomenology* of what Victor Turner called liminality, for my emphasis is on the various ways in which temporal, spatial, personal, and cultural in-betweenness is *experienced* in human life, both through conventional conceptual or ritual manifestations *and* inchoate, oneiric, poetic, and imaginary expressions. Yet I eschew a phenomenology that defines religion in terms of an allegedly sui generis modality of experience or existence, since what is important, in my view, is the unstable *relationship*—the *écart*, the cusp, the broken middle—*between* our experience of immediate and nonimmediate fields of experience—a mutually constituting and fluid relationship that lacks any essence that can be tagged with one particular label. Hence my dissatisfaction with the psychoanalytic notion that religious experience is grounded in a yearning for the sublime, pre-Oedipal phase of fusion or union with the mother, with Otto's notion of "the wholly other" and "the numinous," with Eliade's notion of an "abyss" that divides "two modalities of experience—sacred and profane," and with Csordas's thesis that religious experience springs from a "primordial sense of 'otherness' or alterity." Rudolph Otto, *The Idea of the Holy: An Inquiry into the Non-Rational Factor in the Idea of the Divine in Its Relation to the Rational*, trans. John W. Harvey (London: Oxford University Press, 1958); Mircea Eliade, *The Sacred and the Profane: The Nature of Religion*, trans. Willard R. Trask (New York: Harper and Row, 1959), 14; Thomas Csordas, "Asymptote of the Ineffable: Embodiment, Alterity, and the Theory of Religion," *Current Anthropology* 45, no. 2 (2004): 164.

6. John Dewey, *Experience and Nature* (New York: Dover, 1958), 43–44.

which we draw inspiration and vitality. Though there are countless ways in which any one of us construes and interacts with this nonimmediate realm, James prefers to speak of it in fairly neutral terms as "a wider self," or "the more," or simply "life" rather than as God. As such, it bears a family resemblance to what Freud called the over-I, Jaspers called the encompassing, and Heidegger called Dasein. As a pragmatist, James is less concerned with whether our language actually captures the essence of the elusive world that lies about us, since what is most crucial are the *entailments* of what we say and do for our own well-being and the well-being of others. "Does God really exist? How does he exist? What is He? are so many irrelevant questions," James writes. "Not God, but life, more life, a larger, richer, more satisfying life is, in the last analysis, the end of religion."[7]

Basic to all these reflections is the view that one's well-being depends on one's relationships or connectedness to an "elsewhere" or "otherness" that lies beyond the horizons of one's own immediate lifeworld. This "other" world is sometimes identified with the dead, and ritual labor enables the living to fuse their being with ancestral being in a life-giving union.[8] Sometimes, as in traditional Christianity, it is a realm of divine power and presence, associated with the empyrean.[9] Sometimes it is identical to the natural environment of forest, bush, and stream.[10]

7. James, *The Varieties of Religious Experience*, 382.

8. Among the Yolngu of northeast Arnhem Land, for example, *maarr* is the invisible and ancestral power "necessary for the health and fertility of the Yolngu world, including the environment in which people live." Through ritual labor, members of Yolngu clans cooperate in drawing this power out from the totemic sites where it resides, so that it "can be spread wide and be beneficial and bring a sense of well-being to all who participate with a good heart." Howard Morphy, *Ancestral Connections: Art and an Aboriginal System of Knowledge* (Chicago: University of Chicago Press, 1991), 103. For the people of the Daly River region of northern Australia, ceremony and *wangga* songs "provide the primary locus of human engagement with the ancestral dead," and this ceremony and song are associated "with liminal states of being—dream states, and the states of being in the twilight zone between life and death, or between childhood and adulthood." Allan Marrett, *Songs, Dreamings, and Ghosts: The Wangga of North Australia* (Middletown, Conn.: Wesleyan University Press, 2005), 3, 5.

9. The Indo-European word for a deity is *deiwos*, from the root *diw/dyu* (the bright sky or daylight) and designating a sky god.

10. In the Upper Amazon, the forest stands in the same relationship to people as the moiety from which they receive wives. While the forest provides food,

Although, as Alfred Schutz observes, most philosophy and religion attempt to reduce the extramundane "to a concept, to make it graspable and accessible to accustomed experience, to tame it,"[11] it remains at the limits of what can be thought or said, encompassing our relationships with ancestors, nature, God, foreigners, and even the unborn.[12] Martin Buber speaks of the religious, not as "something that takes place in man's inner life" but rather "between man and God, that is, *in the reality of their relationship*, the mutual reality of God and man."[13] But we have to go even further in our thinking, acknowledging the limits of laws, the limits to which nature can be controlled: the confusion, turbulence, openness, and instability that compose the "liquid history" of the world[14] — clouds massing and dispersing; a thunderstorm breaking and just as suddenly passing; a stream running muddy then clear; the sea leaving its always different rib patterns on the hard ironsand.

Reconnecting

Thirty-six years have passed since I first did fieldwork in Sierra Leone, but I remember as vividly as if it were yesterday the burnished surface of the porch at Abdul's house in Firawa where I installed myself every morning, dunking dry cabin bread in a mug of instant coffee while, in the mist-swathed village, bleary-eyed men with blankets drawn about

---

allies provide women, which helps explain why the forest is said to smell like women, and entering the forest is compared to sexual intercourse. Rules governing the exploitation of forest resources — game, medicines, fruit, and narcotics — are also analogous to rules governing correct sexual conduct. Gerardo Reichel-Dolmatoff, *The Forest Within: The World-View of the Tukano Amazonian Indians* (Dartington, Devon: Themis Books, 1996), chap. 6.

11. Alfred Schutz and Thomas Luckmann, *The Structures of the Lifeworld*, vol. 2, trans. Richard M. Zaner and David J. Parent (Evanston, Ill.: Northwestern University Press, 1989), 101.

12. Ibid., 194–95.

13. Martin Buber, preface to the 1923 edition of *On Judaism*, ed. Nahum N. Glatzer (New York: Schocken Books, 1967), 4 (emphasis added).

14. I am echoing and paraphrasing Michel Serres's *Hermes: Literature, Science, Philosophy*, ed. Josué V. Harari and David F. Bell (Baltimore: Johns Hopkins University Press, 1983).

their shoulders stood around improvised fires, chewing on lophira twigs that served as toothbrushes or murmuring greetings to passers-by.

As the sun came up and the mist began to lift, Abdul would set up his treadle sewing machine at the other end of the porch. I would hear the voices of Tilkolo and Mantene (Abdul's wives) from the backyard as they winnowed or pounded rice. A rooster crowed, a child cried, a mortar thudded rhythmically into a wooden pestle, Abdul's sewing machine rattled into life, and villagers passed by on their way to the bush for firewood or the stream for water.

My fieldwork followed the course of people's everyday lives. Like the local weaver's cotton threads, gathered and anchored to a large stone in the middle of the compound and emerging from his loom as a narrow strip of country cloth, the various strands of my own work were gradually coming together: a detailed genealogy of the Barawa chiefs, notes on a rice-flour sacrifice to family ancestors, a detailed account of a funeral, lists of totemic clans and their far-flung affiliations, data on the composition of labor cooperatives, marriages, and ongoing court cases, not to mention the mysterious relationships that diviners formed with djinn.

All this data afforded me glimpses into the warp and woof of Kuranko social life. But rather than this metaphor of society as a web or net, Kuranko used the image of paths: paths worn into the earth by the traffic of bare feet—evidence of the social connections that linked different family compounds in a village or scattered kin within a chiefdom; paths that led uphill—whose steepness was a metaphor for the difficulty of childbirth and labor; paths that were closed by makeshift barriers, fallen branches, or collapsed bridges—images of the falling out of friends and neighbors; paths that petered out in swampland or darkness—signifying distrust and alienated affections.

The "social death" of paths is a perennial Kuranko preoccupation. Illicit love affairs, conspiracies, and unresolved quarrels, or disrespect between the young and old, women and men, commoners and rulers, clansmen and their totemic animal, "spoil" the amity that ideally obtains among members of a community. Even the months of separation during the rains, when families live on isolated farms in the bush, may cause estrangement. Accordingly, a lot of Kuranko ritual life is concerned with symbolically opening paths, cooling hot hearts, clearing the air, and celebrating what binds people together despite their differences. Yet, as I saw daily—in the white cotton threads placed on the lintels of houses and the thresholds of rooms, in the leather sachets containing suras from the Qur'an that people wore around their necks, or in the various fetishes and magical medicines that enclosed or protected the spaces of one's own body, one's house, one's farm, one's village or chiefdom—the impulse toward transparency coexisted with an equally strong impulse for guardedness, which is why the world beyond oneself, the world of the bush, was symbolically black by contrast with the world of oneself and one's own which was "white."

Though different peoples identify danger in different ways—with witches, terrorists, foreigners, pollutants, germs—this unresolved tension between openness and closure is universal. Consider, for instance, Kuranko views on this subject. Initiation involves sequestering neophytes in a bush camp under the supervision of elders. For weeks on end, the neophytes undergo ordeals and hazings that will transform them from children into adults. Nowadays, however, migration, military service, and schooling are also routes to the same "development," both of self and community. Yet many Kuranko elders who went abroad in their youth, seeking their fortune, now question the wisdom of leaving one's village and speak of modernity as a dubious boon. It is like striking a bargain with a djinn, they argue. Today's advantage will be followed by tomorrow's ruin. It is sheer folly to think that one can take one's life into one's own hands, to be sufficient unto oneself. There is one's own life, to be sure, but it is embedded in Life itself, a life that extends far beyond one's own, encompassing one's lineage, one's ancestors, and one's kind. To place oneself outside the social pale is at the very least to assume a burden one will not be able to bear; at worst it is to invite disaster or madness. Counterpointing this conservative counsel, that simply reveals the older generations' anxieties over losing control over the young, are the stories I heard night after night in Kuranko villages, wherein young men or marginalized women venture into the wilderness, braving its dangers, in order to improve their lot and bring something of benefit home to their more timorous kinsmen. Among Sierra Leonean migrants in London, I saw these traditional scenarios unfold in a very different setting. But the dangers remained the same. As my friend Sewa once put it, "Our elders used to tell us that we should always reconnect back to our home town to get prayers and blessings. The paths are kept open. People who go away from home, they're not safe. Believe me, people who have left home, who forget about home, there'll be rise and fall, things will happen for them but within a minute they'll be down, because that *duwé* is not there, the [ancestors'] blessings are not there." As for those who never make it out of the country, but wind up in Freetown walking the streets, hoping for a lucky break, the news is even more dispiriting. "The street is pain," young people say, alluding to the expensive cars, the fine clothing, the conspicuous displays of imported goods they see wherever they go. "No way, no path. You cannot even afford the price of a fare across the city, or food to fill your belly. The street is pain."

Missed Connections

There were summer thunderstorms all the way from Boston to New York, and my flight was delayed. As a result, I missed my connection at Newark and had to join a score or more of other passengers at the Continental counter where three exasperated assistants were searching their computers for alternative flights to Europe.

Evelyn Ali told me I should wait. They might be able to get me on a Continental flight to Paris. She joked about my name. She said people did the same with her, asking if she was Mohammed Ali's daughter. An hour later, she printed out my new boarding pass and walked me to the baggage claim area downstairs where she ensured that my bag was re-routed, saving me from having to stand in the long queue of frustrated passengers who had missed their connections or lost their bags. Evelyn then handed me a meal voucher and told me how to get to Terminal C. When she shook my hand, apologized on behalf of Continental for the inconvenience, and wished me a happy holiday, I wanted to ask her why she was putting herself out for me when there were so many other passengers desperate to get out of Newark. Was it the name thing? Was this some kind of connection?

The flight to Paris was delayed, and when I finally got my boarding call and collapsed into my seat, I was too tired to sleep. I spent the night watching movies, scribbling notes in my journal, and thinking of Sewa and Ade, Isata and Khalil, and other Sierra Leonean friends I would see in London.

Approaching Charles de Gaulle, we experienced considerable turbulence. Passengers cried out as the plane dropped into air pockets and shuddered back onto an even keel. It was easy to imagine the sickening effects of a real crisis, the panic, screams, and terror. Within seconds of touching down, a spatter of applause spread through our cabin. Sighs of relief. A split second of laughter. Even a few breathless words of thanks to God. For me, it recalled my anthropological reading on percussion and transition, since in all human societies traumatic moments are marked, both spontaneously and ritually, by a shattering of speech, a suspension or reversal of everyday routines, and a replacement of music with noisemaking and din—the so-called charivari with which people react to solar and lunar eclipses or an irregular marriage. At its most mundane, this break from routine, this sudden hiatus and suspense, is marked by the clapping of hands or a burst of laughter. But life itself is a bumpy ride, a turbulent river, a hard road, and in trying to understand how people survive traumatic events—typically described as breakups or breakdowns—I have been struck again and again, in my fieldwork after the civil war in Sierra Leone and in reflections on my own biography, by the limited extent to which abstract ideas inform our actions, help us correct course, or enable us to endure. Despite our commitment to theories of knowledge and theologies, or to concepts of love, heroism, God, and goodness, these abstractions foreshadow but do not necessarily guide our actions. Mostly they emerge as retrospective abridgements and rationalizations of events that unfolded "thoughtlessly" and unpredictably in the no-man's land between ourselves and others. Indeed, we never know exactly what we are doing, or why, and much as we like to impute causative power to our beliefs, they are more like tools that help us cope, after the fact, with events that outstripped our capacity to comprehend and control them.

At Charles de Gaulle I made my way to the Continental ticketing counter. I was jet-lagged. My brain felt like a dead walnut rattling around inside my skull. Waiting in line at the Continental counter I recalled several incidents over the past twenty hours that revealed the ways human beings react when their sense of routine and certainty is suddenly destroyed. On the skytrain at Newark, a woman regaled us, without making eye contact with anyone, with a bitter litany of how, by missing her flight, her daughter's wedding plans would be thrown into chaos, how she couldn't contact her daughter, how her bags with her medication inside had been sent on another flight, and how she had no change of clothes. When, at long last, we received our boarding call, many of the passengers rushed toward the departure gate as if their haste would magically compel the plane to leave more quickly. Now, a young guy was begging us to let him jump the queue. He reckoned he could still make his flight to Frankfurt where he had arranged to rendezvous with some friends before driving to Stuttgart for three days of World Cup games. He'd begun his journey in Tampa, been delayed for three hours in Houston because the pilot, who had broken his leg, had to be replaced, and now he was going to miss the England-Ecuador game. He was in a cold sweat. He'd paid $1,000 on eBay for his tickets. All this he let us know, as he glanced anxiously at the clock on the wall and implored the assistant to hurry. When he finally got his boarding pass he was elated. "If I wasn't married, I'd kiss her," he told us all. "I'm delirious."

Next in line was an Ohio couple with their eight-year-old son. They'd missed their connection to Athens and would therefore miss the first day of their vacation. For this loss they demanded compensation. The woman and her husband took turns to lambaste the assistant, insisting that Continental cover the costs of a suite in a first-class hotel in Paris, plus taxi fares and meal vouchers. And, yes, the hotel *must* have a swimming pool. For these people, bad weather, a pilot breaking his leg, or a malfunctioning jetway were not acceptable explanations for their misfortune. As with the Zande, there was no such thing as a natural disaster, a simple accident, a series of unfortunate events; there had to be *someone* at fault, *someone* to blame, and this *someone* would have to take the rap. As for me, and most of the others in the queue, we exhibited the fatalism of the weary and waited our turn at the counter with little expectation of getting to where we wanted to go, at least that day.

If one human response to chaos is to find a scapegoat who can be punished for causing it, another is to create heroes who can be celebrated for overcoming it. In these ways we perpetuate the myth of human will-power, the fiction that we can transcend our circumstances if only we have a mind to, and cling to the illusion that the world is ours to save, to transform, to transcend.

Tertium Quid

I reached London on the anniversary of the terrorist bombings of July 7, 2005. I had been in London a couple of weeks after these bombings, hanging out with Sierra Leonean expatriates, getting a sense of what was at stake for them. Then, as now, the newspapers were full of references to "Muslim extremists" (the scapegoats), and to local heroes — the ordinary yet defiant Londoners who went to work with "a steely resolve" never to "give way to the bombers,"[15] leitmotifs which would also figure in media coverage of the fifth anniversary of 9/11 in the United States.

I phoned Sewa from Paddington Station. After chatting for a while, Sewa suggested I take the tube to the Angel and catch a 38 bus. He would meet me at the bus stop outside Sainsbury's.

I reached our rendezvous first. But within a minute, Sewa rounded the corner, caught sight of me, broke into a broad smile, and strode toward me. He was wearing a sleeveless black and white country-cloth tunic, knee-length breeches made of dark camouflage cloth, and leather sandals. We embraced, and he introduced me to his cousin Braima who was hanging back, somewhat abashed.

Braima's father, Noah, had been my closest friend in Sierra Leone for many years, but I hadn't seen Braima since 1979 — the year his father and siblings joined my family in Firawa where I was doing fieldwork. Braima remembered how my wife and I renovated the house of the old medicine-master Saran Salia, installing rattan ceiling mats, constructing a porch of mud bricks, and redaubing the walls and floors with clay from the Milimili stream. "Why can't Sierra Leoneans work like that?" Braima asked.

As with many of his countrymen, the war had left Braima feeling disenchanted and ashamed, as if Sierra Leoneans were incapable of creating a viable nation.

I asked Braima what kind of work he was doing in London. He was a "businessman," he said, buying luxury cars at a discount and shipping them to Sierra Leone.

As we strolled toward Thorndike Road, I pressed Sewa for news of

15. "Our Defiance Makes It Another Working Day," *Evening Standard*, July 7, 2005, 6.

his mother and his home village of Kondembaia. "It's a long story," Sewa said. "I will tell you all about it."

At the apartment, Sewa prepared a meal of rice and groundnut stew. As we sat down at the table to eat, Braima, who had fallen silent for some time, suddenly opened up. "We have to get rid of the corruption back home," he exclaimed. "Pay people proper salaries so they don't have to steal in order to make ends meet. And we have to help one another more. Look at the Ghanaians! They have real national pride. But not we. We Sierra Leoneans don't look after each other. We don't care."

These assertions triggered a vehement exchange of views between Braima and his cousin that went on for three hours. I listened, by turns fascinated and bored, as they advanced their arguments for how Sierra Leone could get rid of corruption and develop its social services. Later that night, after I had returned to my digs in Shoreditch, I remembered Braima citing the example of some foreign aid that had been given to build a four-lane highway out of Freetown; the old two-lane road had simply been resurfaced and the surplus money pocketed by politicians. "That's why foreign donors take their money elsewhere," Braima said.

Sewa's response intrigued me. The problem, he said, was not so much the corruption in Freetown; it was what was going on in the provinces. "There is no love," he said. "I can remember growing up in the village. I would go around with my friends, we'd go to each other's house to eat, come to my house and eat, go to the farm together. And in the dry season [*telme ro*] people used to dance. They would call the jelibas [praise-singers] to Kondembaia. People came from all the small villages, beat the drums, the *balanjé* [xylophones], danced all night, cooked food, ate together . . . you see, there was love. But when I went back to Kondembaia last year, everything had changed. That love is not there."

I questioned Sewa a little about what he meant by this lack or loss of love (*dienaye*), a word he was obviously using in the Kuranko sense to mean fellow-feeling, mutual regard, communitas, and solidarity. But I was tired, and decided to take the matter up with him next day when we met, just the two of us, after his shift ended at the Wandsworth cinema.

To fully understand what Sewa meant when he spoke of certain individuals in his natal village "spoiling love" and "bringing confusion between people" it is necessary to know something of the history of the ruling family to which he belonged.

When Sewa's father, Sheku Magba Koroma, was a small boy, a Mandingo Muslim called Sori, who hailed from Karina in northern Sierra Leone, came to Diang chiefdom, recruiting boys for his Qur'anic school. Although Sheku Magba's family had been pagans for as long as anyone could remember, the boy's father's elder brother decided that he should go with the Qur'anic teacher or *karamorgo*. Sheku Magba was not present when the fateful decision was made; he was in the bush with his age-mates, searching for wild fruit. But when he was summoned and told what had been decided, he declared himself happy to go with the stranger and learn whatever there was to be learned from him.

On arriving in Karina, Sheku Magba was introduced to a second *karamorgo*, who told Sori, "This small boy that you have brought with you is a star. You must take special care of him." And so it was that Sheku Magba received special treatment and, unlike the other boys, was not beaten if he was careless or dilatory in his studies.

Twenty-five years passed, and Sheku Magba's *karamorgo* gave his eldest daughter Mami Ami in marriage to his star pupil, and with his teacher's blessing Sheku Magba traveled with his new wife to Kono where he went into business, selling native tobacco.

At about this time, Sheku Magba's father, Chief Sama Magba Koroma, died, and a new chief was installed in Diang. The new incumbent, Mansa Bala, belonged to a rival ruling house,[16] had many wives, and was an ineffectual ruler. The real power in Diang was wielded by his brother, Mamadu Sandi, who was given to assaulting people without provocation, abducting other men's wives, and stealing people's property with impunity.

A certain Alhaji Magba Kamara, who had received some education and was connected to Diang through his mother, saw a way of resolving this situation. Purporting to be Mansa Bala, he wrote a letter to

16. Kondembaia was founded in the late 1880s, following the withdrawal of the sofa invaders from Diang. The first chief, Kundembé, for whom the town was named, was succeeded by his first-born son Kerifa Do. Then followed Kerifa Do's younger brothers, Tina Ferenke and Sama Magba. The rivalry between the two ruling houses reflects the fact that Tina Ferenke and Sama Magba were sons of the same father but different mothers (Tina and Sama), a notoriously vexed relationship known as *fadenye*.

the British District Commissioner, resigning the chieftaincy on the grounds that he was weary of the burden of his numerous responsibilities. The letter was taken to Mansa Bala, who was told it was from the colonial administration regarding some improvements that were about to be made in the chiefdom. These required his warrant. Mansa Bala signed and sealed the letter, and a week later the District Officer arrived in Kondembaia to take the staff from him.

When elections were called for his successor, the rivalry between the two ruling houses—known as the Magbas and the Ferenkes—resurfaced with a vengeance. Although Mansa Bala had accepted the loss of the staff, his brother Mamadu Sandi had not. And when a section chief, whose name was Ma Ferema Kona, suggested that Sheku Magba be nominated as a candidate for the chieftaincy (because some diviners had predicted that the new chief would be a Muslim), the Ferenkes drove the Muslim Mandingos from Kondembaia.

Sewa recalls what happened next.

"Ma Ferema Kona and some other elders, like Pa Bunkure, went to Kono to look for my dad. He was in Tankoro by then. He was living there. They said to him, 'We have come to get you.' My dad said, 'What for?' They said, 'We want you to be our candidate in the elections at Kondembaia.' He said, 'How could I be chief? I'm just a poor man, just doing my business, selling this tobacco leaf to make a living. I'm poor, and my brothers are there.' They said, 'No, this is not about money. You are going to be our chief. We are going to elect you.' He said, 'All right, let's go.' So they went to Kondembaia. Some of his elder brothers were not happy about this. They said, 'What! Over our dead bodies! How can you people come and crown our junior, junior brother Sheku, small, small Sheku?' One of my uncles poisoned himself because of this. There were eight of them contesting for the chieftaincy. By the time of the election, four were dead.[17] But the elections were held and my dad became Paramount Chief. He brought stability. He built a mosque. He started converting people to Islam."

It was strange to hear these details of Sewa's father's story for the first time—to be swept back thirty-six years to when I would visit the renowned storyteller Keti Ferenke Koroma in Kondembaia, aware that

17. In the factional fighting between the Ferenkes and the Magbas, the powerful *korte* medicines were allegedly used, causing these deaths.

he and the chief belonged to two branches of the same lineage, with a long history of bad blood between them, yet not interested enough in the politics of chieftaincy to pursue the matter. I would pay my respects to Sheku Magba II, whom I would almost always find sitting on the high porch of his house, his sandals shucked off, a fly whisk draped over his shoulder, a kettle of water and furled umbrella (which he used as a walking stick in both dry and wet seasons) close at hand. He ruled for forty years, committed to fairness and good governance. When he died in 1995, he was succeeded by his son Sheku Magba III, who had returned home after fifteen years in Washington, D.C., where he had allegedly studied for a degree in mechanical engineering.

Sheku was thirty-six when the June 1996 elections took place after a rancorous campaign that once again pitted the Ferenkes against the Magbas. However, the new chief proved to be as unpopular and divisive as his detested precursor, Mamadu Sandi. Pondering Sheku's lack of respect for his section chiefs and elders, and his decision not to rebuild his father's house (burned to the ground by the Revolutionary United Front in 1998), some villagers took the view that he smoked too much marijuana, others that he had been in the United States too long, others that his father had pampered him too much after his mother died when he was four.

Toward the end of 2005, politically well-placed members of the Ferenke faction began agitating to have Sheku Magba III removed from office. In Diang, people offered a sacrifice of rice flour (*degé*) to the ancestors, swearing that they would accept death if their complaint against the chief was groundless or if they reconciled themselves to his continued rule. Responding to these events, as well as pressure from the chief's most vocal critics, the president ordered Sheku Magba III to vacate the chieftaincy, and he initiated an inquiry into the Magbas' alleged abuses of power.

Some two months after these events, Sewa had a dream in which he was present at a meeting between his late father and some chiefdom elders. One of the elders brought a ram into the compound, a gift for the chief. A second ram was already tethered there, and it backed up, preparing to do battle with the interloper. The rams locked horns and began to fight. "I was the one who succeeded in separating them," Sewa told me, and he went on to explain that the dream "was like a message" from his father, its import being that the chief's first-born son, Yeyeh, had joined forces with the Ferenkes and was now fighting to have the staff taken away permanently from the Magbas. In Sewa's opinion, Yeyeh was old and embittered. By right (of primogeniture) he should have succeeded Sheku Magba II, but during the chief's lifetime Yeyeh had fallen into disfavor. Now resentful and childless—his own line doomed to extinction when he died—Yeyeh had thrown in his lot with Daniel Ferenke Koroma, a disaffected politician presently living in the United States, and was seeking to destroy those he now blamed for his personal misfortunes. Sewa's task was, as he put it, "to separate the warring factions, then bring them back together." Though Yeyeh had sworn that he would never make peace with the Magbas, Sewa interpreted his dream as a communication from his late father, urging him to settle the dispute. "No matter how bad Magba is, or what he's done," Sewa said, referring to his deposed brother, "there's no way you should be joining another ruling house to fight against your own brother. We know that Magba is not respectful of people, but we have to think beyond, and not be thinking about just this one person. Even me, I phoned Yeyeh and said, 'Look brother, I understand.' Because Yeyeh and I were once very close, I said, 'Brother, listen, there's no way all of us can be chief at the same time. This is Magba's time. You've got to accept that. If you don't get along with Magba, all right, but think of the rest of the family, the stepmothers, our great great granddad. They've worked hard for the staff, for the throne. You can't say you are going to join the Ferenkes just because of what Magba has done.'"

The Dead

Sewa and I were alone in the apartment. Ade had left for work, leaving us to our talk of political intrigue and of the dead—for behind everything that occurs in the here and now lies the hidden hand of one's ancestors, of those who have "gone before." In a long-distance call to Yeyeh, Sewa had alluded darkly to this, telling his embittered "brother" that his misfortunes were caused by the ancestors who were outraged at his betrayal of the family. "It's *fo' koe* [lit. 'dead thing' or the action of the dead']," Sewa explained to me. "The dead are always there, they see everything, they know exactly what is happening."

With Sewa's permission I switched on my tape recorder. "So you are saying that the dead have caused Yeyeh's suffering?" I asked.

"Yes, the dead are your *sabu* [cause]," Sewa said. "Right now, Yeyeh has no job, everything is up and down, chasing the Lebanese every day, just trying to get food. There's no respect for him. Even me, I've no respect for him any more. That's *fo' koe*. Imagine someone who was very powerful in the family, who was the head of the family, but now everyone wants to beat up, everyone is looking for just to beat up. He loses his respect, you see."

That the ancestors were able to intervene in the lives of the living, redressing injustices, withholding blessings from the unworthy, favoring those who offered them food and paid them respect, was familiar enough to me from my fieldwork in Sierra Leone. But in many classic studies of the shades in African life, ancestral figures are seen as extensions or projections of kinship relations—especially between parents and children, elders and underlings—onto the "supernatural" plane.[18] As Durkheim argues in *The Elementary Forms of the Religious Life*, "religion is something eminently social."[19] The cosmological is thus simply the social order writ large, and because the ethereal appears to be beyond the earthly, it compels respect and gives legitimacy to the rules governing mundane social life. But by prioritizing the *social* function of beliefs and rites associated with ancestors, these explanations overlook the immediate and affective meaning that ancestors may have for the living. Hearing Sewa speak of his ancestry helped me understand what it actually means to live in the presence of the dead, and how deeply relations among the living depend on ritualized relations with forebears and precursors. To be indifferent to one's ancestors thus implies estrangement from one's kin and community.[20]

18. Meyer Fortes, "Some Reflections on Ancestor Worship in Africa," in *African Systems of Thought*, ed. Meyer Fortes and Germaine Dieterlen (London: Oxford University Press, 1965), 122–44.

19. Emile Durkheim, *The Elementary Forms of the Religious Life: A Study in Religious Sociology*, trans. Joseph Ward Swain (London: George Allen, 1915), 10.

20. This was also a recurring theme in my conversations with Michael Puett at Harvard, since in early China ritual sacrifice meant acting *as if* one could transform "a capricious and potentially antagonistic spirit world into a hierarchical pantheon of ordered genealogical descent interested in its living descendants' welfare." To ignore the spirits or leave them to their own devices was to risk a

The morning after his dream of the two fighting rams, Sewa had phoned his mother Tina in Freetown. Faced with turmoil in the family, she assured Sewa that she would offer a sacrifice to God, asking that the hot tempers be cooled, and the situation resolved.

"Three weeks later," Sewa said, "I had another dream. My father was standing on the porch of his house, with all the brothers and sisters around him. A cow was being killed [as a sacrifice to the lineage ancestors and, by extension, to God]. The people were praying on the blood."

Again Sewa phoned his mother and described his dream to her. This time she traveled to Kondembaia where she offered another sacrifice. The sacrifice, Sewa explained, was "to get blessings [duwé] from the dead." But this sacrifice (saraké) was unlike any other. Called sarakaboi, it was offered every ten years by a family in praise of the ancestors and to "clear bad feeling" among its members. It was therefore imperative that the entire family be present, so Sewa sent two hundred pounds to help people travel to Kondembaia from all over the country, as well as petition the president to investigate the individuals who were trying to wrest the chieftaincy away from the Magbas.

Following the sacrifice, the family's fortunes seemed to improve. The killing of the cow meant that the ancestors began to "take an interest," "to start making things easier," Sewa explained. And on the same day that the cow was sacrificed in Kondembaia, Sewa filled a bowl with cold water, summoned his wife Ade, and begged God and the ancestors to help the Magbas' cause. "I mentioned all their names, the dead. All their names, I mentioned them. I said, 'Please you need to beg God for us. This throne that you worked hard for, they just want to take it away from us. So we are begging you to beg God to direct the right way for us to go.'"

Throughout Africa, God is typically an abstract and otiose figure, having long ago absented himself from the human world. This is why people make costly sacrifices to the ancestors, persuading them to act as intermediaries between themselves and God—a reminder of the universal religious paradox that gods must be otherworldly if they are to

---

world of discontinuity, division, and disorder. Michael J. Puett, *To Become a God: Cosmology, Sacrifice, and Self-Divinization in Early China* (Cambridge, Mass.: Harvard University Press, 2002), 198.

have *authority over* people yet present in some shape or form if they are to have *meaning for* people. In Africa, ancestors and djinn function much like angels, prophets, and holy figures in other parts of the world—as intercessories that effectively narrow the gap between earth and ether without subverting the essential difference between humanity and the gods. All these relationships between heaven and earth are understood in terms of reciprocity. One can expect to receive nothing from the ancestral dead unless one gives up or forgoes something that is vital to one's own well-being, and this means rice (the staff of life) or domestic animals.

"Two hundred pounds is a lot of money," I said, when Sewa told me what the Kondembaia sacrifice cost him.

"It's one million leones," Sewa said. "That money covered the costs of hiring trucks to get people to Kondembaia, provide food for them, and buy the animals for sacrifice . . . it was enough. So now, when I phone my brother, the chief, he says, 'God bless you. I don't know what else to say but God bless you' [Magba had moved from Kondembaia to Freetown where he was living with Sewa's mother Tina, the woman who raised Magba as her own son after his own mother's death].

"Look at me now," Sewa continued. "Me, all the way from Africa, from poverty. Now I'm in England, a supervisor in a cinema, hiring people . . . the dead made all these things happen. I believe that one hundred percent. My luck is open. And back home, things are happening now, things are in our favor. People are starting to join up, give contributions, saying, 'We don't mind if we die but no one is going to take away our birthright.' These are the things the dead will do. They will bring those spirits in you."

Despite the lack of evidence that the situation in Diang *was* getting better, it was clear that Sewa's confidence and spirit had been boosted by the reunion of his far-flung family and their apparent determination to work together for the chieftaincy. Yet rationalists often write off as illusory such magical actions as sacrifice and prayer, ignoring the very real *effects* of these "imaginative" negotiations with the powers-that-be. For Sewa, the sacrifice at Kondembaia and his subsequent dreams had effected a change in his *experience* of the situation back home. A few months ago he had felt that his long-distance efforts to mobilize his kin and save the chieftaincy were doomed; now he felt that his initiatives were inspiring his kinsmen and being recognized by his ancestors. His restored faith gave him both impetus and direction. The next step, he explained to me, was to find two thousand pounds to pay a Freetown lawyer to prosecute the case. To achieve this goal, he was now working two jobs—supervisor in a Wandsworth cinema and night shift security guard in Croydon. To save on bus fares he used a bicycle to cross and recross the city.

I was touched, not only by Sewa's faith in the power of the ancestors but by his conviction that his hard work in bringing the family together—making frequent phone calls home, sending remittances, offering prayers to his forebears, and renewing ties that had become frayed or attenuated—was paying off.

"Even Yeyeh, I am still trying to talk to him," Sewa said excitedly. "I remember when our dad passed away in 1995. We went to Karina, to Yeyeh's uncle. He was an old man. He said, 'Bring a broom.' He put the broom on the ground and took a straw from it and broke it. He said, 'You have seen this, you have seen how easy it is to break one straw?' Then he took the whole broom and tried to break it. He bent it, twisted it, but there was no way he could break it. He passed it to Yeyeh and said, 'You try. You're a strong man. Try to break that one.' He couldn't. He said, 'Do you know why?' He said, 'Divided we fall. When you unite, you stand.' So I reminded Yeyeh of what our uncle told us that time, even though it's ten or eleven years ago now."

Mind the Gap

Because Sewa would be working the next day, I decided to take care of some pressing business, then explore east London and perhaps visit the Tate Modern. Unfortunately, the "business" took longer than I had expected. Having lost my wallet and Green Card somewhere in my travels, I had to get a "transportation letter" from the United States Citizenship and Immigration Services if I was going to be allowed back into the country. But this turned out to be far more complicated than I had bargained for, and as I stood in a dilapidated telephone box near Old Street Station, with porn leaflets and detritus strewn underfoot and the confined space reeking of piss and shit, I thought of Sewa's tales of his daily struggle, during his first couple of years in London, against a bureaucracy that seemed to thwart him at every turn, and a police force that he imagined might detain him at any moment, accuse him of being illegally in Britain, and send him home. After several attempts to work through all the numbered options on the U.S. Embassy's automated answering system, and all the while holding the door ajar so that I could breathe fresh air, I discovered that I could not be connected to the uscis from a pay phone. Exasperated, I hit the street, cursing my luck as well as the threatening rain (for I had no coat), and for a moment or two imagined consigning myself to fate, sitting like the hapless youngsters I saw in the corners of underground stations with their Styrofoam cups or cloth caps filled with a few copper coins, abjectly waiting for rescue or relief. How easy it is to fall through the net or the cracks, as my supervisors at the London Welfare Office for the Homeless used to say, discussing the derelicts and drifters who found their way to our Nissan Hut under Hungerford Bridge where we handed out vouchers for a meal and a night in a Salvation Army hostel. And with what terrible suddenness one could fall from one's ordinary life, like Icarus tumbling out of the sky in Bruegel's great painting, the promise of life slipping from one's grasp because of the betrayal of a spouse, the loss of a job, the onset of illness, or simply the machinations of those who do not think you deserve to live.

The sky was overcast as I trudged to Smithfield Market where I had discovered an Italian café that made excellent espresso. The coffee revived my spirits, and I was soon walking toward the river and London Bridge, determined not to let a transportation letter spoil my day or disrupt my fieldwork—a letter which, it suddenly occurred to me, sounded ominously like the document that criminals might have been given in the nineteenth century, banishing them to the antipodes for the term of their natural lives. It was curious that I should, at that moment, find myself outside the Central Criminal Court Building of the Old Bailey, with the inscription over the great portal—Defend the Children of the Poor and Punish the Wrongdoer—for I, who had once set such store by changing the world for the better, and worked in welfare and community development to this end, had come around to realizing that my vocation was doing justice to life as a writer rather than an activist.

I was soon in Cannon Street Station, where trains left for Lee, and on the spur of the moment I phoned my friends Isata and Khalil, to see if they were home and whether it would be convenient if I paid them a visit. With her usual ebullience and graciousness, Isata urged me to come at once; she would pick me up from the station when I arrived. And so, instead of visiting the Tate Modern and wandering the streets of east London, I wound up in suburbia, talking to Isata about the gap between her life in London and her life back home.

As we talked, Khalil junior watched the children's channel, *Boomerang*, on the TV. Baby sister Moona lay asleep on the settee. The walls of the room were bare except for a framed photograph of Khalil on his graduation day and two reproductions of Edward Hopper paintings. There were bits of chicken bone on the carpet, and discarded shoes and toys. I was reminded of the minimally furnished parlors in Freetown houses—spaces for people to sit together, passing the time in amicable silence, sharing food. A house is for conviviality, not for the conspicuous or aesthetic arrangements of things.

During the course of our conversation, I asked Isata what it was about Freetown that she missed most.

She responded with a story about her last visit home. On the taxi ride from Lungi airport to the city, the driver narrowly missed hitting a pedestrian. Driving on through the thronged streets, the driver jokingly told Isata that it would have been cheaper to kill the pedestrian than "bang" him. If the pedestrian had been killed, the driver would have been liable for the funeral expenses—about 50,000 leones, as well as gifts to the bereaved family. That would have been all. No further complications or obligations. But if the pedestrian had been injured in the accident, the driver would have had to pay hospital costs, costs of feeding the patient's family—who would have to camp at the hospital to attend their kinsman—not to mention the costs of time and hassles. There'd be no end of trouble.

This was gallows humor. Tragedy transformed into farce. In a country where life was cheap, *jouissance* restored one's sense that life was worthwhile. This was what Isata wanted me to appreciate. In Kuranko, one possible response to the greeting, *i kende?* (Are you well?) is "I am as well as hunger," an ironic allusion to the fact that nothing is stronger or more tenacious than the pangs of an empty belly. People listen to local bands that poke fun at politicians ("Two-foot rats" or "big bellies"), saying, "Even though you're poor you can still laugh." They play with words, make light of their situations, turning the tables on tragedy. A sense of bravado and piquancy attends every excursion. But in London, Isata said, she was often depressed by the earnestness and emptiness around her. Many of her colleagues at the private bank where she worked had no families; their talk was all of some program they had seen on TV, a new restaurant they had discovered, a holiday abroad they were planning. On the tube train to the city each morning, commuters hid behind their newspapers or stared vacantly into space, avoiding human contact. David Riesman's "the lonely crowd." Ezra Pound's image: "The apparition of these faces in the crowd / petals on a wet black bough." Isata reminded me of how, in Freetown, greetings were shouted between people who hadn't seen each other in a while. News of births, deaths, separations, and minor catastrophes were exchanged with such enthusiasm that an outsider might be forgiven for concluding that people lacked sympathy and seriousness, that they placed disaster and triumph on the same footing. And I remembered, as Isata spoke, of the social stream that flowed around one, daylong and well into the night, punctuated by palavers, flirtations, requests, and salutations. A veritable picaresque, and a far cry from the artificiality and indirectness of our lives in Europe, where we spend much of the day alone, behind closed doors or in closed cars, glued to a computer screen, reading texts, watching TV, paying bills, signing documents, checking the time. If our workaday routines are interrupted by social pressures, we become irritable and tense. If someone laughs at our seriousness, we are deeply offended. But in Africa, work is an obstacle to social life, and laughter the saving grace!

"But you know," Isata said, "much as I try to be a part of the street life in Freetown when I go back, I am always identified as JC ['Just Come']. If I go to the hairdressers I am immediately called JC. There's no getting away from it. Last time we went, I bought flip-flops, wore a gara-dyed dress, but it made no difference. I was seen as foreign."

"What gave you away?" I asked.

"It's obvious," Isata said. "It's the hands. Your hands. The skin is smooth and unlined."

On her last visit to Freetown, two young men came up to Isata in Garrison Street and asked if she wouldn't mind settling an argument they'd been having. How old was her little boy (Khalil junior) they wanted to know. Isata told them that he was five. They were incredulous. In Sierra Leone a boy that big would be ten. Isata was deeply troubled by this incident, which brought home to her the gap between the rich and poor and made her wonder if the cost of the house that she and her husband were having built in Freetown was morally justified.

I used to anguish about this too and once shared my anguish with Isata's father, S. B. S. B.'s response, I told Isata, was that there was nothing wrong with improving one's lot or even feathering one's own nest, so long as it wasn't at the expense of others. At the time, I had found this answer unsatisfactory, but now I would not venture a judgment; it is for each person to work out for himself or herself what it is to live a moral life.

Khalil was at a mosque meeting, and while Isata busied herself preparing lunch I took little Khalil outside to play. The house was in a close, and assuming the land to be common land I started kicking a ball to Khalil on a patch of dry grass opposite Isata's front door. Within minutes, the neighbor's door opened and an English guy in his thirties ordered me off "his" lawn, explaining that it cost five thousand pounds to lay and we were "trespassing." Chastened and amused, I led Khalil back into the house and told Isata what had happened. "Oh that man!" Isata exclaimed. "He and his wife have no children. They have nothing better to do than fuss over their lawn. They come home from work everyday and pick up dead leaves. They are obsessed with keeping their house spic and span. In Sierra Leone, we always played outdoors when we were kids. No fences, no fuss. Sometimes, I wonder what I am doing here."

A little later, as we were eating, Isata suddenly got up from the table and went to her study, returning with a folder that she placed beside her plate.

"The reason I am home today, Michael, the reason I am not at work, is because . . . well, here, you can read this for yourself."

But as she pushed the folder toward me, Isata began a story of humiliation and hurt that shocked me to the core.

Since my visit the previous summer, Isata had been promoted to the position of private banking assistant in the well-known bank for which she worked. This had entailed a move to another office. Within weeks, the trouble started. A woman who had been assigned to help Isata settle into her new job became agitated and irritated whenever Isata approached her. Before long, Isata felt reluctant to ask colleagues for help. Worse, she would observe them gloating and giggling as she struggled to complete assignments, or they would pretend incomprehension when Isata communicated information in accented English. But the worst she had to endure was racial harassment from a senior banker, who would, within Isata's hearing, loudly announce his preference for size six blondes, would leave bottles of liquid soap on her desk, and once, when Isata returned from a vacation in Sierra Leone, presented her with a surgical mask and another bottle of liquid soap, suggesting she use these in case she contaminated the office with "something you might have picked up in Africa." With no one to turn to in the office, and with a growing sense that she was simply not wanted there, Isata filed a "Dignity at Work Complaint," detailing a series of humiliating incidents and ending with a plea.

> I am a thirty-six-year-old woman who has been made to feel incompetent, threatened, degraded and intimidated. This has had an immense effect on my family life, as I have been going home every night in tears and not sleeping well, worried about going to work. My husband has been extremely supportive and was not happy about me carrying on the way things were, but I was adamant I had to persevere and did not want to give in easily as this is my career. I have been working for seventeen years of my life, apart from my years at university, but I have never been made to feel this way in any job. I have been blissfully married for eleven years with two lovely kids, a loving husband and a very happy home life, but of late I have become an emotional wreck. It was only a few weeks ago that I was so unwell that I could not go to the doctors on my own . . .

I broke off reading Isata's letter. "You are not sick," I said. "It's these colleagues of yours who are sick, and you must not let them or anyone else medicalize this issue."

Isata assured me that though the doctors had prescribed pills to help her sleep and deal with her "depression" she had not filled the prescriptions. She was not going to use drugs. She was going to fight this case.

"I think the bank is a victim of its sense of tradition," Isata said. "Its fortunes are so tied up with this country's colonial past that it has never hired any ethnics. Apart from me, there was only one man, an Indian, who rose to the rank of PBA, and he resigned recently, I think because of harassment. And the bank has a problem with women, too. And being taken over by the Royal Bank of Scotland, a High Street bank, hurt their pride."

That afternoon, Isata and I drafted the letters I would send, on Harvard letterhead, to her superiors, as well as the CEO of the Royal Bank of Scotland, vouching for Isata's "integrity, intelligence, loyalty and generosity of spirit" and urging a quick resolution of the issue. But it was with a heavy heart that I returned to London that evening, for in all my years in Africa I had never experienced racism, had always been warmly received into villages and homes, and had relished the ebullient greetings, recognitions, and stories that made up one's day and that Isata, in saying goodbye to me, said she now missed even more than ever. "I don't want to go back home to make a difference," she said, "I just want to be back home."

The Genealogical Imagination

Sewa often spoke to me of how it was "stressing him" that he was not in Sierra Leone, communicating with his kinsmen face-to-face, warning them against being "brainwashed" by their political adversaries, and encouraging them that "love" was needed if they were to rebuild their lives in the aftermath of civil war. "It's stressful for me to be here, to know that the Ferenkes are trying to take our staff, but I'm the source right now, and money brings people together and makes things happen. I'm the life for these things, you know, so that's why I'm working hard, though it's hard for me being here, going through that pain, phoning them every day, knowing how long it takes for them to do anything. When I'm under stress, I want to go there, I want to show them what I know from experience, from when I used to sit around with my dad. I'm thirty years old now, but you know, my whole life I spent with my dad and my uncle S. B., watching the way they did things. I know politics. Politics is in my future, in my stars. And you know, Mr Michael, how we say in Kuranko, where you throw the stone, there the bush fowl is hiding . . . just as if a blind man said 'I'm going to throw a rock at you' when he already has the rock under his foot, already knows what he is going to do before he does it."

For all his worries, Sewa seemed, for the most part, to be able to narrow this gap between home and away by promising himself that he would return to Sierra Leone sooner rather than later, and in the meantime could keep in touch by cell phone and through prayer.

"Whenever I get up in the morning, I pray to my dad," Sewa said, holding my small tape recorder and resuming his story. "I greet him, '*Eh, m'fa, inwali* [Eh, my father, greetings].' Even my wife knows how to say these words. She's English, but she hears me saying these words every morning, *Eh, m'bimba fore* . . . eh my ancestors, please beg God to open my way, to give me what I need. And it is happening, it's happening . . ."

"You say these words over a bowl of cold water?" I asked.

"That represents, like, to make my heart cool, not to worry. That's the only thing you can give to them here. That cold water means a lot. Whenever we put the cold water, we put some at the door. There'll always be peace in this house, no problems. As soon as I step out of the door my heart will be cool. I'll be coming with a cool heart. Put the cold water in a bowl, pray over it, then sprinkle some under the door and drink some of it. That's what we do, me and my wife."

"Is it the same as putting cotton wool above the doorway back home in the village?"

"Yes. So that no bad things, no bad feelings will come to you."

As I knew from years gone by, the Kuranko reasoning ran as follows: whiteness is like cool, clear, uncontaminated water. The hearts of those who live closely together and trust one another are white. But honesty, trust, and amity are constantly threatened by ill will, either from within the family or from without. Yet, as streams are sometimes muddied but then run clear, so whiteness can combat darkness. The animosity of strangers, or the dark arts of witchcraft and sorcery, are "cleared out" or countered by the goodwill and pure-heartedness they come up against.

Sewa was at pains to emphasize the power of positive thinking. "When you believe in these things, they happen," he said. "These things really happen . . . they are happening for me. My dad is still alive. It's just that I am not seeing him. I only see him in my dreams, like once a month or every two or three months I see him in a dream, but I know he's around me. I have a picture of him in my room. There's one thing he never wants any of his kids to do, and that is drink alcohol. When I go out and drink alcohol, as soon as I come home and step into my room and see that picture, I have to run out of the room again. I want to go and take the picture and put it away, like in my cupboard or box, but I know I have alcohol in my system so I cannot touch the picture. I have to wait for days, days, to take that picture and put it somewhere, so

I can walk into my room and not see it straight away. I know it's just a picture, but it's like it's him seeing me, what I'm doing, you know. You see, I've got all these beliefs. And when I stop drinking, pray to him, ask him for forgiveness, I know that's the only thing I'm doing that my dad's unhappy about."

Ade had suggested Sewa hang the photo of his father in the living room, now bare except for a small lacquered plywood map of Sierra Leone in which different seeds—sesame, millet, mustard, chili, and several species of rice—had been glued to mark the different provinces. "But I can't put pictures in the sitting room. I can't imagine myself sitting here, holding a beer, drinking, when my dad's picture is looking at me. So that's what's stopping me putting the picture up. I can't live in a house where friends will come and want to drink, and my dad is seeing me, I just can't do that. I feel I'm doing the wrong thing, that he doesn't want me to do, even though he's not alive in the real world, I just don't want to do that."

"But you have made so many changes in your life, since coming to England," I said. "Big changes."

"It's true, Mr. Michael. Sometimes I can't believe myself."

"When you and Ade went back to Sierra Leone last year, did people think you had changed?"

"Yes. My way of doing things. JC. They just see me as different. Even my skin looked different. They said, 'This boy's different.' I remember my friends coming up to me at the house where I was staying. They wanted to smoke cigarettes. I said, 'Uhuh, sorry guys, you can't smoke in here.' We used to smoke cigarettes everywhere, even the bedroom. They said, 'Eh!' Then I started washing the dishes! They said, 'Eh! you don change-o, S. B., you don change-o.' So they see these things as very strange—not smoking in the house, washing the dishes after eating food, even my dress code. When I lived in Sierra Leone I used to go more for those American trainers, those basketball trainers, you know. But then I came over here and got a girl-friend, one English girl, white English, and she didn't like the way I dressed. When she asked me out on a date, she said, 'I expect you not to wear those basketball trainers, they're ugly, and we're not going to basketball.' So we went to Foot Locker where they sell those classic trainers, and I asked 'Which are the classic trainers?' The boy pointed at them, those flat trainers. So that's how things started getting changed. And then one day she said, 'Why are you wearing this big shirt, big trousers? Why do you Africans pretend to be like Americans?' So all those things have changed, and when my friends saw me in Freetown, wearing those skateboard trainers, those flat trainers, no baggy trousers, no baggy shorts, they said, 'Eh! S. B., you don change-o, you don turn Englishman now.'"

But for all the changes, Sewa was emphatic that in things that really mattered, he upheld tradition.

"When I think about how I used to go into the bush to find wood, go to the farm, carry loads on my head . . . those things that used to vex me back home . . . I just laugh. But when I am indoors here, I always wear those culture clothes, just for me not to forget who I am, because there's no way I am going to change my culture, my traditions, or my beliefs. That's why I have that map of Sierra Leone on the wall there, and wear this costume that my dad wore, this country-cloth gown."

But his father was not just a role model for Sewa. Sewa had, in many ways, *become* his father. As a small boy, he had been nicknamed "walking-stick" because of the way he followed his father everywhere, dogging his heels, head down, concentrating on placing his feet exactly where his father placed his, literally walking in his father's footsteps. But Sewa had inherited more than his father's way of walking; he had inherited the right to rule and it was his ambition to emulate the political even-handedness and incorruptibility for which his father was known during forty years as Paramount Chief of Diang.

That Sewa was sustained emotionally in exile by the "belief" he had inherited from his father (by which he meant both Islam and a sense of what in Kuranko is known as *bimba che*—ancestral legacy or birthright) was made very clear in the way he responded to my question "Do you think of yourself as a Muslim?"

"I am a Muslim. I was raised in a Muslim home. My father was a Muslim, just as I told you, and my mother too. But I am first and foremost a Kuranko man.

"That child that Ade is going to get for me, he'll grow up seeing his daddy differently, seeing that his clothes are different from the ones they wear here. What I'm trying to do, what I am praying for, is that my son will speak Kuranko. Not Krio, but Kuranko. I want to set that example . . ."

Sewa had already told me that Ade was pregnant, their prayers having been answered after a gynecologist had suggested that Ade may have problems conceiving. Convinced that Ade would bear him a son, Sewa had redoubled his efforts to secure the Magbas' hold on the Diang chieftaincy since if it did not devolve to him, it might devolve to his first-born son.

Ade had told Sewa that if he wanted his child to speak Kuranko, it might be a good idea if he began talking to the child before it was born, and so, Sewa said, "I started yesterday, singing that song the uncles sing to their nephews, but changing the words a bit from uncle to dad. That boy will be called Sheku. Ade likes the name Chelmanseh [the name Sewa's uncle S. B. gave to his last-born son]. We're still discussing that. So the name will be long, like Sheku Chelmanseh Magba Koroma. We definitely have to get that Magba name in, and the Koroma, and Sheku my dad's name. So I started singing this song, even last night, rubbing Ade's belly, saying *Sheku le, i ma de wa yo, i ma de wa Sheku, i ma de wa yo . . . i fa kinkin kuma ma fo la ala ma diye, eh, eh . . .* [Sheku, listen, listen, listen to the sorrowful words your father is saying to you; you don't need to cry . . .].

"That's how the uncles used to sing to their nephews when they were kids, telling them not to cry. So I have that song ready for that child now, and I will tell Ade to tell her family not to be surprised if I am always speaking Kuranko to my son, telling him how we suffer in life, how I suffered, but we should not cry . . ."

That Sewa should adapt the song with which an uncle consoles his nephew brought me to ponder the contrapuntal relationship between a Kuranko boy's relationships with his father and his mother's brother. Insofar as a father pushes his eldest son away from him so as to play down the privileged position of his heir and not show favoritism toward him, the rejected son may turn to his mother's brother as a source of support and affection. Since the mother's brother usually lives in another village, if not another chiefdom, the eldest son migrates, as it were, from where he feels there is too little love to somewhere love is available. Or, should one's father die, one may find a home with one's maternal uncle — which is exactly what happened with Sewa. Thus, the centripetal force that binds the son to his paternal house is constantly countered by the centrifugal forces that give him a home away from home.

The possibility of migration is presaged in such customs, and there is always something already in one's experience — the countervailing forces of town and bush, or of paternal and avuncular ties — that anticipates the way in which one's ultimate journey into the wider world will be understood, and that gives shape to the idea of a limit or threshold where contending forces vie for dominance over one's destiny.

The Penumbral

Late that evening, after transcribing several pages of Sewa's story, I left my digs in Shoreditch and walked along Paradise Street, whose name, according to the street sign, had for some unspecified reason been changed to Clere. Turning south, I passed warehouses of sickly and forbidding brick, rain leaking from a leaden sky, but soon became oblivious to my surroundings, absorbed by the mystery of why Sewa's intense relationship with his late father betrayed no sense of morbidity or repining. Was it because traditional African mourning practices involve a transmutation of the dead in which the idiosyncratic personality is symbolically extinguished—the physical body returned to dust, individual possessions ritually destroyed or given away—and an abstract persona made to take its place—a persona with which the living continue to communicate through prayer and sacrifice, and whose presence is felt in their everyday lives? Is it possible that the prevalence of melancholia in the West might be explained as the psychic price we pay for either seeking absolute detachment from the dead or endeavoring to perpetuate a sense of how they really existed for us in life? While we often allow ourselves to become strangers to the dead, or prolong our attachment to living images of them, Kuranko focus their ritual attention far more closely on a process of idealization that eclipses memories of the dear departed in order to celebrate the abstract qualities they embodied. It seemed to me, for instance, that Sewa's photograph of his father was not so much an aide-mémoire as a means of reminding himself, day in and day out, of the values his father exemplified and the ancestral legacy he held in trust. Sewa's personal loss of his father was thus redeemed in the manner in which the son honored the father's name and moral essence, not the way in which he kept an image of his actual father alive.

In 1965, I returned to New Zealand after many years abroad and found work as a teacher in a rural high school, renting a room in the spacious home of a local widow, Mrs. York. After dinner one evening, some four months after I had taken up lodgings with her, Yorkie asked me to follow her down the long hallway of the house to a room that she nervously unlocked before bidding me, with a finger held to her lips, to enter. This had been her son's room, she explained. He had drowned fifteen years ago, while still in his teens. She had kept the room exactly as he had left it. A shrine, she said, to his memory. She then led me to an immense wardrobe in the corner of the bedroom and unlocked it, releasing into the airless room an odor of naphthalene and dust. Rummaging in the clothes on the rack, she took down a Harris tweed sports jacket and handed it to me with the firm instruction that I should try it on. "It will fit you, I know," she said. And at that moment, I knew that I was lost and would have to find somewhere else to live.

Yorkie's son was a shadow in which we lived, not a living presence. His memory hung like a pall over us, allowing no light or new life to enter the here and now. We could only be absorbed into his shadow. And it was the same twenty years later when I happened to be billeted in the home of Margaret Scott during a period of protest marches against the touring Springbok rugby team in Wellington. Margaret was away at the time, and I found myself in a house of ghosts. Margaret's husband, Harry, had been my psychology lecturer at Auckland University, and when he died in a climbing accident in 1961 I wrote an elegy mourning his loss. But the minute I walked into Margaret's house it was clear to me that she had never gotten over him. An outdated calendar in the kitchen showed a photo of Aorangi, the mountain on which Harry had lost his life. The framed McCahon and Woollaston watercolors on the living room walls were from the brief period Harry and Margaret lived in Auckland in the late fifties. In her bookshelves the issues of *Landfall*, including essays by Harry, came to an end in 1961, either because she had let her subscription lapse or successive issues held no meaning for her without him. Indeed, the house was like a tomb, filled with the fading and unrelinquished memorabilia of a bygone time that seemed to preclude any new departure, any real future.

As these memories drifted through my consciousness, I trudged on through streets and lanes I had first gotten to know when I worked among the homeless in London in 1963. Yet, for all their familiarity these thoroughfares were foreign to me now, not only because the East End had undergone a face-lift, with derelict apartments turned into expensive apartment blocks, blacking factories and boot shops transformed into boutiques, but because the dejection and penury I suffered in those days had passed from me as winter passes into spring. Pavements slimy from decaying leaves and endless rain, or soot-encrusted buildings along the turbid Thames, that forty years ago were metaphors of my inner misery, held no meaning for me now.

It is not possible to fully fathom why it is, when stretched to the limit of one's endurance by suffering, that one person succumbs and another not only survives but discovers a new lease of life. What resources did Sewa and I possess—and that Yorkie and Margaret Scott seemed to lack—that made us survivors? Was it strong and caring parents, whose love sustained us even after they had passed on, enabling us to transform adversity into adventure, making rather than breaking us? Possibly. But in extreme situations, adversity cannot be measured in terms of pain alone, nor even in terms of the degree to which one is supported in one's suffering, for what defines such situations is the complete absence of any freedom of choice, any freedom to move, any hope that things will get better. Immobilized in this state of enforced passivity, one falls prey to one's own worst imaginings. It is perhaps a tragic irony that the philosopher who coined the term "border situation" (*grenzsituation*) found himself and his wife (who was Jewish) in precisely this situation in Germany under the Nazis. After losing his academic position and finding emigration impossible, Jaspers "migrated inwards," recording in his diaries his anxieties over being separated from his wife, his struggle to continue his work, and his arguments for death at his own hands rather than annihilation at the hands of the state. After the war, there was no sense of rebirth; simply a sense that to have survived the National Socialist years, to have lived through the night and seen the dawn, was enough.[21]

Inevitably, all new life requires a death—even if this death is only a forgetting.

I recall how distressed and mystified I was, after my first wife Pauline died and my daughter and I moved from New Zealand to Australia to begin a new life, that I could not conjure Pauline's image in my mind's eye, could not hear her voice, recover the touch of her hand or the

21. Karl Jaspers, "Journal Entries 1939–1942," in *Karl Jaspers: Basic Philosophical Writings*, ed. and trans. Edith Ehrlich, Leonard H. Ehrlich, and George B. Pepper (New York: Humanity Books, 2000), 535–43.

smell and contours of her body. And yet, in the arid landscapes through which I walked every day, I was susceptible to her presence in every change of the winter light, every movement in the grass, every metamorphosis of the clouds over the blue Brindabella range, and out of the understanding that she, dying, lived, I drew the strength to go on.

Of one thing I am now sure — that it is in limit situations and at critical junctures — of birth, initiation, bereavement, or exile — suspended between a familiar world in which we think of ourselves as actors and a foreign world in which we are simply acted upon that we are most alive to what one might call the real or the religious.[22] The words are arbitrary. What matters is only the phenomenon to which they allude — the compression of experience in such situations and at such times, the intense focus that occludes awareness of everything but the moment in which we find ourselves thrown, and yet, paradoxically, may throw us open to new possibilities and new connections, lying beyond the horizons we have hitherto known. This notion of creative destruction is an ancient theme, expressed in the Egyptian and Greek myth of the Phoenix, in the Hindu figure of Siva, in the Christian idea of the resurrection, and in Nietzsche's Zarathustra, who must break with the past in order to be reborn, annihilate in order to affirm. But responding to destruction by rebuilding is one thing; visiting it upon oneself is another.

Like many migrants, Sewa and Isata found themselves between a world in which they did not feel completely at home and a world of homely belonging in which they could "be themselves" — a world of kinsmen and friends who shared the same language, enjoyed the same food, laughed at the same jokes, and had a common background. As with Sewa, you don the clothing of the country that has opened its doors to you (even if those doors have been grudgingly left ajar!), acquiring its language, respecting its laws, yet always constrained by a sense that one is acting out of character, wearing a mask, losing touch with one's real identity. This "stresses" you, Sewa said. "It makes you

22. To speak of limits is practically the same as speaking of experience, since "experience" itself suggests the threshold between private and public spheres — between all that eludes language or slips through the fingers of the mind and what lies within the "homogenizing grasp" of conceptual thought. See Martin Jay, *Songs of Experience: Modern American and European Variations on a Universal Theme* (Berkeley: University of California Press, 2005), 6–7.

feel small." As for Isata, she was at her wits' end, struggling to live with a situation that had reduced her to a shadow of her usually confident and outgoing self.

By the time I reached the river, the rain had stopped, the light now crepuscular, and the Thames flowing into the darkness and an imperceptible sea.

After Midnight

It was after midnight when I returned to my digs. Still restive, and unable to sleep, I searched through the books abandoned by other travelers on the shelves beside my bed.

In Axel Munthe's 1930 preface to his memoir of his years as a physician in late-nineteenth-century Paris and southern Italy, I came upon these lines:

> I am aware that some of the scenes are laid on the ill-defined borderland between the real and the unreal, the dangerous No Man's Land between fact and fancy where so many writers of memoirs have come to grief and where Goethe himself was apt to lose his bearings.

I continued reading for several hours, stopping only when I came to Munthe's account of his journey to Lapland and his description of the Uldra, "the Little People who lived under the earth," who fed bears during their winter hibernation and, if annoyed by human beings, would sometimes steal their children and substitute the Uldra's own. And yet it was the Uldra who bestowed on certain men the shamanic gifts of healing.

The parallel and subterranean social world of the Uldra bore an uncanny resemblance to the world of the Kuranko djinn—capricious and amoral beings that lived beyond the pale of human settlements, a law unto themselves. Djinn embody what one might call natural, wild, or libidinal power. Such power is ambiguous, for it is hard to know whether it will be a good cause (*sabu nyuma*) or a bad cause (*sabu yuge*). One hears plenty of anecdotes about djinn giving a wrestler strength, a dancer grace, a diviner insight, and a musician inspiration, and there are sites associated with djinn in every Kuranko chiefdom, where the unfortunate offer sacrifices of food in the hope that they will be helped, and the fortunate repay the djinn for help received. But an alliance with a djinn often comes at a terrible price. Sometimes, the djinn simply withdraws its favors and disappears. Sometimes, as in European stories of selling one's soul to the devil, such Faustian pacts bring a sordid boon. A djinn that has done you a favor may demand the life of one of your children or kinsmen in return. As the original inhabitants of the land, the djinn may allow human beings to make their farms on condition they make sacrificial offerings at the beginning of each farm season, but even then a djinn may cause a farmer to cut himself with a machete or injure himself with a hoe. A djinn may possess a person, driving him mad or causing fits of delirium. A djinn may appear in a dream in the form of a beautiful woman (succubus) or handsome man (incubus), but the sexual encounter may lead to impotence or barrenness.

In due course I would ask Sewa about the role of the djinn in the Kuranko imaginary, and he would tell me that they figured less in people's lives than they used to. It was a sign of the times. And he made it sound as though the djinn would go the way of the uldra, and of fairies and goblins—remnants of an enchanted world that modernity had rendered superfluous. But though the djinn were exiled to folklore, other antinomian figures replaced them, for the struggle for being continued to involve a struggle between what is simply given to a person—his or her role, temperament (*yugi*), or birthright—and what a person desires, over and above what he or she has or who he or she is. The contrast between town and bush implies a contrast between centripetal and centrifugal forces—the first finding expression in custom and convention, the second in fantasies of what lies beyond what is already established.

To speak of the penumbral is, therefore, to invoke this hazy and indeterminate region between a world where we experience ourselves as actors and a world where we experience ourselves as acted upon. While any social system requires dutiful conformity to ancestral protocols, social life would become empty of meaning unless each person realized in himself or herself the capacity to bring the social world into being. But this capacity draws not only on what is tried and true but on hazardous encounters with extrasocial sources of power—bush spirits, wild places, limit experiences—that lie beyond the pale of what we comprehend and can control.

It is for these reasons that one may draw an analogy between venturing into the wilderness in search of a livelihood or an improvement to one's lot, and migrating to Europe, for both bush and abroad are places of danger where one gains a future only to lose touch with one's past, or ameliorates one's own life only to end up rootless and alone.

Second Skins

There is a Mande proverb, *Ala ma ko kelen da*—God did not create anything single. The implication is that the world is made up of complementary *relationships*—male-female, husband-wife, parent-child, elder-junior, brother-sister, and so forth—not individual entities. The way these relationships are conceived calls to mind Chinese boxes or Matryoshka dolls, since the senior partner, who is symbolically "big," is said to contain, enclose, and protect the junior, who is "small." Being is thus understood relationally, and well-being depends on these vital connections. If they are broken, life is lost.

All this was axiomatic to Sewa, whose existential survival in London so clearly depended on life-giving and confidence-boosting connections with the ancestral dead, as well as his natal community.

Yet migrants are often exhorted to sever attachments to their past—which is identified with the primitive—as well as their extended families back home if they are to achieve "real" citizenship in their adopted homeland. According to this reasoning, it is their mastery of the lingua franca and values of the new world that will guarantee them a future within it.

If only the politicians who make this argument knew what they were asking! If only they knew what it was like to be cast adrift, rudderless in a social environment where one is always on the defensive, struggling either to avoid more than superficial contact with the natives or to pass oneself off as one! If only they realized that Sewa and his cousin Isata, and tens of thousands of people like them, have succeeded in transforming their lives in the first world *because* they "kept their culture," retained vital lifelines with home, and nourished the thought of return.

No one, not even individuals who extol the virtues of self-possession and self-sufficiency, can really go it alone. Not a day passed in London that I did not observe the manifold ways in which people sought to augment, supplement, strengthen, enlarge, or bolster their sense of self—in the clothing they wore, the bodies they built, the apartments and houses they furnished, the cars they drove, the ideologies they embraced, the communities in which they lived, the objects they valued, the friends with whom they hung out and the families to which they were attached, even under the most acrimonious circumstances. And where this enlargement of being was not effected through enveloping objects, ideas, and communities it was sought through the alteration of consciousness—foodstuffs, alcohol, drugs, vertigo, meditation, prayer, and other "techniques of the self." What is ritual, I asked myself, but a way of tapping into the extramundane world in order to augment or make good the degradation of being that accompanies the routines of everyday life?

This question led me to ponder the impact of colonial rule in such places as Africa, New Zealand, and Papua New Guinea, where the colonized, encountering the material wealth and military might of Europeans for the first time, commonly believed their political and economic nullification to be the shameful result of some ancient moral fault that now required ritual redress. With the emergence of cargo cults comes the recasting of traditional myths to explain the radical inequalities between blacks and whites. While some are self-deprecating, others are redemptive, and envision a new moral dispensation based on shared wealth and common humanity. And a recurring motif is that of rebirth, symbolized by the snake that sloughs its old skin and takes on another. Malinowski documented one such myth in his Trobriand ethnography, and the figure of the crippled, ugly, unmarried Tokosikuna who is magically able to change his appearance and make himself young, smooth-skinned, and attractive to women,[23] reappears in Goodenough Island (also part of the kula trading ring) as Honoyeta, who can slough his ugly, abscessed skin and rejuvenate himself, burning as bright as a flame, radiant as the sun. These culture heroes are, however, marginal beings, laws unto themselves, loath to give or share. Honoyeta, for example, is "singular." "Supremely self-contained, asocial and amoral, he is the antithesis of social man who bargains, negotiates, and exchanges in his mundane relations with others."[24]

23. Bronislaw Malinowski, *Argonauts of the Western Pacific* (London: Routledge and Kegan Paul, 1922), 306–11, 322–26.

24. Michael W. Young, *Magicians of Manumanua: Living Myth in Kalauna* (Berkeley: University of California Press, 1983), 73.

And so we come to a paradox: that he who is most capable of trans-forming himself into a new man, as powerful as he is admired, is the least capable of being a man among other men, accepting the time-honored conventions of his society. Which, then, is the real man? The mortal human being, or the one who hides his mortal self behind a mask, bathed in the radiant light of illusion? The question is left un-resolved in the Kalauna myths, even though some people believe that Honoyeta's "real self" is "represented by his beauteous and youthful appearance, while the slough, 'ugly and ridden with sores,' is his dis-guise."[25]

But there is another motif in these Melanesian myths that bears on the experience of migrants everywhere, and that is the power of the dead to transform the lives of the living. This motif is not unconnected to the snake as a symbol of immortality, for, in the social imaginary of Melanesia, the land of the dead is underground.[26] For the migrant, it might be argued, the dead now include all those he has left behind, but on whom he still depends, in the wilderness of the world, for moral strength.

On Not Severing the Vine When Harvesting the Grapes

After completing fieldwork in London, I went to Paris for a few days with my family and, between excursions to tourist sites, completed transcribing the tapes I had made with Sewa. We stayed in an apartment in the 10th arrondissement that belonged to a friend of my wife's, and every morning before walking to a café on the Boulevard Bonne Nou-

25. Ibid., 67.

26. Among the Kaliai of New Britain, the dead were always a vital part of everyday life. "They were accessed continuously, and the gateways to them had to be kept open if life was to remain productive and healthy. To keep the dead close to the living, the dead traditionally were buried beneath men's and women's houses." Today, people still access new magical spells, songs, rituals, and masks through dreams, and through contact with the invisible dead stories and dreams emerge that offer "the potential for a new state of affairs." Andrew Lattas, *Cultures of Secrecy: Reinventing Race in Bush Kaliai Cargo Cults* (Madison: University of Wisconsin Press, 1998), 102, 103.

velle for an espresso I would chat for a while with our *gardien*, M. Lad, who hailed from Benin. He was in his sixties, grizzled like myself, and brimming with energy and wry humor. "Not a year passes," he said, "that I do not go home. One must be careful not to sever the vine when harvesting the grapes."

I would share this adage with Sewa when next I called him, and also something of the conversations I'd had with the young men from Côte d'Ivoire who gathered around the pay phones on rue de Mazagran every evening, to drink beer, swap news, and make palaver. Several clochards slept at night under the wall of the Post Office, and the asphalt stank of urine and bore the stains of spilled wine. A sign on the wall warned *Sous peine d'amende'*: *Défense d'uriner et de deposer des ordures*. Some people sever the vine despite themselves, I thought, and my mind went back to London and all the lost souls I had encountered years ago, in the course of my winter in welfare work, for whom hearth and home had meant not solace but pain, not to mention the embittered expatriates I had met through Sewa who spoke of Africa and England in the same breath, as wastelands that offered one nothing.

One day, I located, in a small park near Les Halles, the lane named for my favorite French writer, Blaise Cendrars, and sat for a while to scribble down the explanatory inscription on the plaque (*Frédéric Sauser dit poète et écrivain*). A guy walked by wearing a T-shirt that said "Vodka Connecting People." And when I wandered off toward the Église Sainte Eustace, I passed a babbling fountain in which a clochard was washing his face. He had parked his supermarket chariot nearby, crammed with grimy clothing and a battered copy of Céline's *Mort-à-Credit*.

Reeling from these synchronicities, I headed south toward the Hô-tel Notre Dame, made famous by Cendrars's poems, where I had arranged to meet my wife and daughter after their sightseeing trip to the cathedral. The streets were thronged with tourists and I was consoled by the thought that many of them found no more sense of connection or satisfaction than I did in the ruins, cathedrals, palaces, museums, and tombs to which they had been inspired to make their pilgrimages. For it seemed to me that the tourist too often expects a place to move her, whereas the resident, whose life has unfolded over many years in the shadows of ancient walls, towers, and tenements, has inadvertently imparted to them a personal meaning that is experienced as a property of the place itself. While the casual visitor is often confounded by the gap between what she believed she would find and what she actually experiences, as well as disappointed in her inability to give this foreign vista any biographical value, the local, who has hardly noticed the history in whose shade she lives, revitalizes this history in everything she says and does.

I found a table on the *terrasse*, and ordered a citron pressé. My senses were so alive that I felt compelled to take notes in an attempt to calm down or, by externalizing everything that I observed, divine its significance. So I described the cast iron table, the aluminum rim around the round, green bakelite top, the rattan chairs, the hubbub of conversation, the clatter of plates, the rumbling of traffic along the *quai*, buzzing mopeds, beeping horns, until it suddenly occurred to me that the past is nothing but an abstraction. There was no real connection or continuity between me and this *quartier* as Chrétien de Troyes or Blaise Cendrars had known it. It was simply now, *profound aujourd'hui*, open to my life and the lives of those around me.

Nowhere contradicted this spirit of free-flowing life more than my visit, the following afternoon, to the newly completed Musée du Quai Branly, also known as the Musée des Arts Premiers. After walking several blocks from the Invalides metro, my wife and daughter and I found ourselves beside a high plate glass wall, beyond which tufts of grass and ferns had been planted. The building, my daughter Freya said, looked like a caterpillar.

Entering it, the first objects one encounters are thousands of wooden musical instruments, shelved, stored, or hanging in meticulous arrays within a curved glass cage. These relics bear a disturbing family resemblance to the hanks of human hair and heaps of footwear you see on entering Auschwitz, and as we moved up the ramp into the body of the museum I wondered if it had been intended that one should see one's own image in the reflecting glass, together with the objects behind it — a visual image of the dissociation of subject and object in European thought, and a sobering reminder of the ways in which we are now doomed to prey conceptually on the decontextualized and insensate things that our forebears tore from lifeworlds in Asia, Africa, and the Americas, along with the slaves, spices, and minerals that made them rich. Or is it that we are simply blind to our own historical relationship with the Other, with whom we still cannot connect as a coeval — as ourselves under other circumstances — but only in terms of the things they made, things we now secret away and study or make sacrosanct yet without a moment's thought for those who gave these objects life?

The first thing we smelled was fiber matting. The first thing we heard was an eerie wind, mingled with vague rummaging and tinkling sounds, as we ascended a curving ramp through sunlit spaces. But the collections were in silence and semidarkness, along sinewy passageways lined with leather-covered walls that evoked the adobe dwellings of Timbuktu or Mopti. You had to strain your eyes to read the signs, such as they were, and the colors evoked earth ochers, potsherds, the underground, or the unconscious—something alien and primitive that one withheld from the light of day. I was reminded of the nocturnal house in a zoo where you peer into dark glass-fronted enclosures in an attempt to discern the bats, kiwis, or night owls. There was scarcely any information on an object's function, and scant effort to separate regions. One moment you were in Oceania, the next in Africa or Amazonia.

The Maori objects in particular unsettled me. Collected in the nineteenth century, these carved house posts, lintels, canoe balers, prows, feather boxes, and weapons gave no hint as to their origins. The labels simply read "Gift of" or "Collection of"—as if the European donors deserved more recognition than the Maori carvers or people to whom these things belonged. I gazed at a greenstone *hei tiki* from the "ancienne collection du roi Charles X," placed on a feather cloak behind glass, and its mournful face and red-rimmed eyes stared back at me as if imploring me to free it from its prison and take it home. As for the pointillist canvases from Central Australia, their subtle surfaces were despoiled by multicolored splotches of light from a nearby stained-glass window. As if to rub in the travesty, a "music box" a few feet away, on whose walls were projected images of dancers from somewhere in Papua New Guinea or Brazil, broadcast the sound of chanting and of drums, as if everything in the museum was all of a piece—emanations of a primeval and timeless otherness to which our only connection was aesthetic.

What bothered me, more than the willful erasure of the lifeworlds in which these objects were fashioned and used, or the greater reverence we sometimes seem to have for things than persons, was the question as to how I was to do justice to my experiences as an ethnographer. I had always eschewed anthropological generalizations and jargons as artificial, comparing them to the light that falls on the masks in ethno-graphic museums, and preferred to celebrate the light that shines forth from the thing itself in its natural context rather than presume to illu-minate it with a light whose source was foreign. There was hardly a passage in Sewa's story that could not be elaborated in terms of cur-rent anthropological theories of transmigration and globalization, yet I clung to the view that the painstaking description of life as it was lived would reveal, at least for an attentive reader, more than my clumsy annotations could.

Corrupted Con-texts

I wrote the foregoing lines a few days after reading, in the *New York Times*, of what Lydia Polgreen and Marlise Simons call "a dark tale of globalization." Four hundred tons of highly toxic petrochemical waste and caustic soda, originating somewhere in Europe, was shipped to the Ivory Coast and secretly offloaded into tanker trucks which then dumped the waste in 128 landfills across the city of Abidjan. Children searching for scraps of aluminum to sell, and people living near the dumps, succumbed to nausea, headaches, skin sores, and nosebleeds. Eight people were already dead and 85,000 had been treated for expo-sure to the lethal chemicals. "Africa has long been a dumping ground for all sorts of things the developed world has no use for," wrote the authors of the *Times* article,[27] prompting me to ask whether the con-nection between our indifference to the lives of Africa's poor and the privileges we enjoy in the affluent societies of the north, including the luxury of marveling at African art objects without having to actually encounter Africa, was something I posited for polemical purposes or something real? And what on earth could one do to prevent such in-justices?

In searching for answers to these questions, I returned to Sewa's and Isata's stories, and their quest for a way of making their way in a world that often bars your entry or treats you like shit.

In his campaign to safeguard the Magbas' position in Diang, Sewa had

27. "Global Sludge Ends in Tragedy for Ivory Coast," *New York Times*, Oct. 2, 2006, 1, 8.

approached the most powerful Northern Province politician, Presidential Affairs Minister Sheku Sisay. "I phoned him up," Sewa said. "He knew I was calling from overseas. He said, 'Eh England man, when are you coming?' because he knows what you are going to ask and he tries to throw you, not talk about the thing you want to talk to him about. So he put me on hold for ten minutes. After that, the phone just cut off, you see? You go to these people, they will smile at you . . . I've seen the way they do things. I've been with my uncle S. B., so I know. They don't want to talk to you, they'll put you on hold, make you wait, tell you to come back at a time they're not going to be there, so I know those things. I rang my mother. I said, 'Forget about Sheku, he is not with us.' You have to be like the ram in my dream. When it's going to fight, it backs up first to get strength, to get force before it runs and head butts the other one. So you have to go home first and organize, to get the strength to fight. Then you come, and you'll succeed."

"So that's what you meant by getting everyone together, making the sacrifice in Kondembaia, joining forces?" I said.

"Yes, that's it."

But Sewa had also emphasized the power of the ancestors and of God, and I pressed him to explain how one struck a balance between prayer and political action.

Sewa responded with a Kuranko adage—there is a lot of water in this world, but the water you drink is meant for you alone. "In this struggle for the staff, it is important that I am in London right now, earning money, supporting the family. That is my destiny. But one day, when the moment is right, I will go home. You see, you have to do what you have to do, and be patient that things will work out. Like with the cinema job, I could see that the supervisor was not hard working. He would phone me in the morning, say 'Oh Sewa, I can't make it, can you go and cover my shift?' I would say 'Yeah, no problem.' Then, come to the summer, he went to Kent and saw his girl-friend, and Kent is far from Wandsworth, so he phoned me and asked if I would do his shift as well as my own. So I knew that one day this fellow would be sacked. It was just a matter of time. And I was waiting, waiting. Even if it had taken two or three years I would still have waited, because I knew definitely that if he went I would be the next supervisor, you see. You have to know what you're doing in life, you have to get focus."

Sewa was far from advocating a fatalistic or thoughtless philosophy.

"When people do things or say things, you have to think twice, think why, why they're doing this, is it because of this? I'm young. I've got to think that even if the [Diang] chief lived a long life or I die, I have kids coming up, and if I have access to the chieftaincy they might be interested, you know. People don't write history, they don't write things down. You have to remember everything. We say, *i tole kina i bimba ko* [your ear is as wise as your grandfather's words]. When my father was young he was listening to the elders talk about things that happened long before his time. Then he told me those stories, and I will tell them to my son. They're not written down, but if you listen you will know them. Those are the things you have to think about, that you have to know deep down. Ade says, 'You think too much,' but I tell her there are things you have to think about, things beyond normal, so that you'll know."

The Broken Heart

Exactly a month after seeing Sewa and Ade in London, and on the same day that the first photos of my grandson Nico arrived in the mail, I received an e-mail from Ade's sister, Sarah.

> Ade has suffered complications in her pregnancy. This began last week when her waters broke, which of course was a major worry because she had only just passed the five-month mark. She was taken to hospital where she has been since. Doctors and midwives had been monitoring her as although this happened it didn't seem the baby was ready to come out. They advised that if she lasted until Monday they would be able to provide some medication that would strengthen the baby's lungs so that it would have a better chance of survival if she gave birth. Ade went into labour very late last night and sadly the baby was not strong enough and has died. They wanted me to tell you it was a boy. As you can imagine they are both devastated. Sewa had kept a constant vigil at her bedside and we the family were visiting daily.

My eyes blurred with tears. I cried out in protest. I thought of Sewa speaking Kuranko to his unborn son, singing his songs to him in the womb, his faith in God and the ancestors, their blessings and watchfulness. I thought back to when my daughter Heidi was born in Freetown thirty-six years ago, and of the diviner whom I had consulted months before, who assured me everything would be well if I made sacrifices of white cloth to people I respected. I made the sacrifices, and all had been well. Sewa had made his, only to have this tragedy befall him.

I walked out into the unseasonably warm mid-September night. Cicadas were stitching in the depths of the garden, but I could not countenance sleep, my soul bruised by what had happened to Sewa and Ade, memories of my own years of grief making me want, unreasonably but desperately, to keep those I loved from this anguish of loss, yet aware that life for us all will include such devastation.

I called the following morning, and Ade answered the phone. She spoke of the faith in God she shared with Sewa, and how it would carry them through this terrible time. Given the confidence that Sewa had drawn from his many sacrifices and prayers, I had half expected that he and Ade would now conclude that God had betrayed their trust, or was unworthy of it. I should have known better. I should have known that when tragedy overtakes us, we do not interrogate our beliefs to see if they hold up to intellectual scrutiny; we turn to something or someone more solid than ourselves—a landscape, an individual that embodies some higher power—the better to get some distance from our grief, to grasp our situation from afar, to reorient our lives. I asked Ade if she had anyone she could talk to, a counselor perhaps at the hospital. The midwives had offered to come to her house, she said, but she did not feel like talking to them. She had withdrawn. She didn't feel like seeing or talking to anyone. "What about Sewa?" I asked.

"He is obsessively cleaning the apartment all the time," Ade said.

When I talked to Sewa, I mentioned the book I was writing, its twinned themes of connectedness and crisis, and how important our conversations in London had been in helping me get this book under way. When Sewa expressed an avid interest in seeing what I had written, I promised to send him my first thirty pages, rough as they were, inviting him to correct or elaborate on anything that did not ring true. Sewa and Ade were going to be staying at Ade's parents' house for a week or ten days, Sewa said. I could e-mail him there at any time. He wanted to tell me more about the Kondembaia story. If it were possible he would return home, but in the meantime he would go home in his mind.

A week later I talked to Sewa on the phone, and asked him what changes I needed to make to the pages I had sent him. Sewa mentioned a few minor factual errors, but what he mostly wanted me to know was how gratifying he found it that I should refer to him as "my friend Sewa," because in my earlier book, *In Sierra Leone*, researched and written when Sewa was working in Freetown as his uncle S. B.'s general factotum, a mere underling at the beck and call of his superiors and despairing of ever realizing any ambition of his own, he had been "small S. B." Now that his uncle S. B. was dead, he could emerge as a political figure in his own right, and be called Sewa Magba, named for his father and not his uncle. Finally he was recognized as the person he really was.

The same week that Sewa and Ade suffered their terrible loss, I happened to be rereading Wallace Stevens's "An Ordinary Evening in New Haven."

> We keep coming back and coming back
> To the real: to the hotel instead of the hymns
> That fall upon it out of the wind . . .

Reflecting on Stevens's beautiful exhortations to seek "the poem of pure reality, / untouched by trope or deviation," going "straight to the transfixing object, / to the object at the exactest point at which it is itself," I knew that reality, for me, lay *between* the hotel and the hymn, on the borderland or threshold *between* bush and town, earth and ether, and at the points where the visible gives ground to the invisible, one season succeeding another like the phases of our lives, the transition from womb to world, existence to nothingness, presence to absence. When Sewa described in phone calls to me the way that he and Ade were coping with their loss, or how the poor in Freetown struggled to keep body and soul together in the face of appalling want, I was brought back to the notion of limit situation in which, as Gillian Rose wrote in her dying days, "a crisis of illness, bereavement, separation, natural disaster, could be the opportunity to make contact with deeper levels of the terrors of the soul, to loose and to bind, to bind and to loose."[28] But the fact remains that moments of existential peril not only open up the possibility of an awakening or rebirth; they are destructive, alienating, and shocking.

28. Gillian Rose, *Love's Work: A Reckoning with Life* (New York: Schocken Books, 1995), 105.

The reason I find little satisfaction in Jacques Lacan's notion of "the real" as a natural state from which we have been forever severed by our entrance into language is because the burning questions for me are not whether it makes sense to speak of a life before language or whether we accept the logocentric view that all experience can be put into words, but rather how we salvage, affirm, compromise, or lose our humanity in the face of catastrophic interruptions to the routines that reinforce our ordinary sense of "normal" existence.[29] Nor am I interested in intellectual efforts to link divinity to some ontologically distinct realm, for the real and the religious mark ambiguous borderlands, not bounded domains—disorienting moments when we feel compelled to speak, but words fail us, and though desperate for understanding, find ourselves lost for words. History, religion, spirituality, culture are shopworn terms, devalued and dulled by the tasks we have assigned to them, the meanings we have made them carry. I prefer the image of life at the edge of language, a shoreline on which the sea washes ceaselessly, shaping and reshaping the coastal littoral, adding and subtracting, exposing and covering—a tidal zone where neither rocky foreshore nor waves holds sway. Ordinary language mires us in language. It is "just words." But great writing, poetic writing, stretches language to the limit and points beyond, helping refresh "life so that we share, / For a moment, the first idea . . ."[30] This is why I like to think that this late meditation of a man who went to Harvard but never graduated, who never left America, and wound up president of the Hartford Accident and Indemnity Company, bears comparison with Gloria Anzaldúa's outline of a *mestiza* consciousness that arises at the "juncture . . . where phenomena collide,"[31] as well as with the classical Greek figure of Hermes—god of the borderlands—and Kuranko images of those times and places where the daylight of ordinary consciousness gives way to night, and the wilderness, unsettling, entrancing, hazardous, and strange, begins.

29. The real "remains foreclosed from the analytic experience, which is an experience of speech." It "may be approached, but never grasped. The real is the impossible." From "Translator's Note," Jacques Lacan, *Écrits: A Selection*, trans. Alan Sheridan (New York: W. W. Norton, 1977), ix-x.

30. Stevens, "Notes Toward a Supreme Fiction," in *Collected Poems* (London: Faber and Faber, 1955), 382.

31. Gloria Anzaldúa, *Borderlands/La Frontera* (San Francisco: Aunt Lute Books, 1999), 101.

Incarnations

"No life is sufficient unto itself. A person is singular only in the sense in which astronomers use the term: a relative point in space and time where invisible forces become fleetingly visible. Our lives belong to others as well as to ourselves. Just as the stars at night are set in imperceptible galaxies, so our lives flicker and fail in the dark streams of history, fate, and genealogy. One might say that we are each given three lives. First is our conscious incarnation, occupying most of the space between our birth and death. Second is our existence in the hearts and minds of others—a life that precedes the moment of our birth and extends beyond our death for as long as we are remembered. Finally there is our afterlife as a barely recognized name, a persona, a figure in myth. And this existence begins with the death of the last person who knew us in life."[1]

When I wrote these lines I was thinking of my maternal grandfather. After a long career as a police constable, first in Yorkshire, then in New Zealand, Fred retired in 1943 and in good weather would spend much of the day in his garden or sitting outside his potting shed, smoking his pipe, lost in thought. If he was forced indoors by rain or cold, he would read novels by A. J. Cronin or Thomas Armstrong, nostalgic for the England in which he came of age, or peruse the *Taranaki Herald* from cover to cover before using the advertising pages as a surface on which to cut and rub his plug tobacco. After filling his tobacco pouch,

1. Michael Jackson, *Minima Ethnographica: Intersubjectivity and the Ethnographic Project* (Chicago: University of Chicago Press, 1997), 137.

he would switch on the wireless to catch the six o'clock news. I can see him now, twiddling with bakelite knobs of the Gulbransen cabinet radio that stood in the corner of the dining room, a pale orange light illuminating its iconic brass clipper ship and suggesting to my young mind that the static through which we heard John Arlott's commentary on the Ashes test at Lords was caused by the surge of ocean waves. On weekends or school holidays I would sit for hours with my grandfather outside his potting shed "down below," and in the afternoons keep him company in the front room of the house among the dark-stained wooden mantelpiece and furniture that my grandmother's brother had carved as a wedding gift for her. Around us hung the watercolors, painted by another of my grandmother's brothers, of the Yorkshire moors and the border town of Todmorden that connected the exiles to the place they still called home. Often as not, my grandfather and I would sit in silence. If we were "down below" I would listen to the river talking to itself as it stumbled over graywacke stones on its way to the oblivion of the sea, or watch white butterflies flap fragile and haphazard above the cabbages. I remember the warmth of the day, wizened seed potatoes spread out on superphosphate sacks to sprout, the smell of blood and bone, the musical lisp and chirrup of a tui, and the babble of the river—background to the stories my grandfather shared with me. His reminiscences become part of my own life, shaping my notions of history, identity, and ethics. Indeed, so deeply did his stories seep into my unconscious that even now, fifty-five years later, I feel as though his life is continuous with mine—the Halifax woolen mill where he went to work at age ten, Houdini's visit to the Halifax police station where he was stationed, his refusal to arrest and baton-charge poor protesters because he understood the justice of their cause, his decision to emigrate to New Zealand, his reluctant return to policing, and his lifelong commitment to protecting the dignity of all men, regardless of the crimes and misdemeanors they may have committed. In keeping alive his stories, I have kept him alive, kept him from vanishing into that penumbral region of myth where facts begin to be fudged or forgotten, where our sense of chronology becomes blurred, where space becomes unreal and the imagination rehashes everything according to its own promiscuous persuasions.

This gap between remembered and mythical time exists in all societies, whether literate or not, because even when written records preserve a partial memory of the past they cannot recall for us a sense of how that past was lived. Of the Nuer of the southern Sudan, E. E. Evans-Pritchard remarked in 1940 that the names of ancestors are lost after five or six generations,[2] which means that "valid history ends a century ago."[3] "How shallow is Nuer time," he writes, "may be judged from the fact that the tree under which mankind came into being was still standing in Western Nuerland a few years ago."[4]

I encountered something similar in my work among the Warlpiri of Central Australia. Though many non-Aborigines believe the "dream-time" refers to primordial events, it is in fact no more distant from the world of the living than the Nuer Eden. Since personal names are put out of circulation when a person dies and all trace of that person ritually swept away for a generation, the mythopoeic field of the Dreaming begins in the immediate past and is, strictly speaking, no more ancient, ancestral, or mythical than the world in which one's parents lived and died. Even so, one can only access the Dreaming and find one's bearings there if one knows the places where one's parents and grandparents were conceived, born, initiated, and passed away. Not to be able to trace these connections leaves one estranged.

Consider the case of Jangala, for example—a man I never got to know well, yet whose muddled origins reminded me obliquely of my own.

My wife and I were working in the Aboriginal settlement of Laja-manu at the time, trying to identify the groups that had rightful claims to royalty money from a gold mine at a place called the Granites. In the company of other middle-aged men, Jangala would boldly draw lines in the dirt to mark the boundaries of Warnayaka—the central area of the Tanami desert in which the gold mine was located. Sometimes the four "corners" of the block would be marked by sticks stuck in the ground, and I would be confidently told that all those born within the boundaries of the block had claims to royalty money, while Ngarliya people (by implication, people from the distant settlement of Yuendumu) had none.

The older men did not disguise their contempt for what they clearly saw as a non-Aboriginal picture of territoriality. "Don't you listen to

2. E. E. Evans-Pritchard, *The Nuer: A Description of the Modes of Livelihood and Political Institutions of a Nilotic People* (Oxford: Clarendon Press, 1940), 199.

3. Ibid., 108.

4. Ibid.

them," Zack Jakamarra insisted. "They don't know. They fibbing. They never walked around that country. They sit here, this Lajamanu. Just because they talk well . . ."

Zack's picture of the Tanami could not have been different. Where the younger men inscribed boundaries, the older men drew circles in the sand as they recited ancestral travels, and connected these sites with lines to signify the traveling tracks. And when they spoke of belonging they referred not just to lines of descent but networks and skeins of relationship that bound different groups together in alliances through marriage (*jurdalja*), adoptive and cognatic kinship, and ritual affiliation. Apart from the people who called a place "father" (the *kirda*, or "traditional owners" of a site), many other people were implicated in any site, and these negotiated ties, variously called *ngurrara jinta, kuruwarri jinta*, or *warlalja* (one mob), made it impossible to define unequivocal and binding principles of identity and nonidentity, inclusion and exclusion.

Jangala must have realized that I was setting little store by what he was telling me. As if trying another tack, he turned up at my camp one day and started talking to me about his origins.

His mother, Napangardi, hailed from Yawurluwurlu, a yam Dreaming site. She had been promised to a certain Jampijinpa who already had many wives. One day, in a jealous rage, several other men killed this Jampijinpa near Paraluyu and took his wives. Napangardi now married the man who would become Jangala's father. But Jangala never knew his name. He knew only the names of his mother's parents, and that his father was *kirda* for Pirtipirti and had passed away at a place called Parntapurru.[5] As a boy, Jangala had been told he was conceived at Pirtipirti (Thomson's Rockhole), the evidence being his "crippled" arms and the lesions on his skin that replicated the wounds suffered by a Dreaming ancestor in a fight with an interloper there. He was born at Wardilyka, to the east of Pirtipirti.

I suspected that Jangala's story might be a ruse for claiming a cut of the royalty money from the Granites on the dubious basis of his

5. Though the names of the dead are put out of circulation for a generation, people often refer to them in terms of the places where the individuals passed away. Thus Parntapurru-wana (literally, Parntapurru-alongside) signifies the place Jangala's father died and is a circumlocution for his name. As Jangala remarked, "We bin lose 'im, right alonga Parntapurru."

father being *kirda* for a place in the general geographical area, and on the strength of his having been conceived in that same country. Insisting that people were wrong in saying his father came from Balgo or Mount Barkly, Jangala told me, "Lots of people are trying to push us away." Then he added, "Our mother's family came from Yawurluwurlu," as if to suggest this also gave him rights at the Granites.

Then he digressed again. Now he was at pains to point out how he was genealogically linked to an age-mate, Jupurrurla, a man who had considerable clout in Lajamanu and was already receiving royalty payments from the Granites. It was a confused story, the main point of which seemed to be to emphasize that Jupurrurla's father had affinal ties with Pirtipirti.

Finally, as if to clinch everything, Jangala assured me that no one was really *kirda* for the Granites. In the past, no one lived there. There wasn't enough water. People only went there to gather wild tobacco.

Next day I was sitting with Zack and some other older men in the shade of some snappy gums near the football oval. When I told Zack what Jangala had told me, Zack dismissed Jangala's stories out of hand. The truth was, Zack said, that Jangala's father came from Mount Barkly. Jangala had been born in the Pirtipirti area, but as for his father, "No name. He bin finish in the bush." Speaking of the Granites, Zack stressed that there were *kirda* for the place, there was water there, and people did camp there.

A few days later I found Jangala eating "damper" with his girlfriend at a windbreak of corrugated iron outside the *jilimi*. I told him Zack had cast serious doubt on his stories.

Jangala did not argue with this. He confessed he had spent a lot of time trying to find out who his father was and where his father's country was located. It had been Jupurrurla who had urged him to play up his matrilineal roots. Older men like Zack had told him he could not claim royalty money on that basis.

"It must be tough not to have a place you can call home," I said.

Sadly, he agreed. All his life he had been looking for his father.

"What of the father who grew you up?" I asked, meaning the man who had seen him through his initiation.

It was old blind Jampijinpa, gangling and gap-toothed, whom Jimmy Jangala led about by the hand. When Jangala was still a small boy, Jampijinpa had married his mother, Napangardi. He accompanied them to the Granites. Later on he lived in Yuendumu and, finally, Lajamanu, where he and his brother took the name of the *kardiya* (European) boss for whom they worked there.

"But," said Jangala ruefully, "I cannot trace my descent to him or to my stepfather. It has to be your real father."

The Matrixial

It was an Indian summer: Michaelmas daisies growing wild along the roadside, pine needles falling, the maples turning russet in the woods. There were fresh apples in a ceramic bowl on the table, and after the exertions of August I succumbed to the languor of the unseasonably warm days.

It was around this time that an old friend of mine, René Devisch, came to Harvard to participate in a symposium entitled "Sites of Memory in Africa." René had happily accepted my invitation to stay in our house, and in the course of our conversation, which seemed to flow on unbroken from where we had left it in Copenhagen almost two years earlier, I told René a little about Sewa's story, and how it had led me to explore the ways in which our lives are embedded in genealogical time. I was particularly fascinated by the fact that while the past continually reappears in our present lives, shaping our destinies, it remains largely beyond our comprehension and control, and we glimpse it, if we glimpse it all, as we might glimpse a specter, fitfully and in fragments. I was thinking, for example, of the criminal excesses of Mamadu Sandi that had led to the Ferenkes' loss of chiefly power, and how two generations later, Sewa's brother Sheku Magba had repeated the mistakes of his forebear and placed in jeopardy *his* lineage's hold on high office. I was also thinking of my own identification with my maternal grandfather, and how, when I wrote my first novel, *Rainshadow*—inevitably a bildungsroman and family saga—I collapsed the generations, so that the protagonist's father is killed in the war and his mother mysteriously disappears, leaving this bewildered child to be raised by his grandparents and struggling to break the conspiracy of silence that surrounds the identity of his ghostly parents. In the orphaning of this child, the grandparents' loss of the "old country" is recapitulated, and this theme of traumatic disconnection was one to which I had returned many times in my writing, as if my own sense of not belonging repeated the alienation my grandfather felt as a young man in a country that offered the poor so few opportunities and begrudged them access to education, healthcare, and a decent living wage.

I was curious to know what René had to say about this systole and diastole of history, its hidden rhythms and repetitions—the rebirth or reappearance of certain traits after a generation in which they seemed forgotten or lost—and I mentioned, as other examples, my wife's frequent comments on the uncanny ways in which our son Joshua seemed to embody her father's mannerisms, though Frank had died many years before Joshua was born, and the recurrence in every generation of my own family of a maverick who turns his or her back on home and settles elsewhere. I told René that whenever I sought to explain this kind of phenomenon, I had recourse to the Kuranko notion of *sabu nyuma* or "good cause" that alludes to the ways in which a significant predecessor or mentor clears a path for us, enabling us to realize certain possibilities in life that were hitherto closed. Or I would fall back on the Warlpiri dialectic of presence (*palka*) and absence (*lawa*)—the mysterious way that experiences, events, and even personality traits lie dormant for a generation only to reemerge in dream, and are then drawn out and reanimated in dance, replayed in the telling of a myth, or reincarnated in a newborn child. Was this what Michel Serres speaks of as topological or "folded time," in which chronologically or geographically distant events come into conjunction within consciousness?[6] Or similar to the relatively unexplored "space between" events that produces the phenomenon Nietzsche called "eternal recurrence"? Could one address these questions without the kind of moral bias that sees the past as a shadow, our parent's unresolved struggles left for us to address, or the iniquities of our fathers visited "upon the children to the third and fourth generation"? And could one also avoid the reductionism in science that argues that the phylogenetic imperatives of selfish genes or selfless memes outweigh the imperatives of individual existence? Could one simply affirm and celebrate, without any moral or epistemological judgment, that the life that flows through us is always more than the life we identify as ours?

Fortunately, my stream of questions resonated with issues that René had been reflecting upon for many years, and he recounted how his

6. Michael Serres with Bruno Latour, *Conversations on Science, Culture, and Time*, trans. Roxanne Lapidus (Ann Arbor: University of Michigan Press, 1995), 64, 70.

initial experiences of fieldwork among the Yaka of southwest Congo in 1971 evoked memories of his childhood on a farm close to the border between Belgium and France and only a few miles from the coast. René's awareness of occupying a borderland, a space of indeterminacy and transgression, was intensified by the everyday switching between Flemish and French and the regional traffic in contraband that embroiled his family.

In the Congo he again experienced the confusion of being on the seashore, fearing the submergence of his identity in "an indefinable and massive otherness." And yet, René was also enthralled by the prospect of being swept away and immersed in something so completely new, "like high tide washing over you as you lie on the beach." Then a strange thing happened. Only ten days after arriving in the village of Yitaanda, the maternal uncle of the ailing Taanda chief begged René, on behalf of the chief, for medicines. His intervention was to no avail, and when the chief died the community was plunged into mourning and plagued by fears that with no ruler to hold together the fabric of the social world it would be torn apart by thunderbolts and predatory leopards. Yet people were mindful of having seen René at the bedside of the dying chief soon after a lightning bolt burned the house of his successor to the ground, and a delegate from one of the highest-ranking lineages argued that René was the reincarnation of the late chief's predecessor, who had been ostracized by the colonial authorities in 1939 for having been active in a millenarian cult and died in exile at Oshwe, in the Lake Region to the northeast of Bundundu. René now found himself received into the Taanda community as an ancestor reborn, and seen as possessing the powers to settle dynastic disputes and divert evil or danger. The irony of his bearing the name "René," literally 'the reborn,' had not, it seemed, entered into his hosts' thinking.

René went on to speak of how the Yaka believe that a person's health (-kola) and well-being (-syaamuna) depends on his or her vital relationship with a web of forces (mooyi) that includes kin and community, as well as realms that are largely inaccessible and inexpressible — the world of witchcraft and sorcery, of strangers and spirits, and of the dead. In his recent writing, René had adopted Brache Ettinger's concepts of the matrixial and borderlinking to theorize this intersubjective flow of emotions, thoughts, and intuitions between oneself and the world beyond oneself. "Matrix," Ettinger writes, "is an unconscious borderspace of simultaneous co-emergence and co-fading of the I and an unrecognized *non-I*,"[7] and this echoed the Yaka worldview, René said, since it assumed that the source of life is ultimately maternal, and the most critical relationships in a person's life are with his or her uterine kin. For Yaka, ill health is a sign of blockage or confusion in the interplay of forces that link inside and outside, or self and other. Hence, healing is a matter of reweaving or re-sourcing this lost connection between the individual and the wider field of being of which he or she is vitally and necessarily a part.

That agnatic descent was also important for the Yaka, I knew from René's published ethnography,[8] but this was not what René wanted to emphasize. Against the phallic principle of uprightness, straightness, dominance, containment, and order, René wanted to give full due to the uterine principle of sympathetic attunement, sensual openness, union, and flow.

As René talked, I found myself thinking of my own father, closing the shutters at the bank where he worked before walking home with me, or exhorting me to tidy up my toys, clean up my mess, and how, by contrast, my mother always seemed more fascinated with the world beyond the confines of our own home.

"It is always discursively difficult," I said to René, "to include in any account of a person's life, *all* the connections that bear upon his or her destiny," and I broached the question of how our relations with grandparents complement our relations with parents, just as our relations with our fathers and their families complement our relations with our mothers and theirs. This led to a conversation about the mystery of why, in societies all over the world, three generations are central to a person's being-in-the-world and how, in his ethnography of the Tallensi of northern Ghana, Meyer Fortes wrote of the "equivalence of alternate generations" in Africa, where grandparents and grandchildren not only share the same name but joke together as though they were familiars.[9] "I have always thought," I remarked to René, "that Lévi-

7. Brache Lichtenberg Ettinger, "Trans-Subjective Transferential Borderspace," in *A Shock to Thought: Expression after Deleuze and Guattari*, ed. Brian Massumi (London: Routledge, 2002), 223.

8. René Devisch, *Weaving the Threads of Life: The* Khita *Gyn-Eco-Logical Healing Cult among the Yaka* (Chicago: University of Chicago Press, 1993), 115.

9. Meyer Fortes, *The Web of Kinship among the Tallensi* (London: Oxford University Press, 1949), 239.

Strauss's notion of the 'atom of kinship' downplays relations between predecessors and successors in order to emphasize the significance of the affinal link between *contemporaries*, and this is a blind spot in his work." But as we talked on, it became clear that for René and me the inadequacy of structural analysis lay less in its attempt to correlate different kinds of relationship within the family (patrilineal and matrilineal descent, and siblingship)[10] with different kinds of affect (+ and −) than with its failure to explore how relationships are played out over time — the oscillation, for instance, between the centrifugal forces within a generation (manifest in sibling rivalry and Oedipal tensions) and the centripetal forces that bring nonadjacent generations together, an oscillation that one may also observe among the first three generations of migrant families as well as other families, my own included, where my mother questioned her parents' values at great personal cost while I bonded with them so deeply that I felt greater kinship with my mother's father than with my own. By the same token, what one generation fails to accomplish another may realize, and what is thwarted in reality may be realized in fantasy and dream.

The light was now beginning to fade, and we fell silent, sitting at the pinewood table in our dining room, the uncurtained windows affording us a view of the garden where, at that moment, two cardinals were flitting through the cedars before alighting on the bird feeder.

A Letter from Athens

A few days after René's departure, and while I was still mulling over the things we had discussed so fervently in Lexington, I received an e-mail from another old friend whom I had first met in the south of France in 1983 at a time when Sofka was a student of anthropology at Cambridge and I was enjoying a year on a literary fellowship, writing *Rainshadow*. The correspondence that followed our fortuitous meeting, and has continued to this day, was born, initially, of a common interest in reconciling literary and anthropological sensibilities, as well as my yearning to forge new friendships in the wake of my first wife's death.

10. Claude Lévi-Strauss, *Structural Anthropology*, vol. 1, trans. Claire Jacobson and Brooke Grundfest Schoepf (New York: Basic Books, 1963), 72, 46.

But other affinities came to light over the years, including our similarly deep identifications with our grandparents and our fascination with what Sofka calls "disreputable genealogical destiny."[11] Sofka was now embarking on the last chapter of her book about her grandmother and namesake, whose privileged childhood in tsarist St. Petersburg was followed by years of exile and upheaval, including four years in a Nazi camp at Vittel where her courage and resourcefulness helped saved fifty Jewish refugees from certain death. Loath to end the story of her grandmother's life on a depressing note, with a catalogue of the "infirmities of old age, stinking bathrooms, aching joints," Sofka was struggling to keep in focus her grandmother's other preoccupations in her final years — the Holocaust, her second husband, Grey Skipwith (who was killed in 1942 while flying with the RAF), the Russian and English poetry that had sustained her in Vittel, and her childhood in prerevolutionary Russia. Knowing what a fine writer Sofka was, I felt sure that a solution to her problem would soon present itself. But in writing to her in this vein, I suddenly found myself remembering my mother, who, despite the amputation of her leg when she was in her seventies and the crippling arthritic pain she suffered all her life, never ceased to affirm that well-being was a matter of accepting both hardship and joy with equanimity. "So the fact that your grandmother remembers an internment camp and her lover in the same breath," I wrote to Sofka, "seems to confirm that the most terrible and the most beautiful are often married in life, like light and shadow, and the real cannot be reduced to a single dimension of being."

After sending my e-mail I went to my filing cabinet and took out the journal my mother began writing when she was seventy-three and kept until her death ten years later.

Emily's Journal

Thirteen years had passed since Emily's death, yet in all this time I had not read what she had intended to be, in part, a testimony to her children. I had assumed that deciphering her not always legible longhand

11. Sofka Zinovieff, *Red Princess: A Revolutionary Life* (London: Granta Books, 2007), 197.

would not repay the effort, or that I would learn nothing that I did not already know. I was wrong. Not only did I find a narrative that was remarkable in its own right; I discovered new things about myself. This was not simply because we had both been raised in the same provincial town and attended the same schools (and were taught by two of the same teachers). So deeply were we shaped by similar influences that I experienced myself as her coeval and contemporary. This conflation of the generations undoubtedly reflected the snail's pace of change in Inglewood over the thirty-one years between 1919 (when Emily was ten) and 1950 (when I was ten), a rate of change that contrasted dramatically with the town's transformations in the thirty years after 1950, when people began to acquire washing machines, electric stoves, refrigerators, vacuum cleaners, television sets, and individual telephone connections. It is also born of that strange sense of identification, sympathy, and loyalty that arises from any sustained and intense relationship with another person, even when that person is the subject of one's research, as when Sofka speaks, in her memoir of her grandmother, of her growing sense of "almost like living with" her namesake.[12]

The event that inspired Emily to begin writing a journal was a sentimental journey she and my father made back to the town where she spent her childhood and where, after several years away, she returned to raise her own family.

"We've been around all the streets we knew," she writes, "past our old house in James Street where the big green gate which D'Arcy made about twenty-five years ago stands crookedly now, with a piece of rope holding it in place. The holly hedge is wild, and it is all a wilderness, with the grey paint washed out and drab, and no memories of our fifteen years lingering anywhere. It is the same all over—the lovely parts, the old houses, are gone. My memories are more real by far—the winter evenings when I walked home to the Police Station with the cold stinging my nostrils, but that wonderful warmth that surged when the mail train crashed round the bend past Trimble's Bush with its glowing red light and rushing sound of excitement. Matai Street was good then. I'd walk from the Police Station past the big boarding house where the Letts used to live. Dorothy was in Standard Three with me, and smelled of unwashed clothing. She sat in front of Jessie Messenger and me and

12. Ibid., 180.

we would look fascinated at her black neck, hardly able to believe it was just unwashed dirt. The boarding house was always mysterious and I would hurry past, fearful of something sinister behind the blurred front windows. Many years later it went up in smoke in the most glorious blaze we had ever seen."

This fire was part of our family lore, and as a child I heard of it many times from my grandfather, who was the local policeman at the time. The fire was deliberately lit, and defied—as had many before it—my grandfather's best efforts to track down the arsonists. But experience had taught him that firebugs get such a kick out of the consternation they cause that they are often the most entranced observers at the scene of their crime, so he moved surreptitiously among the crowd at each blaze, watching for a guilty face or telltale sign. "I can see my father now," Emily writes, "standing straight, with a steely contemplative look in his blue eyes, performing his duty as a policeman."

The breakthrough was his discovery, among scraps of kerosene-soaked cloth and charred paper at a subsequent fire, of a piece of sheet music. The music confirmed his suspicion that two young men—in Emily's words, "quiet, respectable working lads"—were the arsonists, since one of them played in a local band. He interrogated the two boys separately, and by the simple expedient of informing one that the other had owned up, extracted a signed confession from both. After a short jail term in New Plymouth, one of these young miscreants returned home and, when I was a boy, was living a few houses along Rata Street from us, now widowed and on a pension. Whenever I saw him, I would struggle to see in this shambling figure either the young firebrand or the man who, having paid his dues, got married in the Methodist Church but at the wedding reception was about to cut the cake with his bride when, according to my grandfather, the fire siren suddenly sounded in the street outside, so loud that it silenced everyone present and left the bride and groom standing with their mouths open, as if turned to stone. The last time I saw C was at my grandfather's funeral in 1960. After a service in the local Methodist church, the cortège set off for the cemetery. As our car followed the hearse through the cemetery gates, I noticed a group of old men keeping vigil on the opposite side of the road, heads bowed, hats in their hands, among them several men my grandfather had had occasion to apprehend. One of them was C.

Emily moves on in her recollections, past the horse paddock where the boarding house once stood, past the blacksmith's forge with its pungent odor of hoof parings, cinders, horse dung, and sweat, across the Kelly Street intersection to the Railway Hotel where Percy Nops is standing on the middle step, his tobacco-colored waistcoat and fob watch covering his pot belly. As Emily passes, Percy Nops nods, smiles, and gives a twist to his waxed moustache. He lives at the hotel, though has an office nearby. When I was a boy, he had relocated to the other side of the railway tracks, and his daily lunch was a Cornish pasty from Maxwell's bakery two doors away rather than the tin of herrings in tomato sauce that my mother remembers, though his paunch and waistcoat were the same as in Emily's description and his wealth still a well-kept secret. Percy Nops hoarded everything that came his way — the brown paper bags in which he bought his pies or pasties, his newspapers, odd pieces of string, nails, screws, lumber, sheets of corrugated iron, and doors, floorboards, windows, and electrical fittings salvaged from demolition sites and rubbish tips. He owned the first car in Inglewood, and several houses. From his trove of second-hand building material he constructed new houses that he rented out, with no concessions, to Inglewood's poor, including some of the men who worked for him. It is told that one day, on a visit to one of his building sites, he tripped and fell, and lay on the ground like a cast sheep as his hired hands, enjoying their rare moment of advantage, ignored his calls for help. But my father, who was a clerk at the Bank of New South Wales and handled Percy Nops's financial affairs, had another story to tell — of checks regularly and anonymously sent to the Red Cross, of money donated to the war effort, and a will from which few locals benefited but which bequeathed a small fortune to the Barnados Homes.

But Emily is moving quickly on. Past Ern Crossman's saddlery, with its wooden floor, its smell of saddle soap, leather tack, and Western saddles. Past the Billiard Rooms that her mother called a den of vice but her father, my grandfather, discretely made his second home. Past Mate Radich's fish shop with the rippled water flowing forever down the inside of the plate glass window through which I now gaze at the gaping, glazed-eyed red snapper laid out on their white enamel trays . . .

Beginnings

In an essay called "Beginnings," the New Zealand painter Colin Mc-Cahon describes a childhood epiphany without, however, overendowing this "day of splendour" with too much significance. "Two new shops had been built next door," he writes.

One was Mrs McDonald's Fruit Shop and Dairy, the other was taken by a hairdresser and tobacconist. Mrs McDonald had her window full of fruit and other practical items. The hairdresser had his window painted with HAIRDRESSER AND TOBACCONIST. Painted in gold and black on a stippled red ground, the lettering large and bold, with shadows, and a feeling of being projected right through the glass and across the pavement. I watched the work being done, and fell in love with signwriting. The grace of the lettering as it arched across the window in gleaming gold, suspended on its dull red field but leaping free from its own black shadow pointed to a new and magnificent world of painting. I watched from outside as the artist working inside slowly separated himself from me (and light from dark) to make his new creation.[13]

It is hard to spell out the implications of this vision unless you have actually seen McCahon's work, for his landscapes of dark hills with light dawning or dying along the horizon, over which he inscribes passages from the Bible, can be seen as a series of essays that return continually to that iconic window of plate glass in which the gold, black, and ruby lettering overlay shadowy hills and clouds lying beyond the town and the street. At that moment, it is as though the future artist was given a rough draft of what would become his defining work.

For my mother, there seems to have been no such early summons to painting, though she searches her memory for a moment in which she glimpsed her vocation, as though narrative requires it of her.

"I think of the first time I ever attempted a painting. Somehow I had come by a small piece of water-colour paper and some paints. I went into the plantation, a place I loved, and climbed my favourite tree, one with little hard berries that we sometimes pelted at poor unsuspecting people returning from work in the town." From her perch in the tree, Emily could look down Matai Street, and she attempted to paint what she saw. But this proved "difficult and most frustrating" and she "soon gave up and climbed down from the tree." But when she looked again, she saw that she "really had captured a little of Matai Street as [she] saw it, although it was so crude."

13. Colin McCahon, "Beginnings," *Landfall* 80 (1966): 361.

Thirty years later, and despite being overwhelmed by the work of raising five children, Emily was inspired to take up painting by a young art advisor with the Taranaki Education Board. At the same time that Don Campbell was encouraging my mother and other members of the Home and School Association to experiment with oil painting, he was trying to persuade pupils at my school to take a more adventurous and expressive approach to their artwork. The result, at least in my classroom, was pandemonium, and my carefully painted rocket ship trailing fire through a star-studded firmament was soon bespattered by gobbets of paint flicked or flung from the brushes of my anarchic neighbors. Sickened by the impossibility of engaging in serious work, I added some angry and slapdash touches of my own to the now sodden work of tachisme on my easel, achieving the satisfaction that its final destruction had been my own doing, and not something done to me. Don Campbell had red hair, a wispy moustache, a Scots accent, and unbelievably unweathered skin. He stood beside me and commended me for my work. It showed real imagination, he said. Years later, when my mother attributed to the same charismatic figure responsibility for inaugurating her career as a painter, I understood perfectly what she was talking about.

With Laddin Grant, a friend from the Home and School Association, Emily now ventured out on painting excursions, setting up her easel in a field or by a stream and painting the scene in front of her. These small canvases of autumn trees, light and shade on grass, or a river bend are quite unremarkable, and it was not until we went on holiday to Oakura one summer and Emily painted the ironsand beach and boiling surf after a three-day storm that one begins to see evidence of her making the natural world a metaphor for her inner feelings. It is at this point that her art ceases to be an imitation of what appears before her eyes and becomes a transfiguration of what lies beneath the surface, so that her subjectivity now pervades a seascape or landscape so completely that one might say that the world now gives her, as nothing else has given her—religion, fiction, or thought—a means of objectifying her own subjective life.

Emily had, at this time, a very limited knowledge of modern art, and thought of herself as working in the same vein as her uncle Walter, an accomplished but minor watercolorist who had, on at least one occasion, exhibited with the Royal Academy in London. The New Zealand painter Toss Woollaston would remember Walter Tempest's watercolors, the David Cox paper on which they were painted, and the thin slices of bread and butter, served with tea, that he would receive when he visited Emily's parents in Inglewood.[14] Woollaston hailed from Huinga and attended Stratford Technical High School where he befriended the older Crossman boys from Inglewood and often visited them in the weekends. Because Mrs. Crossman and Emily's mother were close friends it was inevitable that Woollaston's and Millie's paths would also cross. "He began to paint scenes of interest in Inglewood," Emily recalls. "They were all small, and were hung in the Crossmans' living room and looked at indulgently by visitors who regarded anyone who painted as quite peculiar. When he said he was going to be an artist when he left school at the end of the year and not take on a job of work, everyone including me really believed he was mad, or else just talking with bravado." Despite his aversion to regular employment, Woollaston left school at eighteen and went to work for Eric Drake, an Inglewood beekeeper. Reading about this period of Woollaston's life in his memoir, *Sage Tea*, I find it uncanny that the big corrugated-iron honey shed and the nearby paddocks where he scythed blackberries should be identical in his memory and mine, despite the thirty years difference between us, and I remember vividly how my sister and I picked blackberries in Eric Drake's paddock, or accompanied my father to fill tins with liquid honey in a claustrophobic shed filled with the simmering busyness of bees, the heavy odor of beeswax and honey, and an unforgettable amber light.

Although my mother never liked Toss Woollaston, his landscapes would influence her profoundly, much as seeing Cézanne's landscapes influenced him. They "inspired me to the core," Emily writes, "and made me begin to paint in a way that was most akin to the way I felt." However, this encounter with Woollaston the painter occurred some seven or eight years after Emily had begun working in oils. Having moved from Inglewood to Auckland, where my father worked several more years for the Bank of New South Wales before taking early retirement, Emily was looking for new ways of interpreting landscape. On her first visit to the Auckland Art Gallery, she found herself look-

14. Letter from Toss Woollaston, August 10, 1977. In *Toss Woollaston: A Life in Letters*, ed. Jill Trevelyan (Wellington: Te Papa Press, 2004), 391.

ing across a blue stairwell at the "magnificent stretches of land and sky painted by Woollaston"—paintings she describes elsewhere as "large and dominating and real." "My heart seemed to leap with joy and I stood spellbound for a long time, going back and forth many times to see again these marvelous things from the greatest distance away. It is the memory of those images that has been close to me in all my painting and I suppose has influenced me greatly and above all others. When I get lost, or more lost than usual, I go back and look at Woollaston or Turner. I used to fear that I would be turning out paintings that were a very poor copy of Woollaston, but I have never actually studied the details of how he gets his effects and I feel that I have emerged as an individual, even though of very small stature."

Such self-disparagement was typical of Emily, and I recall the many times, as we prepared to set off for the opening of one of her exhibitions at a downtown Auckland gallery, when she would complain about the unnecessary fuss she would have to endure and the embarrassment she would feel, standing in the limelight, subject to flattery or praise. This habit of never making an exhibition of oneself, of not being a bother to anyone, is a legacy of our lower-middle-class English forebears, but this self-effacement and false modesty, this contemptuous attitude toward public recognition, was, at least for Emily, as much a product of her family background as of her inner struggle to realize her vision—a struggle she felt, more often than not, that she was losing. But to fully understand Emily's relation with her own subjectivity, one must, I think, consider the link between her painting and her pain.

The Pain in Painting

In August 1987, when she was seventy-eight, Emily wrote: "This [journal] started about arthritis and much as I wished to forget it, it has been perhaps the hardest year for me since the children were all little, and I just hope I am going to come through it. I have so often not really been able to bear the pain, yet knowing I must . . . [the remaining lines in this paragraph have been crossed out, though some lines are still legible] . . . if I can only hold on, no drugs, no Paracetemol, only aspirin and concentration on how to reduce the pain—it is working up to a point and there is no comparison now to the year and a half of those dreadful nights—I am getting through the winter and hoping for the summer to test myself more. My painting has become a millstone too much for me in every way, yet I'm not ready to give up yet. Sometimes I like a few of them, sometimes none, and they certainly do not call forth any favourable comments from anyone who sees them. Like the arthritis I live with them all the time, and cannot escape. I feel sombre and joyless."

The lines that follow explain why the previous lines were crossed out:

"Forget it all! The very next day a most wonderful thing happened to me. I went out to paint and instead of the blaring, loud Olympic voices [my parents were following the Olympics on the radio at this time, though "so much effort, so much endurance and waiting, so much nationalism, so much of everything" left Emily "bewildered and not altogether happy"] . . . all of a sudden some beautiful music began to flow and spread exquisitely to all the corners of the Garden House soothing my troubles and planting me in another world. I painted on and on, never wanting the music to stop. But at last it did and I was full up with tears of joy and reluctant to take up anything else. The piece so perfect, so beautifully composed and played, was Symphonia in E-flat by Mozart.

"We went straight down to Balmoral and ordered the cassette, realizing for the first time that we could now do this, as we owned a radio-tape machine. I have waited twelve days and now must wait till next Friday for the cassette to arrive. But the memory will never go."

How can one say that art brings us close to reality when art is artificial? Is it because reality can only be apprehended obliquely: pointed to, alluded to, suggested, but never completely covered or contained by the means we have at our disposal—words, music, paint, objects? Or should we speak of a meeting, in which the music, say, moves toward us and we move toward it, as if each conspired or colluded in producing this moment of recognition that cannot be explained by reference either to the music or the listener alone?

In the only self-portrait she ever did, and which my sisters found stowed at the very back of her studio after her death in 1991, my mother depicts herself from behind in the act of painting, her brush poised in her gnarled hand, her body leaning toward the landscape on which she is working, yet both she and the smock she wears treated as though they were continuous with the wild hills, the dark bush, the turbulent sky. So it is now, as I reconsider the places she reimagined abstractly in her art—the Waioeke Gorge, the contorted schist outcrops of Central Otago, the papa clay bluffs of the Rangitikei, the volcanic ash and tussock of the Desert Road, the humpbacked hills of Coromandel, a misshapen rock on an ironsand beach west of Auckland—that I realize it is her own body that haunts these works, a body reconstituted in paint or brought back to life by music. "I do not see the landscape from a distance," she observes. "I try to paint myself into every hill, cliff, river, road, bush, cloud and sky, so that when I am painting I *become* for a while the landscape, with its atmosphere and magnificence."

Empathy seems too glib a word to describe what is happening here. Far more is involved than a conceptual or metaphorical connection between self and other. There is fusion. In effect, outer and inner worlds flow together, and become one. It is the same experience Katherine Mansfield describes in a letter to the painter Dorothy Brett in October 1917:

> It seems to me so extraordinarily right that you should be painting Still Lives just now. What can one do, faced with this wonderful tumble of round bright fruits, but gather them and play with them—and *become them*, as it were. When I pass an apple stall I cannot help stopping and staring until I feel that I, myself, am changing into an apple, too, and that at any moment I can produce an apple, miraculously, out of my own being, like a conjuror produces the egg . . . When you paint apples do you feel that your breasts and your knees become apples, too? Or do you think this is the greatest nonsense. I don't. I am sure it is not. When I write about ducks I swear that I am a white duck with a round eye, floating on a pond fringed with yellow-blobs and taking an occasional dart at the other duck with the round eye, which floats upside down beneath me . . . In fact the whole process of becoming the duck . . . is so thrilling that I can hardly breathe, only to think about it. For although that is as far as most people can get, it is really only the "prelude." There follows the moment when you are more duck, more apple, or more Natasha than any of these objects could ever possibly be, and so you create them anew.[15]

15. Katherine Mansfield to Dorothy Brett, October 1917, *The Letters and Journals of Katherine Mansfield: A Selection*, ed. C. K. Stead (Harmondsworth: Penguin, 1977), 84.

The poet Elizabeth Bishop recalls a winter afternoon in Worcester, Massachusetts, when she was seven. She had accompanied her aunt Consuelo to her dentist's appointment, and during her long wait for her aunt, the little girl leafs through the *National Geographic* magazines on the table in the waiting room, studying photos of erupting volcanoes, a corpse slung from a pole somewhere in Melanesia, babies with bound heads, and Congolese women with their elongated necks "wound round and round with wire like the necks of light bulbs." Suddenly, as if from somewhere inside her, the child hears a small cry of pain. It is her aunt who has cried out, but for the child her aunt's cry and her own are one.

> What took me
> completely by surprise
> was that it was *me*:
> my voice, in my mouth.
> Without thinking at all
> I was my foolish aunt,
> I — we — were falling, falling,
> our eyes glued to the cover
> of the *National Geographic*,
> February, 1918.
>
> And then the child asks herself:
>
> Why should I be my aunt,
> or me, or anyone?
> What similarities —
> boots, hands, the family voice
> I felt in my throat, or even
> the *National Geographic*
> and those awful hanging breasts —
> held us all together
> or made us all just one?[16]

16. Elizabeth Bishop, "In the Waiting Room," *The Complete Poems, 1927–1979* (New York: Farrar, Straus and Giroux, 1984), 159–61.

Paths

When Brian Boyd published the first volume of his critical biography of Vladimir Nabokov, *The Russian Years*, in 1990, Emily's enthusiasm for her son-in-law's work made it abundantly clear that the Russian writer's views on art and life gave voice to her own—particularly, I think, the question that Nabokov confesses to have bewildered and harassed him all his life: "what lies outside the prison of human time, our entrapment within the present, and our subjection to death?"[17] Brian Boyd captures brilliantly his subject's central preoccupation—the "breach between the limitless capacity of consciousness and its absurd limitation"—and shows how Nabokov's answer was art. Not only does art bring home to us "the marvel of consciousness—that sudden window swinging open on a sunlit landscape amidst the night of non-being";[18] it enables us to escape the confines of our own time, place, and personality, so that even pain is transcended—since it is recognized as also being the pain of others. So it was that Emily could articulate, through Brian's account of Nabokov's work, something of the freedom she found in art, and of the movement that art made possible, from the pain that pinned her down in her own delimited subjectivity to a world apart, of landscapes, journeys, and other possible lives.

These reflections were much on my mind as I read of Emily's discovery of Woollaston's landscapes, for on the very day she encountered these breathtaking works she also saw, for the first time, several works of Colin McCahon from his gate and waterfall series. "I could understand neither," Emily writes. "They were too deep for me then. But [I] was impressed in some way, so that many years later when I saw these paintings again, I appreciated them to the full, especially the waterfalls—I realized how strongly the subconscious image of them had lain in my mind over the years."

This sense of a path not taken, or which she was not prepared to take, is evident elsewhere in her journals, particularly when she recalls what it was like to grow up in a world in which options and opportunities

17. Brian Boyd, *Vladimir Nabokov, the Russian Years* (Princeton, N.J.: Princeton University Press, 1990), 9.

18. Nabokov in a letter to his cousin Sergey Sergeevich Nabokov, March 15, 1959, in *Vladimir Nabokov*, 11.

for young women were very limited. She begins with a recollection of helping her father at the Police Station, filing statistics on farm acreages, crops, and stock numbers. "I could gladly have settled for a permanent job of office work," she writes, "but somehow I got the message that with my education the only two suitable jobs were nursing or teaching. Girls who did not have High School training or matriculation stayed in the town, and worked in shops and offices. There was even one woman in the bank, a position I found very enviable. To be a nurse was unthinkable, to teach was not pleasing in any way, but the chance to go to [Teacher's] Training College and maybe part-time to University was the only thing that held some hope, and this I did.

"How I longed to go to university full-time, but only those with rich parents ever could. I loved the atmosphere, the lectures, the students, the beautiful old library, and the dances. But Training College was utterly boring and I learnt nothing except from the art and music lectures, though I enjoyed my life at Friends Hostel where I was always up to some sort of mischief. Despite doing well in my teaching sessions at Miramar, Thorndon and others places [in Wellington city], I always felt I was wasting time. I had a year at Stratford after college, teaching Primer Three, and tried to put my whole energy into it, getting good reports, enjoying the children, but never really happy, although not knowing what I did want to do. However, the Depression came, with cuts in salaries, one or two term's work at the most, and permanent jobs very scarce. All the married women teachers were sacked, and all one thought of was a relieving job, anywhere, with very low pay."

Emily did relief teaching in a number of isolated King Country and Taranaki towns between 1932 and 1935 before landing a permanent position at Norfolk Road a few miles south of Inglewood. Memories of those years in boarding houses fill several pages of her journal— of rooms without electric light, drunken workers and wife-beatings keeping her from sleep, and the winter cold so severe that the water pipes and lavatory cisterns iced up every night, the ink froze in the inkwells at school, and Emily's breath on the blackboard turned to ice.

After a term at Norfolk Road School, Emily moved to Wellington to marry D'Arcy, my father, who had himself been persuaded by his mother not to pursue his father's trade as a carpenter and cabinet-maker but get a white collar job for greater security. I suspect that this overbearing woman was, however, less concerned with her son's well-being than her own struggle for respectability and desire for wealth, and my father never found much satisfaction in banking, spending all his free time in his radio shack or workshop, employing the tools he inherited from his father and designs from *Popular Mechanics* to make toys for his children and additions to our house. As for Emily, she felt no qualms about having to give up teaching. "I exchanged that life for one of housework and bringing up children, and although it was harder than I could ever have dreamt (mainly because of the arthritis), I never had a single regret or felt even a stir of frustration."

Parallel Lives

As a boy, I was intrigued by what drew people to their various trades and destinies. What led Mr. Trigger to take up butchery, and his brother to become a chimney sweep? What unspoken gratification did Mrs. Peters, our draper, derive from the curiously magnified sound of her scissors on the wooden countertop as she sheared through a yard of cotton, and what, in her foreign past, presaged the skill with which she pulled a length of silk from a bolt and laid it along the calibrated brass edge of the shop counter? What, I would ask myself, were the secret links between their invisible and visible lives? There was, of course, less mystery than I imagined. Eric Drake had become an apiarist, for example, not out of any sense of calling, but because he had been invalided home during the First World War and advised to take up an outdoor occupation that would not tax his strength. Moreover, at a time when most kids left school after getting "Proficiency" in Standard Six, and when working-class families simply could not afford to send their children to high school (they needed them to supplement the household income), one simply accepted whatever work was on offer.

But Emily was not someone who could simply accept "what was on offer." She wanted more. And in her journals she recalls two households to which she gravitated as a child, as though they afforded glimpses into a world that her own staid and rule-bound home denied her. The first was the Crossman house, where Toss Woollaston also found his second home—a place Emily describes as "so much a part of my life." There were six boys in the family—Oswald (Ossie), Ronald (Ron), Norman (Norm), Clifford (Cliff), Vincent (Vince), and Harold. Their father, Ern

Crossman, owned the local saddlery in Matai Street, and Emily was as terrified of him as were his sons. "He looked thin and made of wire. His razor-strop hung on the wall by the kitchen table, a real and constant threat to all, [though] I never saw it in use and suspect that Ern's apparent toughness concealed a very soft heart. I stayed there several times, and loved every minute in spite of the contrast to the Police Station. I played with the four older boys so much—we tore through the jail yard at the old Police Station—a banned area, of course—and reveled in Cops and Robbers, Cowboys and Indians and other wild games which I loved. The little jail was barred and locked and not one of us ever went in, but we saw my father putting the hot meal cooked by my mother through the pigeon-hole for the prisoner, and the empty enamel plate being returned later. The yard was overgrown with weeds and was a lovely, sinister place to rush about in. Cliff was always my partner in crime, and we led the others on. There was always the big paddock at the back to play in if we couldn't get near the lock-up (as it was called). The paddock went right back behind the fowl yard and shed (which contained a garage and a big loft) right to the next street, and the inner side had a row of tall trees belonging to the Gudgeons. Beyond these boundaries was the plantation which ran from Matai Street half way to Windsor Road, and was full of tall full-grown trees, and a deep ditch, with the houses set back from the road (including the Crossman house). This was a poor smallish house bursting at the seams with six boys and mother and father, but full of life and vitality.

"The lavatory was at the back of the section and there was a stile there over which we climbed to go blackberrying in the neighbouring paddocks. The back door of the house opened straight into the kitchen—a long narrow room with a large table, benches instead of chairs, and a coal range. The floor was covered in cracked and faded linoleum. One door led to a tiny bathroom with an old rusty tin bath; another opened on to a square living room containing an old gramophone which I loved, and on which the boys would play their few rollicking records if I pleaded enough.

"One day, Oswald dared me to climb the highest tree, which was directly outside their house. I started up, while he jeered raucously and willed me to give up. When I reached the top, that was not enough—I had to tie my handkerchief to the topmost branch, and on doing this, I heard faint shrieks from far below where the tiny figure of Mrs. Crossman stood on the path, calling 'Come down Millie, whatever will your mother say!'

"Oswald had osteomyelitis as a boy, and spent a year in hospital where half the bone from the ankle to the knee was cut away. When it grew again, the other half was taken out. There was no penicillin then, and seldom a cure, but Oswald survived and grew into a red-faced, coarse boy whom I never liked very much. He had none of the jollity of the other boys and when we had finished our training as teachers and were probationers together at Inglewood School, he was very lascivious. I was very innocent and ignorant, but I had enough natural loathing of his advances to keep him at bay. Cliff and Harold also became teachers, and Cliff was at one time an All-Black. He was always very popular, jolly like his mother, and my best friend of all of them."

In complete contrast with the Crossmans', the other household in which Emily felt at home was a place of cultivated manners and educated taste. "My greatest treat," Emily writes, "was to visit the Messenger house and spend a day with Jessie [a class-mate and close friend]. There was space, paddocks, a big lovely garden, with many trees, and a grass tennis court. Inside, the house was old and charming, with polished tables, a piano, and lovely ornaments. We had meals with crystal cruets of salt and pepper, vinegar and mustard, table napkins starched stiff and glossy, and delicate china and fine cutlery. It was a magic world to me. We would discuss the books we were reading and at school Jessie and I would always get first or second prize for our work."

As the old adage goes, the grass is always greener on the other side, and many children happily imagine that their best friend's home is freer and more fascinating than their own. Emily's craving for mischief, vitality, and culture was partly a reaction to her mother's "narrow Methodist outlook." "My parents did not approve of dancing," she writes, "and it took many years for me to prevail upon them and be allowed to go to dances, and also to go to the swimming baths, and even cards were frowned upon by my mother—any form of gambling was quite sinful. Sundays were the one miserable part of every week. They were dull and boring—we weren't allowed to play cards or other games, or even spend a penny on an icecream. We went to Sunday School or Bible Class in the morning and to church at night. I never listened to the sermon or readings from the Bible, or joined in the singing of the hymns. After looking around the church and ascertaining that all the same people were there, looking pale and wan and uninspired, I would go through the hymn book and count the hymns with the initials C.M. above them, which to me stood for Clive McGonagle, my boyfriend. Sundays always finished with our evening meal set out in the sitting-room, at the big gate-legged table covered with a white cloth and laid with the best china. As I can remember, it was always a dish of pink salmon, a dish of tomatoes, with white bread and jam. I longed to become an Anglican, which I later did, being confirmed in the Church of England before I was married, though I later came to reject all conformist religion. This happened suddenly after my first lecture at university on evolution. But the shackles didn't fall easily and weighed me down for a long time—perhaps to this day a little."

One Sunday, writes Emily, Clive McGonagle appeared at church, wearing dark trousers and a snow-white shirt, and when the congregation left the church after the morning service and was standing in small groups, exchanging small talk before dispersing, Emily was aware of Clive staring at her. "I didn't realize then that he had come to see me, because he was a Presbyterian really. We saw each other at school and at the baths, but hardly ever spoke to each other—it was worship from afar then. We used to swim together in the Dual Relay Race and Clive's father was always there, coaching him to swim faster and faster. This was all at Primary School, and I remember Clive refusing to lead the Grand March with Marjorie Julian, as he wanted me for his partner. But of course I was in no way suitable as the tallest children were chosen for this rather dubious honour. I think it all ended with Bill Morrison, another of my admirers, marching with Marjorie, who was regally dressed as 'Rule Britannia.' When I went to High School and Clive went to Auckland to join H.M.S. Pilomel [a New Zealand Navy 'Pearl' class Cruiser] we were thrown into different worlds, but he used to write to me, knowing the letters would be opened and censored by my father. When Clive came home on leave, he told me in a letter that he would be traveling to New Plymouth and would pass through Inglewood on a certain train on a certain night, and I should be at the station. So my father took me to the station and stood with me as we saw Clive looking longingly, as the train stopped in Inglewood, for a few words. But I stayed by my father's side, like glue, of course, and that was the last time I ever saw Clive. One day, as I traveled to Stratford Technical High School on the train, I suddenly heard his name mentioned, and the voice of Una Lile telling the girls that Clive McGonagle had died of meningitis. The shock was terrific, but I kept silent and went to school and never a word was said until some weeks later a photo came in the post from Mr Ayling who was Scout Master in Inglewood and evidently knew of my friendship with Clive. I never forgot the comfort of this, even to this day."

Every family is, in some respects, a world unto itself, with its own moral codes and its fixed ideas as to what is and is not proper or possible. This preoccupation with protecting hearth and home reinforces a view of the outside world as a place of danger, corruption, and chaos. Emily's mother was particularly prone to this fear that foreign forces inimical to purity, goodness, and order were always seeking to invade the small and fragile space she shared with those she loved, and one of Emily's first memories is of a factory siren sounding and her mother crying out "The Germans are here." "It was the first inkling I had," she writes, "that the Germans might come, and it is hard to realize that so many of our fears were completely unfounded," including the "Yellow Peril"—the threat of invasion from China—to which her mother would also frequently allude.

Amy's trepidation undoubtedly had a lot to do with the trauma she had experienced when she left her own genteel life in Yorkshire to marry my grandfather, whom she had known briefly before he migrated to New Zealand. Emily would remember her mother Amy as "a shy but lovely person, very reserved, with a narrow Methodist outlook, as had my father." Amy was "the only girl in a family with two brothers, both of whom worshipped her, and she received a good education, trained as a teacher and elocutionist, and could sing well as a soprano." "I loved my mother," Emily continues, "but I would be exasperated when on asking to be allowed to do something or other she would always say 'We'll see,' which always meant no. And there were always the dreadful things that would happen to one, if one wasn't good or wasn't prudent." By contrast, Emily's father "was much more outgoing." A largely self-educated man, he was, in my mother's words, "much more extroverted" than the woman he married, "and although strict and narrow in many ways, loved many things that his religion banned, such as a bit of a gamble, or a game of snooker or billiards. He loved all card games and I would play draughts with him, then euchre and five hundred, and he always had a twinkle in his blue eyes and a mischievous look. He also had a reputation for 'speaking his mind' which got him in a lot of trouble with the local farmers, but he was 'honest and straight as a die,' to use his own expression.

"In those days, the very worst thing that could befall a girl was to get pregnant while unmarried. It was the ultimate and irrevocable mistake, never to be forgotten or forgiven. Although I did not know this, and less still how to get pregnant even if I wanted, I realize that my parents must have always dreaded this 'quite impossible thing' to happen. I remember standing in Moa Street one day and gazing up at the window across the railway line in Matai Street where behind the high curtained window Alice Coles spent her days. Some of us had heard that the dreaded thing had happened and Alice was going to have a baby. The fact that she married Clarrie Nicholls the father, had several other children in due course and led a seemingly happy and respectable life, was quite incidental. But I can understand my parents' protectiveness. Once my father forbade me to go out with Cliff Hill, an English Flock House student who worked on a farm, ever again. We had been to some Parish Hall hops on Friday nights and he would come to the Police Station sometimes and sing his song, 'I hear you calling me' to entertain us all, and teach me how to play chess in a very amateur way."

Gunner Jenkins (who manned the North Egmont Mountain Gate and was reputed to have fired the first shot in World War I) had evidently told Emily's father "something about Cliff to his discredit—I never knew what—but as I liked him I rebelled and went walking through the streets of Inglewood as before with Cliff on his day off in town from the farm, until of course the day that I saw my father approaching in the distance. We eventually met in what I expected to be a face to face encounter, but as I looked fearfully aside I saw my father's granite face, with never the flicker of an eye from the front as he marched stolidly and silently past. I told Cliff all about it. He said something I could not understand or believe at the time. 'It will be the same with whoever you go out with, girl.' Soon after, he left Inglewood for another farm on the Flock House scheme and I never saw him again. He was eighteen and I was twenty-three, and it was only a nice friendship anyway. And D'Arcy had already started coming to the Police Station with my brother Jack, though that is another story."

Reading of these long-ago episodes, I think of Colin McCahon's lines, with which Emily would undoubtedly have agreed:

Sin is anything that separates us from reality . . . whether it is the reality that is called God or the reality called Man (who created God in his own image!) or the reality of the world about us.[19]

There are always other stories—the lives we might have lived, the paths not taken, the family secrets, the events swept under the rug because they challenged the ethos one cultivated, polished, and presented to the world. Such was the story of Emily's father's brother, who had followed Fred out to New Zealand. Loathing his job in the woolen mills, he started a grocery business in Petone that soon failed. One night, Emily heard her father and mother whispering furtively and anxiously together before Fred hurriedly packed his bag and left the house by taxi. No explanation was given. A couple of days later, Amy showed her daughter a newspaper article, holding her finger on the text Emily was to read. Arthur Longbottom of Petone had attempted to kill himself with his razor, but was recovering in hospital. In fact he died of pneumonia before Fred's taxi reached Wellington and, in Emily's words, "a veil of silence was drawn again," even after Arthur's widow Louie and her two children came to live in Inglewood and Louie went to work as a housekeeper.

My Lunch with Arthur

I had lunch with Arthur Kleinman in the Faculty Club a few days after reading his recently published book, *What Really Matters*. I wanted Arthur to know how important I considered this work, and how wholeheartedly I shared his view that our hold on life is always tenuous and our struggle to live generously and decently almost impossible. I had learned from living and working in West Africa that life was something to be endured, not a predicament we can be saved from or transcend. One strives to place the rough and the smooth on a similar footing, making the most of what one has. Life is a gamble. There are no guarantees, no binding moral codes, no center that always holds. For Arthur, this did not mean that one gave up on the idea of the good;

19. Cited in Marja Bloem and Martin Browne, *Colin McCahon: A Question of Faith* (Amsterdam: Stedelijk Museum; Nelson, New Zealand: Craig Potten Publishing, 2002), 41.

rather one conceived a moral life as something that had to be struggled for. And it was at the most dangerous and difficult moments of our lives that this struggle is momentarily won or lost—when we become monsters or saints.[20]

It was inevitable, I suppose, that we should get around to talking about the dangers of being too open to the world, in particular the risks that often attend doing fieldwork in far-flung places. One's ethnographic passion to understand how others see the world sometimes blinds one to the situation one places oneself in. Ethnographers are a little like war correspondents, who will heedlessly risk their necks to get a good story, a scoop. Many of us are driven, less by ambition or bread than by an insatiable desire to go beyond ourselves, to be remade by new experiences, reborn in the fires of the new. We sustain losses in doing this, I told Arthur, for the new always entails the eclipse of what we have been, of what we thought was true or certain before. Arthur said we should do a book together on bereavement in two cultures, how people go on in the face of devastating loss, and this led to us talking about therapy, how a doctor or psychiatrist must convey to a client that he or she really cares about the client getting well. Technique is one thing, Arthur said, but unless it is a vehicle for this deeper concern, this genuine concern for the client, the therapeutic transformation simply cannot occur. There are not many people who have this gift, this disposition, he said. And then he took me aback by saying how much he liked and admired me. I was rock solid, he said. I was real. I carried this aura of sincerity and reality around with me. It was instantly obvious to anyone who valued such things. At Harvard, Arthur said, one runs into a lot of people who are playing games, academic games, power games, mind games. And then you meet someone who seems to know exactly what is worth doing, and is steadfast in his or her commitment, who cannot be bought, distracted, or bent.

As Arthur spoke, I was thinking about another friend who used flattery to secure one's fealty. Was Arthur using the same ploy? I said I wasn't sure about all this. I was as vulnerable and as much a moral coward as anyone. If I had stuck to my last (the expression was one Arthur had used) it was only because I had gotten into the habit of writing as a child, seeking refuge from a world I did not feel at home in. My secure

20. Arthur Kleinman, Introduction, *What Really Matters: Living a Moral Life amidst Uncertainty and Danger* (New York: Oxford University Press, 2006).

base was very narrowly defined. I did not risk departing from it for fear I would be lost. "Besides," I said, "you have had the same steadfastness of mind, the same sense of what William James called 'genuine reality.' Leaving medicine because it seemed to you to lack any perspective that embraced culture or experience. Then departing from the anthropological straight and narrow by calling into question the extent to which everything in life is culturally determined, or cultural in character, your strong sense of the existential, that I share, and of well-being as something irreducible to physical health, wealth, or status."

"It is true," Arthur said. "One cannot make of a phenomenon anything you want to. There is, in every phenomenon, something that resists interpretation."

My thoughts began to drift, then, as I realized the irony of having this conversation in the Faculty Club, for when I came to Harvard a little over a year ago to explore the possibility of taking up a job offer in the Divinity School, I stayed several days in the Faculty Club, and during those days, when it was too cold to venture outside for very long, or I found myself alone in my room, watching TV, writing in my journal, or pondering the wisdom of leaving Copenhagen where I was reasonably happy, I kept returning to the question of what was real. I had met people at Harvard who seemed to want to possess both humanity and power, as though the two could be combined, seeking to have a hand in Washington policy making and yet be seen as public intellectuals in the tradition of Zola, Sartre, and Russell. I had met others whose excellence in their own particular fields left one speechless with admiration, but mystified—for they seemed to have left entire dimensions of their being uncultivated in the course of achieving their particular expertise. One night, I woke jet-lagged at three and turned on the bedside light. I could hear the hum of the central heating, but felt cut off from the world. Vivid memories of northern Sierra Leone overwhelmed me, of the heat and dust, of my friend Noah's house by the swamp in Kabala, of the day we set off on foot for Firawa and my first ethnographical fieldwork. In my journal I scribbled: "Something deep within me opposes being here—craves to be in the real world, hard up against it, no home comforts, no bookish isolation or soundless, heated rooms with classical music on the radio." And then I asked: "Why do I abhor wealth and privilege so much. Why do I flee from it that sometimes does me seek?"

All this passed through my mind in a few seconds, as in a dream, and then Arthur and I were talking again about the ethical question of whether we let ourselves be guided by our loyalty to persons or our regard for principles when the two come into conflict. I wanted to hear Arthur's views on how or even whether or not we are guided in our actions by moral principles. Can abstractions govern our behavior, or is it that they derive distantly from someone who was a role model for us in early life, in which case they are not really abstractions at all? They are, in fact, like people we regard highly, and do not want to disappoint or betray. "We should do a book on this," Arthur said. "We should do something together." And he asked me a question then that I had no good answer for. "What is it about certain people, that we tend to say of them 'they are real'? These are the people we trust implicitly, in whose hands we would place our lives."

The Wellness Narratives

Arthur had mentioned, over lunch, that when his book *The Illness Narratives* was published in 1988 the medical establishment totally failed to understand it. Instead of seeing it as an indictment of medicalization—a critique of the technicist approach to medicine that reduces the patient to a symptom, a dysfunction, or a problem that can be resolved—doctors read it as a contribution to how medical practice could be refined by adding to a patient's clinical chart, with its ECGs and temperature and blood pressure readings, another set of facts that might guide them in determining the most medically effective course of action.

In fact, "illness narratives" could just as well be described as wellness narratives, because even an ill person is well in a way, just as a dying person is living. One could as well say a half-empty glass is half-full, to avoid the morbidity of always seeing absence where there is simply a struggle for presence.

In my mother's journal for 1984 there is a section headed "My Life with Arthritis."

She begins, "I thought it might be a good idea to record something of my ever constant companion for over 50 years. It is a subject I have never talked very much about—mainly because people who talk about illness are such utter bores, and also because I could never see any good coming from it. Complaints and diseases do not make interesting topics of conversation, and are never understood anyway by the listener, who is usually immune. There is even a slightly ashamed feeling that goes with physical disability and illness—one *should* be well and healthy if one follows the rules, but this turns out to be an illogical idea somehow. Yet there is always the lurking thought that one could have avoided it all. When a child, I liked sweet things, and these were given to me. I liked vegetables, but there were never many of these somehow, except for long overcooked ones—our diet was not well-balanced or even interesting. My mother slaved over the coal range, producing a roast of overcooked beef every weekend, sometimes with Yorkshire pudding, and apple pie and sponge to follow. The stews were dry and overcooked and never tempting. My meal was heated up for me when I came home from school at the end of a long day, and I can still remember the taste, or maybe the lack of taste—I couldn't eat it. But it did Jessie, Jack and Herbert [Emily's siblings] no harm apparently, so I can't blame that. We accepted what we were given and knew no difference. I never drank milk or ate much fruit, and was rather a delicate child. Perhaps my memory is bad—my father loved his meals, especially tripe and onions, which he got from the Rivetts at the fruit shop every Saturday night.

"I always had aching legs above the thigh, as long as I can remember. I could never sit at 'the pictures' [the movies] without pain and discomfort. I would go every Saturday night with Kath Coles to see Hoot Gibson and hear Mrs Devereaux playing the piano with great gusto and much flourishing—and when I walked around the town with my mother, I still remember the aching legs. When I was in my twenties and playing tennis at the Inglewood Club, enjoying it so much and being a good player, I suddenly found that when I got home my knees hurt unbearably every time. Then I went away to [Teacher's] Training College in Wellington, waving from the window and trying to get a last glimpse of my mother and father standing on the platform, my father straight and tall in a long dark coat and my mother small and tearful in coat, hat and gloves, bravely saying goodbye. I felt sad and lost, going into the unknown world. I didn't want to be a teacher—I would rather have worked in an office somewhere, but there was so little choice of what a girl could do, and with my secondary education it was 'the thing' to be either a nurse or a teacher. However, I knew that by going to Training College I could go part-time to Victoria College [later renamed Victoria University of Wellington], and this was the great consolation. There was no way of earning money then by part-time or holiday work for students, so we accepted our salaries of £8.16.8 a month for girls, and £10.16.8 for boys, although with resentment at the unfairness. I paid £6 a month for board at Friends Hostel in the Glen and had £2.16.8 a month left for books etc. My mother and father bought my clothes and helped as much as they could. Our one treat every week was going down in the Cable Car to DIC and having morning tea for one shilling and listening to the guest pianist. Dances at Training College and University were free and no transport was needed, and sometimes I went to a film with the girls, or was treated by a young man who had a little money. One even used to produce a box of chocolates which appeared on my lap—this was the ultimate mark of a successful evening. The trouble was that I didn't enjoy his company and was totally unattracted to him, so no great romance came of that.

"I met Bruce Bell at the Freshers' Ball—the boys lined up at one side and the girls on the other, to take partners, but Bruce leapt out of line and grabbed me and we had a wonderful evening. We were thrilled to find out that we both came from Taranaki, I from Stratford Technical High School where I was Dux and he from New Plymouth Boys' High School where he was Dux. He was very clever and full of fun—with a lame leg, but he was also a marvelous dancer and so was I. We finished the evening by sitting on the one bench on Victoria Hill in the moonlight, with romance all around us. After that we often danced together and he would come to Friends Hostel for the dances there and we would sit out on the porch sometimes between dances. We never went out anywhere else together, and after my two years at Training College never met again until 1982, in the New Plymouth Hospital ward where Noel [Emily's sister-in-law] lay ill, and Bruce was visiting an old friend. But I don't think either of us had ever forgotten that romantic time, so innocent and so lovely.

"I first noticed the pain in my big toe when walking down Lambton Quay and it kept on hurting for years. I had spent so much time rubbing my father's feet with methylated spirits and olive oil when his pain was so bad and had always dreaded the thought of ever getting rheumatoid arthritis, which was the diagnosis for my father. His hands swelled on the knuckles where rheumatoid arthritis usually starts, and he could not even cut a slice of bread—then the pain was everywhere and he suffered dreadfully—I would sometimes hear him crawling up the passage on all fours to bed at night. In the evening the pain would often ease and we would play three-handed Bridge or Euchre—he went to New Plymouth Hospital for periods and looked very ill, but his joints never became crippled or misshapen and I don't think now that he had rheumatoid arthritis.

"But when my pain increased in my early twenties, and after I was married, I at last went to the doctor in Nelson. He took one look at my swollen knuckles and said, 'You have rheumatoid arthritis.' I was stricken to the core with the shock, and he said 'Go home and *drink* a full glass of Condy's Fluid every day.[21] There is nothing more to do.' I was pregnant with Gabrielle, and knew very few people. When I got home, I felt I must share this blow with someone, and thought of Mrs Hurrell, who was a neighbour we had found to be very nice to us. She came to the door and I went in and told her what the doctor had said, rather tearfully. The room was carpeted, very comfortable, and reassuring with its velvet curtains and other trappings of an established house owner who has reached the status of not having any more money worries, with a husband at retiring age. Mrs Hurrell said a few cold conventional words, I can't even remember now what they were, but she was obviously not over-impressed by what I then felt to be the blighting of my young life—perhaps she had a cake burning in the oven, I don't know—but she herself was cold and all I wanted was to flee to our own house and wait for D'Arcy to come home, which I did, and the subject was never again mentioned between us (I mean Mrs Hurrell and me). While I waited for D'Arcy I managed to do some thinking and come to terms with things. 'Twenty years, then it will burn itself out, maybe before,' said Dr Storey Johnson. I faced the obvious, I had it, and must live with it—at least it wasn't a death sentence, and I would drink the Condy's Fluid and hope for the best.

"This I did for some nauseous months, with no results. We were now living in Acton Street and with pregnancy advanced beyond four

21. Condy's Fluid is a disinfecting solution of sodium and potassium permanganates that was used in pre-antibiotic days—for example, during the 1918 flu pandemic in New Zealand—to prevent viral infection. A weak solution was gargled, and patients, especially children, were warned not to swallow the fluid, which contains a corrosive oxidizing agent. It is inconceivable that a doctor should recommend it be drunk, especially by a pregnant woman, hence my mother's underlining of the word "drink."

months the pain decreased, and gradually disappeared—I felt well and energetic and the dreadful pregnancy sickness went too. When we were living in Vanguard Street the pain in my hands was so dreadful that I would get up and walk the floor at nights, sitting around the kitchen range in the mornings almost unable to bear it, until by midday, or soon after, release came and I would walk the long desolate street into town. Dr Johnson had said even then that we must move from Vanguard Street as it was in a cold damp valley. So we hunted around and found our old house in Acton Street, opposite a little foot-bridge which spanned a stream lined with weeping willows, the Convent across the road, and the Central School further along. We put our three suites of furniture in the sitting-room, bedroom and dining room, with our two carpet squares and some odd mats. The dining room was a lovely big room with a fireplace, and large windows through which we reached out and picked peaches from the tree. We had our dining table of dark rimu, four chairs and a sideboard—later a piano from D'Arcy's mother, a wooden couch with squab, a radio on a makeshift table curtained below, and two fireside chairs. We spent our winter evenings in there, by the fire, with a rug tacked in round the door to keep out the draughts, a big dish of apples, and the chess set. We were secure from the cold, and thought about Gabrielle coming, and were happy."

After some detailed recollections of the house, Emily speaks of the "ecstatic event" of giving birth to her first child, Gabrielle, in Te Rangi Hospital, then returns to her arthritis, now "becoming even worse."

"Things were very hard, though I never felt unhappy, although at times rather despairing. But I always felt that things would get better. When the other four children came, the same thing happened each time—the pain and swelling disappeared for six months or more, then returned worse still. I told the doctors this, to their uninterest, except for Dr Rutherford who investigated and tried to obtain blood transfusions from a pregnant woman, but was unable to match the blood. He said something had been done about this in Germany. After Michael was born, D'Arcy was sent relieving sometimes to Blenheim, and I felt things getting too much without him there. One day when he was away, Issy Cameron, whose husband was in the Bank of New South Wales with D'Arcy and about our age, came to visit. I was at the end of my tether (a state I've been at for much of my life I sometimes think) and when Issy appeared I burst into tears and couldn't stop crying at the thought of the vision of help and comfort before my eyes. But Issy grabbed me and shook me, saying, 'Tell me what happened, tell me, tell me?' I think she thought a tragedy had happened, and when at last I tried to explain a little of how everything was too much, she dismissed it with a shrug of anti-climax and went away as soon as possible. I think perhaps from that moment I realized that there would be no help from anyone outside, and that I must bear my troubles alone and not inflict them on others. And from then I found I gathered strength and a new perspective and learned that the fatal thing is to feel sorry for oneself. If ever I begin to feel like that, I think of how lucky I am compared to so many others who suffer far worse things. So I have never talked about my arthritis—it would be boring and non-stop, and useless. Also I learned never to fight it, as I soon realized it was to be my constant companion, part of my life, probably forever—so I thought to live with it, and be happy, and be happy in that it was nothing worse—live my life to the full just the same, rather than waste time seeking the ever-promising cure which reason and knowledge told me was non-existent. Luckily I could do this as my love of life and all the little things, as well as the joy of a family and love for them, could never be diminished.

"Reading this over, it sounds so boring and 'goody-goody'—I can hardly bear to go on. However, it is the truth, whatever it is not.

"When I became pregnant again, with Juliet, I went to Dr Lucas, as Dr Johnston had retired—I presume gone to a haven where he never saw, let alone ate, an onion (he always told his patients never to eat them). Dr Lucas was young and forthright and immediately suggested an abortion, which really shocked me. I asked him if the reason was because rheumatoid arthritis was hereditary, then if *my* life was in danger (which I knew it wasn't anyway) and he said 'Definitely not!' But he wanted me to go to Rotorua Hospital for months, up to a year, and not have this baby. To me this was absolutely unthinkable and I told him so, at which he got rather angry and said that if I didn't listen to his advice he predicted I would be in a wheelchair within twelve years. I didn't really believe this but continued to go to him until we left Nelson during the war years, transferred to Inglewood."

Inglewood happened to be Emily's hometown, and the move seemed to her "a retrograde step in most ways and yet comforting to be back in some ways." D'Arcy enlisted in the air force, but his employer, the Bank of New South Wales, applied on his behalf for an exemption from war service on the grounds that he had a young family and a wife who suffered from rheumatoid arthritis. After the birth of Juliet in 1943, Emily's doctor suggested that she undergo a tonsillectomy. Even though she had had her tonsils removed when she was eight, she entered New Plymouth Hospital and underwent a procedure that left her "unable to swallow anything for weeks, and in great pain." She then suffered a miscarriage. A year later her fourth child, Bronwen, was born. "I would get up in the mornings, see the children [Gabrielle and Michael] off to school and settle Juliet and Bronwen to their day, then sit on the high stool in the kitchen and wonder how I was going to do the dishes, make the beds, do the washing and cooking. It all seemed like the gargantuan tasks set for the heroes of fairy tales. I used to love particularly the story of the little mermaid—now I knew how she felt when she exchanged her fish tail for feet, 'like walking on swords,' and when I walked I felt just the same. Also I was desperately tired. I used to long to lie down and go to sleep.

"Before Bronwen was born, or even on the way, we had been reading the books of Dr Ulric Williams, a dietician who had been struck off the medical register for his unorthodox behaviour and beliefs. We were greatly impressed by all he said and firmly believed that diet was probably the only answer to my troubles. In Nelson I had gone to the hospital three days a week for a good while, taking Gabrielle and Michael to a woman near the hospital to be looked after while I had my treatment. I had 'ionization,' 'diathermy,' 'infra-red' and even 'ultra-violet' rays and massages, but no good came of it and I felt even worse. After the treatment I would walk home with the children as the bus times didn't suit, and it was very tiring."

I remember as a small child the infrared lamp my father made, and the Ulric Williams book shelved next to "Mothercraft" and various Plunket Society publications in our living room. I also remember the Epsom salts in which my mother would bathe her feet, the copper bracelet she wore for a while, the cod liver oil she took (and made her children take as well!), the wheat germ sprinkled on our porridge, the fresh orange juice. She even carried a potato in her pocket for weeks on end, no doubt in response to a neighbor with more compassion than good judgment. But it was Ulric Williams who spoke most directly to her own inchoate ideas about health.

After completing medical training at Cambridge and Edinburgh universities, Ulric Williams (1890–1972) worked as a surgeon at Wanganui Hospital for fourteen years before undergoing a midlife religious conversion that led him to postulate that illness was a result of "refined, adulterated food," "smoking, abuse of liquor, lack of exercise and fresh air" as well as "negative emotional states." Arguing against the medical orthodoxy that acute diseases could be cured "by poisons or violence"—words which surely resonated with my mother's experience of doctors—Williams advocated that people stop imposing clinical labels on diseases, that they cultivate an optimistic disposition, and subtract from their life all the negative elements that produce illness. "Your body has a healing power that will heal you when you stop making yourself sick."

My mother and father resolved to meet Ulric Williams. My elder sister Gabrielle would stay with a family friend while they were away, while Juliet and I would be taken care of by our grandparents. This must have been in 1944, when Williams was at the height of his fame.

"I was keyed up to meet the great Ulric Williams," my mother writes, "but from the very first sight of him my heart sank slowly, and I closed up at his coldness. Unlike his books, he was apparently unsympathetic, rather contemptuous, and so very cold. 'Stand up straight,' he said to me straight away, and though I didn't know that I wasn't, he kept on saying, 'Put your shoulders back, hold your head up!' Then he asked a few questions with clinical detachment, and outlined the diet I must follow strictly. This diet needed a juice extractor, which we didn't have, and as it was during the war, had no hope of getting, which I pointed out rather timidly. 'You can get anything you want, if you make up your mind,' he said harshly. We paid our bill and left, his last words echoing in our ears as we walked the streets of Wanganui looking for a juice extractor, which we now expected to leap at us from somewhere, but in vain. At last in an old second-hand shop, D'Arcy found a tin punctured with nail holes and a wooden gadget with a handle, which he bought and used for many long days.

"When we got home we settled to our routine, buying sacks of carrots from a farmer. D'Arcy would get a bucketful and squeeze the juice from his slow-working gadget, and I would drink a quart every day, feeling very nauseous the more I drank. Each morning I would drink down *quickly* a quart of warm water with a dessert spoon of Baking

Soda in it, quite an ordeal. During the day I had a cup of Glaxo, a dish of dried apricots and a salad—no meat, no eggs, no bread. I used to long to eat a crust from the childrens' sandwiches, but didn't, and so I went on for six long weeks, getting very weak, but able to get into the bath unaided, which I hadn't been able to do for a long time. Then I realized that Bronwen was on the way, and after confessing this to Dr Rutherford, who suggested an abortion, I wrote to Dr Williams asking about the diet, receiving almost immediately a very nasty letter, saying how could I be so stupid, and he would suggest nothing for me. I had to eat now to keep up my strength—I was so thin that even after Bronwen was born the doctor said I *must* put on some weight. Once again the rheumatoid arthritis went into remission until after the baby was born, and so it was later with Miles whom the doctor again advised an abortion, in vain—this I could never do, although my ideas on abortion generally are not really definite. I think each person must decide for herself—for me it was out of the question."

Emily ends with an account of various other doctors she consulted. Dr Law advised her to go to Rotorua Hospital for treatment. When Emily expressed the view that the small gains she might make did not justify leaving her children for weeks at a time, Dr Law said, "You are a very near-sighted woman, I fear." Law's successor, Dr Whittle, proved a more sympathetic human being, and when he suggested the possibility of surgery, Emily consented to see Dr Isdale, head of Rotorua Hospital, who proved to be a "lovely person who listened to my own ideas and how I found it best to cope." Indeed, this was the first time any doctor had agreed with the choices Emily had made, saying she "had done the very best possible thing and to keep to it." This was, Emily notes, "so surprising, but so very comforting," and the possibility of operating on her hands was not broached. Years before, as her hands became clenched up, she had tried a clawlike contraption that she wore at night and that forced the fingers to straighten. Later, she tried a molded plastic splint strapped to her hand, but this was as ineffective as the metal claw and as excruciatingly painful.

Emily's account of her life living with rheumatoid arthritis is brought to an abrupt and telling end.

"I'm tired of all this talk of R.A.," she writes in 1984, "and although there could be much to tell, I think it is far too boring. Of course, Dr Caughey [her doctor through the early and mid-1980s] said he found me remarkable etc., as so many people do, but I said: 'It's a matter of living or not living, there's nothing wonderful about it.' I chose life instead of invalidism, and a family of five children, three of whom would have been aborted had I listened to the doctors—I told him this too. When I told him about going to bed wearing splints with wires to stretch my fingers out, and later plastic ones moulded to the shape of my outstretched hands, he seemed rather upset and disapproving, and asked what doctor had suggested that."

It would be consoling to think that medical science has now got it right, that new drugs and genetic techniques will soon offer us a cure for rheumatoid arthritis, and that doctors are more understanding of the patient now than they were "then," but this is, to some extent, beside the point. For we will never be able to escape pain and adversity, and what I find so illuminating in my mother's story is the way one learns not to give one's energies to the allocation of blame or the search for causes but to a renewed determination to live within the limits set. She speaks of "getting through the winter and hoping for the summer to test myself more," and of life being "very hard, though I never felt unhappy, although at times rather despairing." Writing about Holocaust survivors, Dan Bar-On observes that fear and hope are "deeply interwoven" in their lives, oscillating between the terrors of the past and the hope of a new beginning.[22] To some degree, this observation holds true for most people. Stretched to the limits of her endurance, Emily "always felt that things would get better," and this hope, springing eternal, countered despair. But what I find most edifying about Emily's memoir is that her resilience has little or nothing to do with any moral code. She never speaks of overcoming obstacles because she has her children to think of; she is never sustained by a sense that her suffering may have meaning in the sight of God; she never sees her actions as principled, as heroic, or even as worth commenting on. Living is simply what one does; there is neither virtue in it, nor meaning. Ethics are autonomic. One is not reducible to one's pain, one's condition, ability or disability, any more than one's being is rendered transparent and explicable by identifying one's color, class, or creed. My mother was pitied by some—who saw her as crippled and therefore compromised in her humanity—and praised as extraordinary by others, who extolled her grace and resolution in the face of adversity. But she was equally

22. Dan Bar-On, *Fear and Hope: Three Generations of the Holocaust* (Cambridge, Mass.: Harvard University Press, 1995), 1.

impatient with both responses, for life did not consist in the reality of pain or in her disease, nor even in what she had made of her life, in raising a family, in surviving, in reinventing herself as a painter after her children were grown and domestic chores were less oppressive. As for illness, it was a "companion," something you lived with, nothing more. It was neither a cause for congratulation if you overcame it, nor a cause for criticism if you succumbed. Nor was it to be made the central subject of one's life, an occasion for philosophizing. It was something you accommodated as best you could, not something you talked about. One talks about the things that make life worthwhile, not the things that detract from it. And yet I am struck by the way in which her every moment of well-being is made so by its closeness to the corrosive force of pain, as if the one were conditional on the other, a gift salvaged from a wreck with which life can be rebuilt. Nor do you look back. What is done is done. Regret is a waste of time, a misuse of scarce resources and vital energy. One looks forward, always forward. Hoping for the best. Or to use one of her favorite phrases, "hoping that everything will work out in the long run." In silence life is honored. For Emily never visited her pain on her children. Like a story from the Holocaust or hell, why would one want others to share this terrible burden?

Nothing, however, is without its cost. I dislike the vulgar expression "trade-offs." Yet for everything one resolves to do or say, something will not be done or said. Except perhaps within the secret pages of a journal, to be read only after one's pain has ceased with the ending of one's life.

"I think perhaps one of the worst parts of it all is the loneliness. No one, doctors or family, can possibly understand, and I couldn't bear to join groups such as the Arthritis Foundation. Even I, when I feel a little better after a hard, impossible, seemingly endless spell, cannot quite understand myself, or feel the agony—it has gone and left me in the same state as after childbirth—pain forgotten, life renewed."

Night

Reading Elie Wiesel's *Night* and Judith Sherman's *Say the Name* in the same week brought me back to the perhaps unanswerable question: what on earth can one do, being a creature who *must* act, who *must* speak, when one is thrown into a situation that absolutely prohibits one to do or say anything except on penalty of death? On his second day in Auschwitz, Elie Wiesel's father suffered a colic attack. Appealing to the barracks Kapo, he asked in polite German: "Excuse me . . . Could you tell me where the toilets are located?" The *blockälteste* stared at the man for a long time, "as if," writes Wiesel, "he wished to ascertain that the person addressing him was actually a creature of flesh and bone, a human being with a body and a belly. Then, as if waking from a deep sleep, he slapped my father with such force that he fell down and then crawled back to his place on all fours."[23] In this hell on earth, there is nothing one can say, nothing one can do, that will affect one's fate. One's body—the body that craves food and sleep, that suffers lice, and cold and pain—is a liability. As for one's soul, it is in ruins, for even almighty God does nothing, says nothing, gives no sign. Beaten and abused by ss guards, Judith Sherman asks, "God, how are we so visible to them and so invisible to You? You owe us visibility—."[24] And on the eve of Rosh Hashanah, as he hears thousands of lips repeating the bene-diction "Blessed be God's name," Elie Wiesel, who had once believed in salvation and prayer but now finds himself alone in a world that God has abandoned, asks, "Why would I bless Him? Because he caused thousands of children to burn in His mass graves? Because he kept six crematoria working day and night, including Sabbath and the Holy Days? Because in His great might, He had created Auschwitz, Birkenau, Buna and so many other factories of death?" In such places, at such times, humanity is in the hands of those who have no humanity, while those who suffer, and are all too human, are stripped of everything that would suggest to their tormentors any kinship, any common ground. Though the prisoners are compared to animals, it is not ordinary ani-mals that the ss have in mind—for these are useful and even lovable—but a degraded and useless species or collection of things—*figuren* or *stücke*, dolls, woods, merchandise, rags. "Move faster, you filthy dogs," the ss bellow. People are herded into cattle trucks. Police dogs tear a man apart. Those who survive become like animals, scavenging for a

23. Elie Wiesel, *Night*, trans. Marion Wiesel (New York: Hill and Wang, 2006), 39.

24. Judith H. Sherman, *Say the Name: A Survivor's Tale in Prose and Poetry* (Albu-querque: University of New Mexico Press, 2005), 49.

crust of bread, a scrap of cloth, a pair of shoes. Sometimes it is only an animal that is capable of recognizing the humanity of these degraded beings, as Emmanuel Levinas recalls, describing how, for a few short weeks during his long captivity, a stray dog entered the lives of the Jewish prisoners among whom he numbered. On their way to work in the forest each morning, the prisoners would be observed by German civilians in whose eyes, writes Levinas, they were subhuman, no longer part of the world. And then, one day, this cur that lived in some wild patch near the camp came to meet the pitiable rabble as it returned under guard from the forest. This happened many times, the dog greeting the prisoners at their dawn assembly and on their return from work, jumping up and down and barking with delight. "For him, there was no doubt that we were men."[25]

And yet the most urgent question may be not the question of what a prisoner could say or do inside the Lager but what, if one happened to survive, he or she could say or do afterward. Elie Wiesel finds it difficult to answer this question. "Did I write so as *not* to go mad," he asks, "or to *go* mad in order to understand the nature of madness? Was it to testify to events we must never forget, lest they happen again? Or was it simply to preserve a record of the ordeal I endured as an adolescent, at an age when one's knowledge of death and evil should be limited to what one discovers in literature?"[26]

That these questions cannot be answered unequivocally attests to the poverty of our belief in our power to foretell our future or decide our own destiny. If I take any lesson from the testimonies of writers like Elie Wiesel and Primo Levi it is that human existence is largely a matter of contingency, not design, and that there are strict limits to our ability to know why things happen as they do or in what ways our words and deeds influence our unfolding fate. We like to imagine that we act rationally, or on principle—as if the ideas we hold in our heads are scripts that guide and even determine our behavior. But I have learned that we attribute reason and morality to our actions in retrospect, and that for the most part we act thoughtlessly, unconsciously, habitually, or despite ourselves.

25. Emmanuel Levinas, *Difficult Freedom: Essays on Judaism*, trans. Seán Hand (Baltimore: Johns Hopkins University Press, 1990), 153.

26. Wiesel, *Night*, vii.

What arrests me, reading these survivor tales, is not the brutality of the SS or even the fact of genocide (for despite all our dreams that things might be different after Auschwitz, history has decided otherwise) — but that *anyone* should survive that limbo that lay between memory and ash. Two days before the Red Army reached Buna, the SS evacuated the camp. In blinding snow, the thousands still able to walk were force-marched away from the front. Chilled to the bone, famished, and at the very limits of their strength, these living dead were nonetheless able to march twenty kilometers, sometimes running, before being allowed to rest in a gutted brick factory. The dead lay in the accumulating snow like logs of wood. Yet the living pressed on, driven by the SS who shot whoever stumbled or fell. "Our legs moved mechanically," writes Elie Wiesel, "in spite of us, without us."

It may be no more possible to find a reason for writing about such things than it is to explain why the majority of these prisoners did not give up the ghost, but went on. One did so because this is what human beings do. This is what we do even when we see no reason for doing it.

Is it, then, also human to go back over the ground we have traveled, often in abject misery, and recount our experiences? Is it human to tell stories? For it would seem that storytelling is as ubiquitous and inevitable as the actions of breathing, speaking, eating, and mating. Some say we write to find meaning in what has befallen us, to restore our sense of agency when it has been overwhelmed by events we did not choose and could not control. Others speak of the imperious demands of bearing witness to evil.[27] Still others say that we have recourse to stories to spell away the overhanging night, or escape the ignominy and difficulty of our lives. But maybe we tell stories because we have no choice. Perhaps storytelling is part of the curse of consciousness.

In my version of Genesis, God expresses his anger and displeasure at man's disobedience by cursing humankind with consciousness. Thenceforth this creature is in thrall to its imagination, able to envisage lives it cannot lead, remember the terrors of the past, contemplate death long before it comes, pose questions that cannot be answered, and entertain

---

27. Primo Levi, *Moments of Reprieve*, trans. Ruth Feldman (London: Abacus, 1987), 9; Primo Levi, *The Drowned and the Saved*, trans. Raymond Rosenthal (New York: Vintage, 1989), 174.

all manner of hopes and aspirations that other animals are blissfully incapable of conceiving. Though perpetually dissatisfied with their lot, human beings discover that this capacity of consciousness also provides them with a way of getting back at God. They can imagine a world in which God does not exist, through wishful thinking deny their own mortality, and conjure justifications for their wildest dreams. They can even find value in the most unlikely places, the most unassuming things, and even create their own version of His creation. This, we call art.

Outside the Window

"Yesterday," Emily writes, "Juliet drove me to Avondale to visit her Osteopath who was to give me some 'muscle balancing.' I am not an easy person to deal with in these cases, I know, and I have always been rather skeptical of a number of mysterious and unexplained or unproven things. I think I am, strangely enough, very logical, and I loved the study of Logic and Ethics at university more than anything else. I appreciated Juliet's goodness and concern and know how deeply she believes in her diets and muscle balancing etc. but I just can't do it myself. I tried many treatments and diets when I was in the early years of arthritis but came to the conclusion that if I were to live and have a good life I must disassociate myself as much as possible from sickness and ignore it in the main. Otherwise I would be chasing cures all my life, reclining on couches and being a dreadful nuisance to everyone, as well as being bored and miserable. So now, at seventy-six, I can't go back and compromise—I must stay alive as long and as vitally as possible. I wanted to go yesterday—for Juliet's sake, as I did to the homeopath a year ago, as I did forty years ago for someone else, when I put a potato in my pocket and kept it there till it shriveled up supposedly taking my pains away, but ending up in the washing machine—when I drank cod-liver oil and orange juice, went on elimination diets, wore copper bracelets till my arms were black etc. etc.

"Please forgive me Juliet dear for being an unbeliever and not trying hard enough. But I found my attention wandering throughout the interview, looking through the window at the lovely distant view of the sea and beach and the life of spring everywhere. The little room was like a prison. The steep steps to the front door led to a small room with a couch, chairs and table all about six inches from the ground, and like a dwarf's opium den, into which I, the giant, was intruding. Ross looked worried and uncertain, and I felt no warmth between us—I suppose my not being able to get up the steep steps was a setback for him. He came out carrying two yellow telephone directories, very disdainfully and hopelessly, and disappeared into the house when I accepted them to climb the steps. When I came down again later with the directories and D'Arcy's help, I put my foot down tentatively from the top step, looking intently at the small yellow space upon which I must stand as a go-between when the black printed words written on the Directory cover leap into my vision, 'Disaster is Impending' causing me to pause for thought before moving another inch—slowly I descended until I stood on 'Disaster is Impending' on the lowest step and alighted with great relief. The humour of it made me feel good and I am none the worse, really, although surer than ever that I am the master of my fate. If my life ends soon, or a little later, what really does it matter. I've had a wonderful time, a wonderful family, and the pain is nothing in comparison with all the wonder and beauty of my life."

"What Really Matters"

Conventional definitions of religion tend to emphasize the rituals, practices, doctrines, ethics, laws, symbols, and experiences associated with beliefs in spiritual, extrasocial or "supernatural" beings. Such definitions are substantive in character and presume that religious *experience* can be directly inferred from beliefs and practices. But if this were the case, someone like Emily, who from her earliest childhood felt no affinity for the religion of her parents, and was bored and disenchanted by church, would be seen as lacking any experience that one might call religious. That this is patently untrue—despite Emily's avowed atheism—suggests that we need to approach religiosity without a theological vocabulary, repudiate the notion of religion as a sui generis phenomenon, and distance ourselves from the assumption of a necessary relationship between espoused belief and subjective experience. Adhering to the precepts and practices of a particular faith does not mean that one shares, to the same extent and in the same measure, the experiences of other adherents. Nor does depth of commitment or intense "revelatory" or mystical experience of the divine constitute an onto-logical proof of it. For these reasons, I am skeptical of the idea that we can grasp the truth of any experience from the ways in which it is con-ceptualized. Methodologically, this means construing terms like God, heroism, good and evil as *potential* ways in which we retrospectively gain some purchase on shattering experiences or acknowledge that the ways in which events overtook us appear to confirm the truth of our conventional ways of describing the world. A theological language is, of course, part of the culture in which we grow up. Even when it is not a conspicuous or focal element in our lives, it is available to us as one possible way of making sense of events that outstrip our comprehen-sion and control, which is why we will cry "Oh God" when in shock, or have recourse to prayer as a way of bolstering hope. But limit ex-periences do not necessarily bring us to religion, as Emily's story makes clear, and "spiritual" resources are not the only resources available to us in crisis, despite our tendency to use a quasi-religious language in describing experiences that confound and overwhelm us.

Though approaching the question of "religious" experience from very different vantage points, my colleagues Robert Orsi and Arthur Kleinman arrive, though not straightforwardly, at remarkably similar conclusions. In his earliest work, Orsi is at pains to get beyond the tra-ditional definitions of religion I have just alluded to by emphasizing people's "ultimate values, their most deeply held ethical convictions, their efforts to order their reality, their cosmology." These, he writes, constitute "their ground of being."[28] Unfortunately, this conception of religion remains wedded to the idea that our lives are grounded in our worldviews, and that the meaning of our lives can be therefore divined from our moral conceptions of who we are, where we have come from, and where we are going. Perhaps this is why, twenty years after his initial formulations, Orsi redefines religious experience more dynamically and contentiously, not as "a web of meanings but of rela-tionships between heaven and earth," occupying an ambiguous space betwixt and between established codes and extreme experiences, a do-main of intersubjective struggle rather than moral maps.[29] Yet there is

28. Robert A. Orsi, *The Madonna of 115th Street: Faith and Community in Italian Harlem, 1880–1950* (New Haven, Conn.: Yale University Press, 1985), xvii.
29. Robert A. Orsi, *Between Heaven and Earth: The Religious Worlds People Make*

one phrase in his earlier work that compels attention. "Simply stated," Orsi writes, "religion . . . means 'what matters.'"[30] Here he seems in perfect agreement with Arthur Kleinman's thesis in his book *What Really Matters*, where the moral is not made identical with the moral codes we commonly associate with religion but with deeper existential imperatives that find expression *not only* in religious doctrines but in vernacular and secular idioms as well. What is at stake are those critical experiences, unfolding between what we take for granted and what we find we cannot control or comprehend. Whether we refer to these experiences as intimations of ultimate reality or of the divine is beside the point; what really matters is not how we name them, but how we live through them, though naming the new is always an important tactical response to it.

Can we live without the languages with which we name our experiences? Can we do without the words we take to be identical with the world? Can we avoid the dangers of seeing our representations of the real as repositories of reality, aspects of its very nature, essential to its existence? Can we at least accept the arbitrariness of names, so that in communicating our experiences to ourselves and to others we waive the signifiers, the better to get a sense of what is signified, hopefully glimpsing the common ground that our signposts have obscured? My own approach to these questions is to reexamine the notion of transcendence. In the Sartrean sense, transcendence is a form of surpassing, overcoming, or going beyond (*dépassement*). This implies, first, that human beings strive to go beyond the circumstances into which they are thrown by the contingencies of history, the accidents of birth, the twists of fate, and the unpredictable course of relationships over time. It is human, all too human, to try to transform what is given into something over which we *appear* to exercise some degree of choice and control. Second, human beings strive to go beyond *themselves*, consummating their singularity in relation to universality, variously construed as the social, the cosmic, the historical, or the ideological. Third—*and it is here that the twin leitmotifs of this book, connectedness and crisis, come together*—in limit situations more than at any other time,

---

and the People Who Study Them (Princeton, N.J.: Princeton University Press, 2005), 2.

30. Orsi, *The Madonna of 115th Street*, xvii.

human beings turn to *ulterior* objects, ideas, words, and persons as ways of gaining some purchase on the thoughts and feelings that elude their grasp. And so it is that I discover in my mother's journal the essence of my own worldview, and where it comes to religiosity feel that she might have felt a kinship with Martin Buber, who writes that "what really matters is not the 'experiencing' of life (*Erleben*)—the detached subjectivity—*but life itself*; not the religious experience, which is part of the psychic realm, but religious life itself, that is, the total life of an individual or of a people in their actual relationship to God and the world."[31] That Emily never invoked God, nor framed her existential struggle in religious terms, does not mean that her experience was *essentially* different from the experience of those for whom life's intelligibility and ultimate meaning are expressed through the language of a faith. It may be impossible to ever know why the wilderness of this world brings some people to a knowledge of God and others to a knowledge to which they assign quite different names, such as Ultimate Reality, Enlightenment, or Truth. But it would seem that for all human beings, regardless of their worldviews, it is in border situations when they are sorely tested, where they come up against the limits of what they can control, comprehend, and cope with, that they are most susceptible to those epiphanies, breakthroughs, conversions, and revelations that are sometimes associated with the divine and sometimes simply taken as evidence of the finitude, uncertainty, and thrownness of human existence. If there is any argument against preferring one interpretive vocabulary over others, it is that some mistakenly imply epistemological claims, appearing to privilege one way of representing reality by depreciating others. What matters, what really matters, is that our experiences always remain, to some extent, transparent, so that our particular ways of comprehending the world do not prevent us from seeing that no one person is ever in a position to grasp *the* human. "The whole," writes Theodor Adorno, overturning Hegel, "is the false."[32]

31. Martin Buber, Preface to the 1923 edition of *On Judaism*, 8 (emphasis added).

32. Theodor Adorno, *Minima Moralia: Reflections from Damaged Life*, trans. E. F. N. Jephcott (London: Verso, 1978), 50.

3. ELECTIVE AFFINITIES

Knots

In a characteristically aphoristic vein, Theodor Adorno observes, "The person is the historically tied knot that should be freely loosened and not perpetuated," adding that our conventional notions of the person are evidence of "the ancient spell of the universal, entrenched in the particular."[1] Clearly, Adorno is alluding to a modernist European conception of the person, and it probably did not occur to him to consider seriously African, Aboriginal, or Asian traditions of thought that have never tied the knot of the self as tightly as we are inclined to do, thereby avoiding the "ideological mischief" of seeing persons as worlds unto themselves, defined within the bookends of birth and death. But while we might applaud Adorno's criticism of philosophers who deconstruct the notion of a bounded, enduring, identifiable self only to replace it with a personlike abstraction such as Existence, Being, Subjectivity, or the Social, we might wonder how any human being could conceive of the world except in human terms. Who is ever in a position to see the world as a salmon, a fly, a ghost, an ancestor, or a stone might? Rather than rail against personalism per se, perhaps it is more feasible to aim at loosening the knot of our *own* particular point of view—to which we are inclined to cling, claiming it as ours, if not definitive of who we are, and defending it to the death (often of others) as the only right and reasonable way of seeing the world.

It is to Goethe that we owe the analogy between human and chemical

1. Theodor Adorno, *Negative Dialectics*, trans. E. B. Ashton (New York: Seabury, 1973), 276–77.

bonds. In *Elective Affinities* (1809), he borrows from chemistry the term *wahlverwandtschaft* and makes it a metaphor for the "chemistry" that ignites or inspires a sense of affinity between seemingly different people. Of such "elective affinities," the Captain in chapter 4 of Goethe's novel remarks: "Those natures which, when they meet, quickly lay hold on and mutually affect one another we call affined. This affinity is sufficiently striking in the case of alkalis and acids which, although they are mutually antithetical, and perhaps precisely because they are so, most decidedly seek and embrace one another, modify one another, and together form a new substance." In response to the Captain, Charlotte observes that "it is in just this way that truly meaningful friendships can arise among human beings: for antithetical qualities make possible a closer and more intimate union."[2] The term "elective affinities" may be extended to encompass all our relations with others—singular or collective, human or extrahuman—since in all such encounters we stand to lose *and* find ourselves; some aspects eclipsed, others thrown into relief. And since *something* transpires in the course of every encounter, leaving one slightly changed, human existence is always, to some extent, a living beyond oneself.

To be social is inevitably to both risk losing or compromising the things one calls one's own *and* to gain something more than one is, has or can accomplish alone. Human existence is thus a continual oscillation between quite different modes of being—from the singular (ipse) to the universal (idem). As Charlotte, Eduard, and the Captain observe at the beginning of their conversation, human beings are like drops of water, oil, or quicksilver—one moment discrete, the next merged with others. This is why we sometimes say that we show different sides of ourselves to different people, even though we cling to what we take to be abiding conceptions of who we *really* are or the inalienable and "sacred" symbols of our particular identity. Viewed from one's own standpoint, one is the sum total of all that one calls one's own, including material belongings, social relationships, physical attributes, and psychological traits.[3] Viewed from the standpoint of others, we

2. Johann Wolfgang von Goethe, *Elective Affinities*, trans. R. J. Hollingdale (Harmondsworth: Penguin, 1971), 52–53.

3. William James, *The Principles of Psychology*, vol. 1 (New York: Dover, 1950), 291.

are equally manifold for, as William James puts it, "*a man has as many social selves as there are individuals who recognize him* and carry an image of him in their mind."[4] Despite the plasticity of human identity, people are generally inclined to give more credence to the substantives they attach to themselves and others than to the transitive experiences they undergo in the course of their social interactions over time. This is as true of folk culture as it is of anthropological analysis. Yet what unfolds in the course of a relationship may be far more relevant to understanding the reality of that relationship than the identity terms with which individuals insist on characterizing it. Despite the great store we set by such values as maternal love, filial piety, and kinship solidarity, the realization of these concepts is never guaranteed by the passion with which they are espoused. Indeed, their determining power is far less than their symbolic power in retrospectively acknowledging that a particular relationship has "worked out," so confirming the value as well as giving the impression that it was the reason or cause of the positive result. In other words, the *idea* of a good relationship does not necessarily create a good relationship; rather, a good relationship is a by-product of what transpires between people in the course of time. "Good" is simply an ex post facto compliment we pay to the happy coincidence between what we hoped would happen and what actually eventuated.

These aporias between self and other, moral ideal and lived experience, mean that emotions of anxiety *and* exhilaration arise in every interaction. Accordingly, face-to-face relations may be thought of as border situations par excellence, for here more than anywhere we risk confirmation or nullification, and are made or unmade. We are thus, in a sense, all migrants. Every day and in every encounter we cross the dark sea that lies between the known and the unknown, embarking on journeys in which we hazard all that we are and from which we return transformed. This is not primarily a struggle to find God or to come home, but a struggle for being itself, in which we are sustained by the faith that life will either be found or will find us. When tragedy befalls us, we sometimes say we are "undone" or "shattered," and "fall apart." We stretch our bodies, minds, or senses to the limit, so that we may escape the confines of ourselves. We still the mind and steady the

4. Ibid., 294 (emphasis in original).

body, altering our sense of who we are. We enter into relationships that change us utterly. We travel, and see ourselves as if from afar.

Marina del Rey

With nine hours to kill before my onward flight to Auckland, I took a shuttle to Marina del Rey, wanting to smell the sea and soak up the sun. In a supermarket near the marina, I bought some sushi, a couple of bananas, and a bottle of water and wondered what conclusions a Martian anthropologist might draw from seeing all the provender and people in that place. A woman in her late forties with long blonde hair was playing her harp near the coffee counter—tunes like *Greensleeves* and *Chanson dans la Nuit*. Nearby, several customers were dunking free strawberries in a fountain of liquid chocolate. Everyone was dressed casually, in sandals, sneakers, shorts, and T-shirts. The store sold everything from takeout food to candy, cell phones, huge chocolate cakes, cold meats, and "lifestyle books." *The Da Vinci Code* was ubiquitous, as were the usual selection of books on how to succeed in life, if not in business. *Winning. Performance Excellence. A Powerful One-Step Plan to Live and Finish Rich. Closing Deals. Beating the Market.*

On the corner of Admiralty Way, a Mexican guy wearing an iPod was jiggling a sign with a large arrow and the words *Condos for Sale* on it. I headed down to the water where Latino families were barbecuing their lunches, the kids playing ball or cycling along the paths. I could hear the 747s taking off with a surging roar in the distant heat haze. Across the water came the sound of speedboats.

I passed some of my time drafting the short speech I would be expected to give when I received an honorary degree in Wellington in a few days' time. I had found it hard to accept this honor, in part because I suspected it was more in recognition of my Harvard position than my books, which had always had an anti-establishment edge to them. I was also acutely aware of the gap between my life now and the relatively low-key if not anonymous life I had lived in New Zealand, and the many idle moments I had spent wondering whether I could ever go home again. For though I had lived abroad for many years, moving often in search of work and becoming more and more estranged from my homeland, New Zealand remained my *turangawaewae* (place to stand), the place to which my thoughts always gravitated when I wanted to remind myself of what was real.

This notion that what is historically prior or biographically antecedent is more causally compelling than any event or experience that comes after may be rephrased existentially as a contrast between events that befall us without our awareness or assent, and events we have a hand in choosing, for we attribute to primordial events a determinative power and moral authority that we would seldom claim for ourselves.

In the Maori myth of human origins, the primal ancestors, Ranginui (sky) and Papatuanuku (earth) are initially clasped in such a close embrace that their five progeny are compressed in the dark gap between the parental bodies, barely able to move. Tu-matauenga—the ancestor of war—argues for slaying the parents; four of his brothers—Tane-mahuta (ancestor of the forests), Rongo-ma-tane (ancestor of cultivated foodstuffs), Haumia-tikitiki (ancestor of uncultivated foods), and Tangaroa (ancestor of fish and reptiles)—argue for forcing the parents apart. Despite their best efforts, only Tane succeeds (which is why, in Maori carved art, the trunks of forest trees, pushing against the earth, hold up the sky). The fifth brother, Tawhiri-matea (ancestor of wind and storms), is so angered by this violent separation of the parents that he assails his brothers with hurricane-force winds, thunderstorms, and hail. All succumb except Tu, who now turns on his weak and cowardly brothers, devouring them—an act that carries the symbolic meaning of rendering them "common" (noa), and making them articles of food. Tawhiri alone withstands this onslaught, so that in today's world warfare and storms are the forces that prevail.

What is compelling to me about this myth is not only the way it spells out the correct relationships (tikanga) between all things for all time; it presumes that human beings not only chose to bring light and life into this world but that they disagreed about how best to achieve the task, and proved to have very different capacities when they applied themselves to it. Moreover, unlike the reluctant births in Oedipal myths from all over the world, where an ancestor or god impedes the arrival of his successor or the heir delays his own maturation, the Maori myth embraces the idea of aggressive heroism and celebrates the energy and will of each new generation's right to life. But there is a real existential difference between voluntary and involuntary exile—the first being something we can live with because we have chosen it and can, in theory, reverse; the second visited upon us, often with traumatic suddenness, by circumstances or forces beyond our comprehension and control.

In Limbo

On my flight from Los Angeles I was seated across the aisle from an elderly woman who seemed to be having difficulties with her remote control. "Can I help you?" I asked. Without saying anything, the woman allowed me to show her how to operate the remote. "Is this your first time flying to New Zealand?" I asked. "Oh no," she said, "my daughter lives in California, in LA. I visit her every winter to get away from the cold. I've had cancer, you know. I almost died. I spend half the year in California with my eldest daughter, and half in New Zealand with my youngest daughter. They take care of me. My daughters say I was a good mum to them; now it's their turn to look after me."

"So you get the best of both worlds?" I said.

She watched movies long into the night. As most passengers slept, and I lapsed into reverie, she watched movies. I glanced over at her from time to time, as if I was under some obligation to take care of her in this limbo between her daughters' worlds. Then I realized that she was watching the same movie over and over again. *Last Holiday*, starring Queen Latifah, about a store assistant with a passion for fine food who learns that she has only a few weeks to live and splashes her life savings on a stay at a luxury ski resort in the Austrian Alps, determined to realize her dreams before she dies.

In Media Res

Liberated from mundane routines and requirements, I slipped further and further into reverie. Though close to sleep at times, lulled by the drone of the aircraft engines and the subdued light in the cabin, my thoughts keep returning to the idea of the penumbral, and the meaning of limit situations, and the question of how I might do justice to such phenomena in my writing. Then, as arbitrarily and instantly as in a dream, I was suddenly back in Provence, the mistral blowing out of a clear sky, playing havoc with the dry leaves, and howling at night in the stone chimney of our house.

My wife and I had rented the *mas* for the summer with two close friends. For five days, as the mistral blew, we were confined indoors. Over glasses of brandy after dinner, Tom regaled us with stories of frayed nerves and gruesome crimes, forgiven because of the wind. But on me it wreaked a very different change, and for the first time in many years, I turned my hand to poetry.

> It breaks into the gap
> left by the day before yesterday's calm.
> Like an arm bent, a hand hardened
> by work in the lilac earth
>
> It helps itself to us
> harvesting our thought
> teasing out what lies hardest on our hearts.
>
> I walked toward the hill this morning
> buffeted by it and built
> a stone wall for shelter.
>
> Moths and grasshoppers flickered
> in the stubble and juniper;
> the whole hill was moving in the wind.
>
> Was it like this for Van Gogh
> during his last days at Arles
> this sinewy arm of the mistral
> with a clenched fist hammering
> the table in an arid yard
> for something he could not give?

I had thought that my discontent stemmed from my academic job or, rather, the balance I had lost between the ivory tower and the gritty reality of the world. One Thursday afternoon, I was sitting in the back of the seminar room as one of my colleagues vigorously chalked a diagram on the blackboard—a couple of boxes, connected by squiggly lines and various arrows. One box was called epistemology, the other was called ethics. I thought: *So this is what we do. Create these simplistic simulacra of the real world, make connections between them, and through a sleight of hand imagine we have grasped life in its essence, in its entirety, attributing to the world a systematicity that is a figment of our own ratiocination. In fact, we have lost touch with the world, we have lost it.* I found myself gazing out the window at the rain, wondering when I last felt completely alive. When I had last experienced a world drenched in sunlight and mystery. When life lay before me, boundless with promise and possibility? I remembered an estuary north of Wellington, the wild screech of gulls at night as I walked down the steep path through a shell midden to Sam's cabin on the foreshore, and then the creak of macrocarpas in the wind, the sawing and scraping of branches against the cabin wall, the blankets that smelled of woodsmoke, and sleep overtaking me as the fire died in the grate. I remembered walking a dusty path in northern Sierra Leone that was haphazardly punctuated by whorls of ash from the fired elephant grass . . . and, in the Congo, a blind boy on the roadside playing a thumb piano (*mbira*) on his head. But my colleague was droning on, and I was in prison, serving an indeterminate sentence. Books defined my world. A padded cell of printed pages. For years I had labored under the illusion that I might write my way out of the darkness that enveloped me. My father used to say I had the gift of the gab, that I could talk myself out of a paper bag. I thought that words would set me free. But now, like Don Quixote, I was about to be buried alive beneath them. Pitch darkness. The stale odor of monographs and treatises, and endless shelves. Words offered no way out. The world of books was windowless and closed, like Marcus Bennett's two boxes.

At La Boissière, the light flooded back into our lives. The dentelles of Mont Mirail were like a broken comb of ivory. In the courtyard of the *mas* the light seemed to issue out of the stones. Our bodies glowed. As night fell, we drank to our happiness. When Tom and Sylvia took our children away for a few days, to see some theater in Orange and reconnoiter the countryside, visiting vineyards and ruins, my wife and I found ourselves alone for the first time in many years. We moved our bed closer to the open window so we could see the stars. We lay awake, with the milky moonlight flooding the room. We inhaled the night air, heavy with the smell of dry earth and vineyards.

In the morning, I was preparing a breakfast to take out to the terrace. My wife was in the bathroom. Our radio was tuned to Luxembourg. Suddenly, the room was filled with this haunting music. I stopped what I was doing, as if my slightest movement would break the spell. As I was standing there, in the middle of the kitchen, eyes half-closed, listening to this song, my wife came from the bathroom, drawn to the music, as mesmerized as I. Neither of us said a word. My wife had a white towel around her. Her body was still wet. Globules of water on her shoulders and neck. Her hair lank. We stood together as the music transported us to some distant landscape, one moment steeped in shadow, the next in light, as the voice of the singer, by turns exultant and bereft, carried us further and further away.

As the song came to an end, my wife brought a finger to her lips, wanting to hear the title of the song. *Zajdi Zajdi*. A Macedonian folk song. I had never heard its like. But who was the singer?" I asked her.

"Nadya, Natania . . . something . . . I didn't really hear."

When the announcer moved on to the next piece, I turned down the radio. My wife began to dry her hair slowly, her hand holding the compressed towel against the side of her head for a moment, as if she had momentarily forgotten herself and the music again held her in thrall.

Months later, in London, I found a copy of the song, and identified the singer.

Sunrise, sunrise, bright sun, sunrise sunset
and you, clear moon—
go away, drown in the water.

Dark mountain, sorrowful sister,
we two sad ones
you for your lost leaves, Sister Mountain
me for my youth.

Your leaves, Sister Mountain, will return
my youth, sister mountain,
can never return.

In the shade of the fig tree, we sat side by side on the stone steps, with bowls of café au lait, planning our day. I could smell the rosemary, planted along the wall. The buttered croissants.

My wife packed a lunch—a baguette, some goat's cheese we had bought in the village yesterday, some arugula, a bottle of mineral water.

We struck out across a stubbled field. Two days ago, a combine harvester had come up the road. The kids ran after it, as if it had taken the mistral prisoner and it was now rattling in protest inside the lumbering machine. That evening the wheat was gone.

It was like walking into one of Cézanne's paintings of Monte St. Victoire.

As we climbed the sheep track through stunted holm oak and juniper, my wife slipped her arm through mine. After so many days of unrelenting wind, the stillness was uncanny. When I stopped to catch my breath, the blood was singing in my head.

From the crumbled stone wall of the terrace we looked out over the valley, the farmhouses obscured by cypresses. We hazarded names for the colors. Sky—deep cobalt; Payne's Gray near the horizon.

"The shadows of the grapevines are lilac," my wife said.

We leaned back against the sun-warmed stones. I closed my eyes. I could smell the warm earth. Hear the buzz of flies, the tinkle of a pebble dislodged by a lizard scuttling into the shadows of the stones. My wife's voice came to me with my own thoughts: "If only we could stay on here," she said. "Just do nothing but let this landscape seep into us. Just dissolve away in this blue light."

"How could we survive?"

"We wouldn't survive. We would live."

I opened my eyes. The screen on the seatback in front of me showed that we were now a thousand miles from the California coast. But I was not in time or space at that moment, but adrift, and suddenly aware of what I had been missing: the experience of music carrying one beyond oneself. The seemingly uninterrupted, seamless relationship between one's own body and the body of the land. Those transfiguring moments when one enters so fully into the being of another that the relationship is all there is . . .

In Wellington

I was staying with old friends in Roseneath. The house overlooked Evans Bay. Cedars and pohutakawas framed my view of the wind-abraded water and the hills beyond, scabrous with gorse and matagauri. Jennifer and I were sitting at a rimu table in the front room, sharing stories.

I was telling Jennifer about my fascination with the way in which certain traits, sensibilities, and identifications transcend the limits of space and time. Of the stream of life to which our own particular lives are tributary.

When I was living in Wellington in 1998, a passing acquaintance, Barbara Sumner, shared with me a story about her adopted half-brother. The young man was in his thirties, a vacuum-cleaner salesman, deeply unhappy, in a rut. One day, according to Barbara, her brother broke down and cried in front of her, confessing that he missed his "mummy," though he had never known her. Within two days, Barbara was able to trace the mother and arrange a meeting between her and the son she had given up for adoption. The young man then talked to his birth mother on the phone, saying that he would bring his wife, who was Indian with him to their meeting. There was a stunned silence at the other end of the phone, and the young man wondered whether his birth mother was racially prejudiced. But to his astonishment he now learned that his birth father, who died when the boy was one year old, was Indian. He had always thought of himself as white, and no one had ever suspected or suggested that his ethnic background was other than European. Yet, when he looked closely, he now began to discern, or imagine, an Indian cast to his features, and he reminded himself that the only women he had ever dated were dark-skinned; indeed, that he had, for many years, used his job as a door-to-door salesman as a pretext to meet and seduce Indian women. And then, of course, his wife was Indian.

"Meeting his birth mother and uncovering the truth about his origins transformed his life," I told Jennifer. "He migrated to Sydney and went into business, selling water filters in poorer neighborhoods. He became a millionaire. Apart from anything else," I added, "I like the symbolism. The vacuum cleaners picking up dirt. The water filters removing impurities. The sense of order and of cleanness when we know where we come from, who we are, and where we are going."

"If only it always worked out so well," Jennifer said. And she recounted the story of a minor writer she had met briefly a few years back. This man was in his forties when his parents died. When the will was read, he discovered for the first time that he had been adopted at birth. Stunned by this news, he set out to locate his birth parents. It turned out that his father had passed away several years before, but he tracked down his mother in a small South Island town. He knocked on her door. When the door was opened, he explained to the woman (whom he instantly recognized as his own flesh and blood) who he was and what he wanted—a few moments to talk, a little time to ask some questions. The woman said, "I don't know what you're talking about and I don't want to know." She closed the door in his face. Within a few weeks, Jennifer said, this man had multiple sclerosis. He went into sudden and terrible decline. For fifteen years his children watched their father degenerate into a wheelchair-bound, finally semivegetative, invalid.

We continued swapping stories about loss. One, in particular, remained lodged in my memory—the sad tale recounted by Barry Humphries in his memoir, *My Life as Me*.

A child of parents with plebeian tastes, Barry Humphries managed to accumulate, by the time he was in his early teens, a small and precious library that included Sunday School prizes (*Kidnapped, Bevis, Masterman Ready*) and a few rare, illustrated editions (*Arabian Nights* and *Mother Goose*). One day he returned from Camberwell Grammar to find that his books had disappeared from his room. On being asked by her breathless and distraught son what had become of his books, Barry's mother casually replied, "Oh, those. You'll be pleased to hear I gave them to the nice man from the Army. They'll go to poor Protestant children who haven't got any books."

"But they were *my* books," Barry protested, now in tears. His mother laughed. "But you've read them, Barry," she replied. And as she dried her son's eyes with the corner of her handkerchief, she added: "I hope you're not going to grow up to be a selfish little boy."

To this "early traumatic incident" Barry Humphries would attribute "the occasional savage bouts of bibliomania" that afflicted him all his life, scouring out-of-the-way secondhand bookshops and, more recently, the Internet, for exact replicas of those "volumes confiscated by the Salvation Army, with [his] mother's charitable contrivance."[5]

I then asked Jennifer a question that I had never been able to answer to my own satisfaction, perhaps because it was too general. "Do you think this endless search to reconnect with something or someone you have lost, and that you feel is absolutely vital to your existence, is also

5. Barry Humphries, *My Life as Me: A Memoir* (London: Michael Joseph, 2002), 75–77.

characteristic of people who were enslaved or colonized, who had their lands confiscated, their language and customs denigrated, their rights denied? And being treated like shit, or shunned as second-class citizens, are they then driven to recover their roots, find their original parents, and angrily insist on being given back what they are missing, even as they mourn it, even as they pass on their grief generation after generation, until it becomes a way of life?"

One answer lay in front of us — a book that Jennifer had recently published to mark the sixtieth anniversary of the forced resettlement of the entire population of Barnaba or "Ocean Island" to Rabi Island in Fiji in 1945. Jennifer's book was largely made up of Banaban stories — their recollections of time-honored practices such as the catching and taming of frigate birds, of life under the colonial regime, and the move to Rabi. Like Nauru to the west, the high atoll of Banaba consisted almost entirely of superphosphate. No sooner had the British made this discovery in 1900 than they set local and indentured laborers to quarrying it for export. Despite the Banabans' attempts to have mining restricted to certain sections of the island, to have the phosphate replaced with soil and trees replanted, the island became, by 1945, almost uninhabitable. Having endured the horrors of Japanese military occupation, the Banabans lost their homeland.

"Banaba is our mother," said Nei Makin Corrie Tekenimatang. "She brought us up."[6] And tears well up in the eyes of the old people as they recall the devastated landscape of their natal island, the contaminated water, the once bountiful mango, papaya and coconut trees. They speak in the same breath of the homeland lost and the "second land" they found. "We look on Rabi as synonymous with Banaba . . . it's becoming like that,"[7] said Taomati Teai.

Others speak less of the past than of the hardships of the present, explaining "the loss of laughter and joy" in terms of the struggle for a living wage, the difficulties of "putting food on the table every day,"[8] and problems such as getting access to markets and health services.

6. Jennifer Shennan and Makin Corrie Tekenimatang, eds., *One and a Half Pacific Islands: Stories Banaban People Tell of Themselves* (Wellington: Victoria University Press, 2005), 128.

7. Ibid., 127.

8. Ibid., 115.

But one story affected me more deeply than all the others. Kabunare Koura, who was eighty-three years old when interviewed in 1999, was the sole survivor of a Japanese massacre on August 20, 1945. On that day, some 150 Gilbert Islanders, who had been brought to the atoll to mine phosphate, were rounded up and taken to a cliff top high above the sea. Blindfolded and with their hands bound, they were then bayoneted and kicked from the cliff. Many died on the razor-sharp rocks below. Others were killed by the soldiers firing shots into the fallen bodies. Despite his wounds, Kabunare made his way to a sea cave and after 104 days in hiding presented himself to the Australians who had now occupied the island. Fifty-four years later, he would explain how he could cut toddy, but "no longer from the highest coconut trees." "Life is good," he said, referring to his nine children, twenty grandchildren and four great-grandchildren. "The past is gone."[9]

The Enigma of Anteriority

Is a person's life a seamless whole, a single story?[10] Or do we lead several lives at once—the life we author in our imaginations, and the life that is authored by others? And for those of us who have traveled far from our original home, how can we remain faithful to our beginnings, and is there any essential self than can be said to be the measure of who we truly are? How do most of us live? Samuel Beckett's answer: "By aporia pure and simple? Or by affirmations and negations invalidated as uttered, or sooner or later?"[11] Beckett goes on to ask if it possible to be *consciously* ephectic—habitually suspending judgment, adopting a skeptical attitude, living betwixt and between. My own view is that we live this way whether we know it or not, and that our identity is at the same time a shifting outcome of the relationships we are presently in and a residual memory of every relationship we have ever known.

9. Ibid., 71.

10. The phrase "the enigma of anteriority" is Paul Ricoeur's. Paul Ricoeur, *Critique and Conviction: Conversations with François Azouvi and Marc de Launay*, trans. Kathleen Blamey (New York: Columbia University Press, 1998), 100.

11. Samuel Beckett, "The Unnameable," in *I Can't Go On, I'll Go On: A Selection from Samuel Beckett's Work*, ed. Richard W. Seaver (New York: Grove Weidenfeld, 1976), 332–33.

This is why we often experience the present as a vague and spectral repetition of the past of which we retain only a distant memory (déja vu), the original forever slipping from the grasp of the mind even as it reappears enigmatically in the here and now under the guise of what Paul Ricoeur calls "the always–already–there." 'What' the past actually is can, therefore, never be disentangled from the question of 'who' is recalling it, and why.[12] I think this explains my fascination with those penumbral regions that lie outside the settled area of the self, where we see the world as through a glass darkly, glimpsing aspects of ourselves that seldom see the light of day yet offer the possibility of understanding others.

Forty years ago, during a brief stay in Munich, I discovered the paintings of Lovis Corinth (1858–1925) in the Neue Pinakothek. His earliest works are often staid and orthodox portraits, none of them particularly memorable. But from 1911, when Corinth was fifty-three and suffered a stroke that left him partially paralyzed on his left side, his style and subject matter undergo a sea change. Not only does landscape figure more prominently but the vision is now expressionist, the brush strokes betraying the unsteadiness and emotionality of an artist struggling with the compounded aftereffects of a stroke, alcoholism, and manic–depressive illness. So disturbing are some of these large canvasses that it is easy to understand why the Nazis considered them degenerate. But they spoke to me with such immediacy that I felt that if I were a painter, this is how I would paint. This man—"enormous and bumptious" according to one description, "like a polar bear with small red eyes" in another—was in some mysterious sense an avatar of myself.

I experienced the same thing when I first heard the music of Alexander Borodin (1833-87)—*In the Steppes of Central Asia . . . Prince Igor.* It wasn't that I thought of the music as the work of genius; rather that I felt a deep kinship with the composer, whose twofold life helped reconcile me to my own.

Borodin was illegitimate, and his father Luka Gedianov had his offspring registered as the legal son of one of his servants, Porfiry Ionovich Borodin. Though mother and son remained together and were passionately close, Avdotya could never officially recognize her son, and always

12. Paul Ricoeur, *Memory, History, Forgetting*, trans. Kathleen Blamey and David Pelauer (Chicago: University of Chicago Press, 2004), 5–6.

referred to herself as his "auntie." As for Borodin's biological father, Gedianov, he provided generously for his mistress for as long as she lived, though we have no record of how he regarded his ill-conceived son.

Would the divided loyalties of a child growing up under these circumstances translate into a sense of having mutually negating destinies?

Borodin was, like many musically gifted individuals, precocious. His first known work is a polka in D minor, composed when he was nine, the same year that he fell in love for the first time! There followed studies of the piano, flute, and cello, and further compositions. But from as early as 1843, Borodin developed a passion for chemistry that equaled his love of music. What began as attempts to make his own fireworks developed, by the time he was thirteen or fourteen, into serious scientific work, which Borodin conducted in a home laboratory. After graduating in 1855, Borodin's interest in chemistry deepened, possibly as a result of the inspiring lectures of Nikolai Nikolaevich Zinin—the grandfather of Russian chemistry—that Borodin had attended at the medical Academy of Physicians. Yet, as he became more and more engrossed in science under Zinin's mentorship, he continued his musical education, composing and performing as well as meeting and working with other young musicians. Zinin took a dim view of his protégé's disparate interests, and told him so. "Mr. Borodin, it would be better if you gave less thought to writing songs. I have placed all my hopes in you, and want you to be my successor one day. You waste too much time thinking about music. A man cannot serve two masters."[13]

It is tempting to relate this notion of two masters to Borodin's dual parentage, and perhaps also to see Zinin as the father that the young man had not had. In any event, at twenty-three Borodin became a medical practitioner in a military hospital, pursued research in biochemistry, and, a year later, met Mussorgsky, a foppish and somewhat mannered aristocrat with a way with the ladies, who was then an officer in the Preobrazhensky Regiment appointed to guard duty in the hospital where Borodin was house surgeon. The two hit it off, though it wasn't until three years later, in the autumn of 1859, that the two friends met again. Mussorgsky had now left the army, and had got rid of his af-

13. Serge Dianin, *Borodin*, trans. Robert Lord (London: Oxford University Press, 1963), 16.

fectations. It had been impossible, he confided to Borodin, "to combine a military career with music," and it was music alone that mattered.

The rest, as they say, is history. Borodin abandoned his medical career and devoted himself to scientific research, both in Russia and France, while continuing to write music. In 1861, he met the young Russian pianist who would become his wife, traveling and performing all over Europe with her. A year later, he met Balakirev and became a member of a circle of young Russian composers that included Mussorgsky and Rimsky-Korsakov. It was in this milieu, and under the influence of Balakirev, that Borodin's music began to achieve the maturity, originality, and Russianness that would gain the composer international renown.

Contrary to the opinion of Professor Zinin, one *can* serve two masters.

There is a wonderful passage from Rimsky-Korsakov's memoirs that captures the excitement of this double life. "When I went to see him, I would often find him at work in the laboratory next door to his flat. When he had finished what he was doing, he would come back with me to his flat, and we would play together or talk. Right in the middle he would jump up and rush back into the laboratory to make sure nothing had burnt or boiled over, all the while making the corridor echo with incredible sequences of successive ninths or sevenths; when he came back we used to pick up the music or conversation from where we had left off."

Survivor Guilt

When I think of chemists who were also artists I also think of Primo Levi, whose books were a series of suicide notes by a man who, even before his incarceration in Auschwitz, doubted his very humanity and, though a survivor, would die like Lorenzo "of the survivors' disease."[14] Not only did he feel guilty at having survived Auschwitz, he felt guilty that his books about the gray zone should bring him honor, riches, and fame, and that the "things that imperiously demanded to be told" had

14. Levi, *Moments of Reprieve*, trans. Ruth Feldman (London: Abacus, 1987), 149, 160.

fallen upon deaf ears. Moreover, to his dying day Levi was haunted by the "doubt" that, despite his survival being accidental and not providential, he was unworthy of the reprieve he had been given, since only the "worst survived, the selfish, the violent, the insensitive, the collaborators of the 'grey zone,' the spies." "I might be alive in the place of another," he wrote, "at the expense of another: I might have usurped, that is, in fact, killed."[15]

Primo Levi's terrible self-incriminations came back to mind during May 24 and 28, 2006, as I read reports in the Auckland newspapers of Mark Inglis, a double-amputee, who on his way to the summit of Everest had passed a dying climber huddled under a rock shelter and done nothing to help him. Sir Edmund Hillary was appalled. "On my expedition," he said, referring to his ascent of Everest with Tenzing Norgay in 1953, "there was no way that you would have left a man under a rock to die. It simply would not have happened." Mark Inglis countered that his climbing party could do nothing; the dying man had neither oxygen nor proper gloves. "Trouble is," he said, "at 8500m it's extremely difficult to keep yourself alive, let alone . . . anyone else." Hillary was not so sure. "You can try, can't you?" he said, "At least you can try to rescue the life of a man who is obviously in a distressful situation." And he went on to criticize the commercialization of Everest, and the gimcrack preoccupation with record breaking and making one's mark that involves the exchange of large sums of money for the dubious honor of being dragged up the mountain by Sherpas.

As for me, I asked myself the question that gnawed at Primo Levi: Can one ever rid one's mind of the question, escape the shadow of a suspicion, or avoid the sense of shame that comes of being "alive in place of another," each one of us "his brother's Cain?"[16]

As Mark Inglis defended himself in the press over the next few days, showing the frostbite he had suffered on five fingers and his stumps and expressing anger that his "phenomenal achievement" was being undermined by the negative publicity, I was arrested by a single phrase. In describing the condition of David Sharp in the "Death Zone" 300 meters below the summit of Everest, Mark Inglis said that the English-

15. Levi, *The Drowned and the Saved*, trans. Raymond Rosenthal (New York: Vintage, 1989), 82.

16. Ibid., 81.

man was "effectively dead." This was the exact phrase a New Zealand publisher had used in a letter to me, rejecting the manuscript of *Pieces of Music* in the early 1990s. I had been living abroad for too long, I was an unknown in New Zealand now, it would be well-nigh impossible marketing any book by me: I was effectively dead.

But it was not the rejection that hurt but the sudden realization that I had left a life in my homeland in order to lead another life abroad, and that, whatever success I enjoyed, I would be haunted by the thought of the life I had not led, the road not taken.

Curiously enough, it was another event on Everest that enabled me to write about this experience of losing touch with one's natal country, and helped me resolve it in my mind.

THE DISCOVERY OF MALLORY'S BODY

Why, I do not know,
but I imagine it is myself
they have found frozen
under the summit of Everest,

the braided and bleached
climbing rope still coiled
around the torso, skin
as white as marble,

upper body wedded to the ice,
and the broken leg
with its perfectly preserved
hobnailed boot.

Why do I see these as
the misidentified remains
of my own life
and crave to be lost

to consciousness again,
a letter from my wife against my heart,
the weather closing in,
and then the dark

in the utterly unconscious space
of Everest? And why do I peer

like a voyeur at the web page
called mountainzone

the news relayed
by satellite, the photo
and the name,
unless I want to retrieve my life

from where I left it
all those years ago
when my first wife's death
sent me snowblind

into a place of whiteouts
and thin air.
Now I come back
like Mallory

to a world I barely
recognise, lives
that have passed me by,
old friends for whom

I am as good as dead.
Better perhaps to lie
back broken in that
oblivion, one's body

ageless in an icefall
than return to where
one imagines it is possible
to make it to the top

without oxygen
leading one's own anonymous
life at the end of a rope
climbing nowhere.

Ventifact

I was living in Denmark at the time, and it was Bill's son Karl, phoning from London, who gave me the heartbreaking news. Bill, who had been in good health and high spirits when I visited him in Bournemouth less than a year ago, was now dying of lung cancer in a Bournemouth hospice.

Although my departure from Copenhagen was hurried and anxious, I had the presence of mind to take a wind-weathered stone from my desk and put it in my pocket before leaving. Dave Irvine, a mutual friend of Bill's and mine, had given me this stone in 1998—a memento of the decade in which we had all lived in the Manawatu. Dave had found the ventifact on a wild stretch of ironsand beach north of Tangimoana, and you could see on its dark brown surface the miniscule striations left by the rasping of wind blown sand. Moreover, it was neither smooth nor rounded like a stone tumbled in water, but keeled and faceted, and it was warm and comforting when held in the palm of one's hand. I called it a touchstone, not knowing at that time that the word denotes a siliceous stone with which the purity of gold or silver is assayed by seeing if the precious metals leave a trace when rubbed against it. This meaning is apposite, for when I saw Bill in the hospice where he was already on a morphine drip and only vaguely aware of my presence, I pressed into his hand this wind-eroded stone as a confirmation of all that we had lived through together, all that we shared.

Who would have suspected, back in the 1970s, when we were drinking beer and playing snooker together, or writing books without much hope of having them published, that Bill's life would end so prematurely, that Dave would also die before his time, and that I would wind up teaching at a divinity school at Harvard and writing a book about border situations and transmigrations that included these reminiscences of our friendship?

For a long time I knew Bill only fleetingly. Though we frequented the same Wellington hotels and ran into each other at the same parties, we exchanged few words, though Bill remembered us meeting at Victoria University in 1961 when we were students. "Everyone at the cafeteria table seemed to be wanting something—dope, contraceptives, identity," Bill wrote me in a letter twenty years later. "But you stuck out, because you did not appear to be after anything at all. You just *were*.

You assumed you *were*. You demanded you *were*. 'This is my table,' you said. We didn't know. But I noticed the difference between you and the others."

My memory is of being often drunk, in settings where one shouted belligerent and incoherent opinions at one's fellow drinkers or simply focused on downing as much beer as possible before the pub closed. This was a culture concerned with the rough and ready idioms of mateship, not intellectual depth. And yet there was something extraordinary about Bill Maughan, and he reminded me strongly of a character in one of Edwin Arlington Robinson's poems.

> Whenever Richard Cory went to town
> We people on the pavement looked at him:
> He was a gentleman from sole to crown,
> Clean-favored, and imperially slim.
>
> And he was always quietly arrayed,
> And he was always human when he talked;
> But still he fluttered pulses when he said,
> "Good-morning," and he glittered when he walked.

In early 1973, after living abroad for several years, my wife and I returned to New Zealand with our preschool daughter, Heidi, and settled in the Manawatu. Unbeknown to us, Bill had resigned his job at the Treasury in Wellington only months before and also moved, with his wife Lesley and small son Karl, to the Manawatu. Bill's aim was to get away from the brouhaha of the city and devote his energies to writing fiction.

Within days of learning of their whereabouts, Pauline and I drove into the hills beyond Colyton, looking for the farmhouse Bill and Lesley had rented. It was a still, sunny autumn day, yellow poplar leaves drifting to the ground, magpies gurgling in the paddocks, and we had a clear view of the distant sea and of Kapiti Island floating like a sperm whale in the haze. Pauline got out of the car and unbolted the gate. Then we descended the dirt track that circled the head of a small valley and came to a red-roofed bungalow with white weatherboard walls, backed by a row of wind-racked macrocarpas. Lesley spotted us from the kitchen window and was the first to greet us. Then Bill, who had glimpsed us through the castor-oil tree, emerged from the house with Karl. Even before we sat down to a cup of tea and began reminiscing, it was clear that we were kindred spirits, elated to have found one another in the same relatively isolated place.

After that initial meeting, we got together most weekends, rambling the hills, gathering mushrooms, and discussing everything from the geology of the Pohangina Dome to Bill's latest rejection letter from the editor of *Islands*. And always we would return to the farmhouse, to warm ourselves in front of a fire of pinecones and macrocarpa logs, enjoy a hearty meal, invent practical jokes to play on pretentious acquaintances, tell tall stories, and listen to Bill's old LPs of Kid Ory and Bix Beiderbecke, acquired during his undergraduate years in the Victoria University jazz club.

Bill had already written a satire on the civil service called *Good and Faithful Servants* and a picaresque novel whose title was from a Leonard Cohen song—"Like a bird on a wire, like a drunk in a midnight choir, I have tried in my way to be free." I envied Bill's Dadaist knack of writing tongue in cheek. He was working on *The British Empire for Two and Sixpence* at the time, and everything was grist to his mill, his childhood in England, my experiences in Africa. Even the typescript was a work of art, each chapter headed with a postage stamp from a former British colony.

Over the next couple of years we recruited other fellow travelers to our circle, none of whom would have been out of place in one of Bill's books—the panel beater who read Nabokov, the landscape architect who knew that cabbage trees were lilies and drove like a rally driver the trade unionist who argued that the *Titanic* was a microcosm of modern society. We played a lot of snooker, drank a lot of beer, had a lot of fun, and tried to get our acts together. We were nonconformists, and uneasy with the provincialism that hemmed us in, yet we shared a crazy energy, and nurtured in each other, often without knowing it, our intellectual and literary ambitions.

Gradually, however, a darker side to Bill's antinomian tendencies began to emerge, notably when he was drunk. I should have seen it sooner, for even on our first visit I had noticed, wedged in the branches of the Judas tree that had been planted outside the back door of the house the dismembered pieces of a painted wooden sculpture that Bill had done of Lesley. On subsequent visits, I became disturbed by the self-destructiveness I saw in my friend. The way he would seize one of his precious jazz records from the gramophone and throw it into the fire, where the vinyl curled and sizzled and gave off an acrid black smoke. And I wondered if this was in any way connected to the motorcycle accident in which he had smashed his knee so badly that he now walked with difficulty, and in pain, or the beer glass stain on his son's drawing of a forest clearing, or even his own writing, brilliant as it was, that seemed destined for rejection.

I soon found it impossible to keep up with Bill's drinking. Perhaps I was finding it hard to see where his wild energy was leading him. For though I was well aware from my own unruly past that every rebirth requires a death, and that the new is born from the ashes of the old, I could discern nothing creative in Bill's tirades and fugues. It was fun for a while, cooking up practical jokes that would, on one occasion, take the form of a fake letter of invitation to an exhibition of Rembrandt etchings at a house in the remote Wairarapa (a colleague I disliked took the bait and duly reported on this "exclusive" event to which he and his wife had gone), and on another, a spurious letter from the Royal Society of British Phonology and Etymology that we created for Robin Dudding, the editor of *Islands*, thanking him for his letter of inquiry and providing him an irreverent etymology of his surname. But how could I work at my own writing with a hangover every Monday morning that took two days to dissipate, or the smoking that went with the drinking? When I took up Iyengar Yoga as a way of correcting course, I became, in Bill's eyes, an apostate, and we saw each other less and less frequently. Ten years later, reviewing our estrangement in a series of letters, Bill wrote:

> I am not sure why I write—this letter or my books. Perhaps it is that only in the written word can I talk properly, free from the superficial unity of a character which does not suit/fit me well. I understand—and understood—your dislike of my drinking and of the repetitious idiocy that often followed, but I shall always drink in the company of all but a few people whom I totally trust. I try—and tried—only to drink with those who enjoyed drinking, but when you ceased to drink I became of course desperate and irritated at the loss of contact. How *can* a drunken man talk to another who stands on his head? Still—all that is in the past and our common respect for words allows this conversation now.

Bill was an odd mix of irreverence and morality. When he renounced fiction and took up a position as agricultural economist at the same university where I worked, wearing a necktie, behaving diplomatically (even, at times, sycophantically), I thought it was partly to escape the anarchy he associated with art. Classical scholarship and science entailed order, but—like the gardens his wife Lesley was beginning to design and his son Karl would soon begin to paint—an order within which creative chaos found a place.

Not long before my wife Pauline's death brought my years in the Manawatu to an end, Bill took six months' leave from his university job and returned to writing.

When he showed me the result of his semester's labor, I was taken aback. *Not a Novel but a Letter* was, as the title suggested, a lengthy missive in which Bill explains to an old flame, whom he is about to meet after many years apart, the course his life has taken since they were lovers. The "letter" contained long sections about his friendship with Pauline and me, about Lesley and Karl, about his efforts to write and his present situation.

"Was it true?" I asked him.

He confessed it was. He had never gotten over Maggie. He was in love with her. "Lesley *is* love to me," Bill said, but he was *in* love with Maggie.

Bill's casuistry left me cold. And when he compared Pauline and Lesley in the same breath, saying *they* "complemented each other"— "the intellectual" and "the bird"—all I could think of was that a deep symmetry has been incomprehensibly and irreversibly knocked awry.

Years after Bill left Lesley for Maggie, and they went to Florida to make a fresh start, thence to Bournemouth in England, I visited them and found it difficult to reconcile the Bill I thought I knew with the bourgeois trappings that he seemed to have so fulsomely embraced. But despite appearances, the same creative destructiveness that once brought us together bonded us still. In a letter from this time, Bill asked me:

> Do you remember standing one day on a hilltop at Waiata, looking over the plains? It was late evening and the light was burnished. It made me think of Cleopatra. I don't know what we had done that day, but earlier in the week I had helped a novice to blow up one mile of muddy ditch (The explosives had given me a headache but I was pleased to be involved). I told you of the car in which the explosives came—a Lotus, in which there were four and a half cases of gelignite, a half mile of cortex, forty anti-tank mines, and a sack of ammonium nitrate soaked in diese-

line—and I said that after the big bang I was disappointed that the river in the farm next door still ran muddy. Perhaps, I suggested, we should blow that up too. "Why not?" you asked. "Dynamite your way across the plains to the sea" (This last was an imperative).

Why not? I ask myself as I read your letter: the old mud of the past needs blowing up, is blown up, but the problem is, as always, to dynamite one's way, ever wider, towards that golden burnished sea.

I haven't solved the problem, but I know it, and I reply to you who knows it, and who has taught me that we both (you and I) know it. . . .

Years after Bill's death, I talked with Lesley in Auckland about those long-ago years, and the mysterious war that raged in Bill between respectability and rebellion.

His parents were English working class, Lesley said. His father joined the army and rose to the rank of lieutenant-colonel during the Second World War, but after the war courage and acumen on the battlefield counted for less than class, and Bill's mother's unrefined accent had been the subject of unkind comments in the officers' mess. When Bill's father left the army, he was a disillusioned man, and this undoubtedly left its mark on Bill, who vacillated, Lesley said, between a sense of loyalty to his working-class origins and a desire to win the kind of social acceptance that had been denied his parents. "In all the years we were married," Lesley said, "Bill would never agree to a mortgage, seeing it as a bourgeois institution that deprived one of one's freedom. And yet," she added, "he would leave me and buy into a life with Maggie in upper-middle class Bournemouth!"

A couple of days later, Bill's and Lesley's son Karl, who had become a close friend, insisted on driving me to the airport. We talked a little about this unresolved conflict in Bill, and how he had, in the end, repudiated art and embraced the comfortable life of a scholar.

Karl said that Bill had inherited his father's campaign medals and war diaries, but told Karl he would not pass these on to him lest he lose them. He then ceremoniously gifted them to the Regimental Archive and had a photo framed for display on his mantelpiece, of himself and Maggie shaking hands with the co at the special ceremony.

"It is strange," I said to Karl as we approached the airport, "that you should have inherited in such large measure Bill's artistic gifts, his vitality and generosity of spirit, and be so free of the ambivalence that bedeviled him."

Waiting for my flight, I gazed across the Waitemata harbor to the hills near the headland where smoke from two fires was rising into an empty sky. I took out my journal, and began writing. *It takes three generations to slough off the burdens of the past, but in all that time one is borne back into the past, haunted by a sense that that is where one properly belongs, that it defines who one really is, and that it is what one should settle for . . .*

My train of thought was interrupted by an announcement from the PA system. "The flight from Wanganui has been further delayed." Then, the final call for Flight 8803 to New Plymouth filled the Koru Lounge, and for a moment I thought of changing my flight, of returning to Taranaki where I lived as a child, of seeing my hometown again. But I had outlived it. There was no going back. I would not find the person I once was there. Again I gazed out at the harbor, a mailed hand whose wrist wore an amulet of grass, the smeared water waiting to be cut by the flensing knives of the next ship heading out to sea. "Passengers are reminded to keep their belongings in sight at all times. Any untended items will be removed by Aircraft Security and possibly destroyed."

Measured Talk

In Sydney, I spend the best part of a day talking with Kathy Golski. Kathy and I had known each other since 1984, when we met through mutual friends in Canberra six months after my first wife Pauline died of cancer and three years after Kathy's husband Olek had been killed by a hit and run driver as he was cycling along the Tuggeranong Highway. Invariably, when Kathy and I get together after months or years of separation we are drawn back to these critical moments when our first lives came to an abrupt end and we began again. Kathy was telling me about a remarkable book she had recently read by Jacob Rosenberg, called *East of Time*. Rosenberg was born in Lodz, Poland, in 1922. In 1939 he and his family were confined in the Lodz ghetto. They were sent to Auschwitz, then Gross-Rosen. Jacob alone survived. He met his future wife in a displaced persons' camp in Italy in 1945. Esther had taken part in the Warsaw Ghetto Uprising and had survived eight camps. In 1948, Jacob and Esther migrated to Melbourne, Australia. He fell in love with the country as soon as he saw it. And their first daughter was born there.

In the granite quarry at Mauthausen, prisoners had to climb 186 steps with fifty-kilogram blocks of stone on their backs. "There was no past and no future," Rosenberg writes, "only the now, the instant . . . You lived and died between a yes and a no." But in Australia he reentered time. There was a future again. But he urges his reader to remember that "a story without a shadow is a sad tale . . . Good writing . . . is a meeting of heart and mind, of storm and calm. Here the sun may set and rise at the same time."[17]

Kathy talked about how she survived the loss of Olek, how the will to live overrides the urge to throw oneself into the grave, into the darkness, at one with the person you have lost and without whom it does not seem possible to go on.

Kathy marveled at the way my daughter Heidi had survived her mother's death.

I told Kathy that Heidi had once confided that her mother remained in a side room in her mind, a place she could always enter, always be. But this was not a living room. Life required a different space. A clear space.

After Kathy had made a pot of tea she began talking about her son Mishka, who was slightly younger than Heidi but who also gave the impression of never losing his cool, never allowing a situation to get the better of him. At the beginning of one very difficult school year, Mishka was summoned to a conference with the principal. Angrily and condescendingly, the principal attacked the dilatory Mishka. "You going to work this year, Golski? Pull ya finger out? Put ya head down?"

"Yes sir, I'll certainly try . . ."

"You lying to me, Golski? You lying?"

Mishka pondered the question for several seconds. "I wouldn't put it quite that way, sir."

After Olek's death, Kathy remarried Wojcieck Dabrowski, another Pole, and with three-week-old son Rafal and her three children from her first marriage, Kathy went to live in a remote area of the Western Highlands of New Guinea where Woj was beginning a two-year stint of anthropological fieldwork. Though Mishka was only ten, the locals saw in his measured way of speaking, his calm disposition, his thoughtfulness and fearlessness, the qualities of a big man, and Mishka was given

17. Jacob G. Rosenberg, *East of Time* (Blackheath, N.S.W.: Brandl and Schlesinger, 2005), 27, 25.

a coffee garden in the expectation that he would cultivate it wisely and well, and in time draw from it a bountiful and profitable harvest from which everyone would benefit. When Kathy and Woj returned to Australia, Mishka was twelve. "Whenever I went to the supermarket with him," Kathy said, "he would find his way to the coffee grinder. He loved the aroma of coffee. He was fascinated by everything to do with coffee—the roasters in the espresso bar down the road, the espresso machines, the cups stacked on top of them, the steamer, the sacks of PNG beans stacked in the corner. I sometimes thought that the smell of coffee was what connected him with his New Guinea friends, who called him Dokta Miki because of his medical skills and reputation as a curer." Having acquired a box of instruments such as tweezers and scissors, as well as various dressings, disinfectants, and curative leaves, Dokta Miki would coolly attend to minor wounds, infections, and burns with the aplomb of his late father. Indeed, Kathy would write in her memoir of how amazed she was "to see the sudden connection between the young Dokta Miki and his dead father, Olek, a real doctor—the same calm concentration in the face of illness and distress, the same warm humor, banishing panic in its wake. He even looks the same. He advances upon the scene with the same measured gait and inspects the problem with a specific tilt of the head of which I am suddenly reminded, seeing it again."[18]

Heaven and Hell

Two years ago bushfires had devastated the National Park. South of Sydney, the casuarinas were like sooty witches' brooms, though the fire-blackened wattles and charred eucalypts were returning to life. When I stopped the car I was immediately deafened by the indefatigable stitching of cicadas—a lull, and then a million miniature rattles like seedpods in the trees, urgent, insistent, intensifying, before they fell silent again and you heard the squawk of a bird, the hush of tires on the road, or the blood coursing in your veins.

At Thirroul, I asked a clerk in the post office if he could give me

18. Kathy Golski, *Watched by Ancestors: An Australian Family in Papua New Guinea* (Sydney: A Sphere Book [Hodder Headline Group], 1998), 40–41.

directions to the bungalow that D. H. Lawrence and Frieda rented in 1922. He said he was unsure, but told me to drive back along the main street and take the first left. "You drive down Bath Street until you get to the beach, then you gotta go a fair way down the coast. The road twists and turns a bit. I dunno zactly where the house is but you kin ask."

I did. A woman climbing out of her car with two plastic bags of groceries nodded toward the high fence across the road. And there it was, number 3 Craig Street, a pine tree, a cactus growing against the wall, a disheveled oak, and a glimpse of the sea beyond. "There's that little park, too, if you're interested," she sang out, nodding again toward the big araucarias at the end of the street.

The park, named for DHL, had been created in 1998. After reading the brass plaque, I scrambled down to the rocky foreshore and made my way to the foot of the sandstone cliff from where I could see, perched above me, a deck, the back of the house, but little more. I returned to the park and sat on a bench, scribbling notes. The ocean churned on the rocks. Far out it was dark blue, and scarified by the wind. I thought of Lawrence's quest for renewal and naturalness, faithful to that dark interior sun that makes us burn with a passion for life, a life far from the abstractions and traditions of Europe, that can be touched and tasted and smelled, like the wind-lacerated water on which a lone windsurfer in a wet suit is blown seaward, the oak bent and beaten by the wind, the weathered araucarias and the pine. And I wondered whether our dreams of a utopia on earth are born of the same desire that throws up images of heaven, and that the distinctions we make between the secular and the sacred are artifacts of language, not facts of pure experience.

One of the best examples I know of this indeterminate relation between how we *have* an experience and how we *apprehend* it is to be found in Agehananda Bharati's work on mysticism and "zero-experience":

> One night when I was about twelve, it happened for the first time. I was falling asleep, when the whole world turned into one: one entity, one indivisible certainty. No euphoria, no colours, just a deadeningly sure oneness of which I was at the center—and everything else was just this, and nothing else. For a fraction of a minute perhaps, I saw nothing, felt nothing, but was that oneness, empty of content and feeling. Then, for another five minutes or so the wall with the kitschy flowers reappeared,

and the fire crackled in the large brick stove. But I knew it was One, and I knew that this was the meaning of what I had been reading for a year or so—the Upanisadic dictum of oneness, and the literature around and about it. *I did not think in terms of God, atman, brahman, nor, strangely enough, in terms of having found fulfillment*—I was just struck by the fact that I had not known this oneness before, and that I had kept reading about it very much as I read about Gaul being divided into three parts, or elementary Sanskrit grammar.[19]

Back in Sydney, at a New Year's Eve party, I was introduced to Anne Whitehead, whose book *Paradise Mislaid* interleaves a chronicle of the 1893 utopian socialist settlement in Paraguay called "New Australia" with the author's own journeys between Australia and South America, tracing and interviewing descendants of the original colonists, and seeking to understand why the socialist dream proved impossible to realize.[20] "I was fascinated by this drive in all of us to start afresh," Annie told me, "to break with tradition and create a new world. It's like the search for the Holy Grail, for the elixir of life. But you can't create a new world without recreating yourself, and this was the stumbling block. For all their ideals of gender equality and a classless society, the settlers could not kick their engrained habits. Old habits die hard."

"It reminds me of D. H. Lawrence," I said. "He wanted this new life-form, wanted to slough off his old self and create himself anew. Didn't he come to Australia, thinking this might be his Rananim? Is that the word?"

"Exactly," Annie said. "He wanted to open himself up to Australia, to make a go of it here, just as he did later in Mexico, but much as he railed against the staleness and heaviness of Europe the poor sod couldn't break free of his own past. All that talk of his in *Kangaroo* about the white unwritten atmosphere of Australia, the tabula rasa, the new leaf, the new unspoiled country, untainted by authority, he simply couldn't get rid of the old world in himself, and his own need to dominate the world with his own vision."

"You know *Kangaroo* better than I do!"

"I should. I wrote a screenplay from it."

19. Agehananda Bharati, *The Light at the Center: Context and Pretext of Modern Mysticism* (Santa Barbara: Ross-Erikson, 1976), 39, emphasis added.

20. Anne Whitehead, *Paradise Mislaid: In Search of the Australian Tribe of Paraguay* (St. Lucia: University of Queensland Press, 1997).

I hesitated to tell Annie about my pilgrimage to Thirroul, or the mini-essay that I was sketching about utopian dreams, in case she concluded that I was stealing her ideas, and I thought of the last line of Ecclesiastes: "Is there anything of which one can say: this is new?"

Manifest Destiny

I gaze out at fallow fields, rooks clamoring in leafless oaks, gulls facing into the wind. I am as anonymous as anyone on this train—commuters behind their papers, others slumbering, nibbling a bar of chocolate or, like me, staring out the window before looking away, realizing that we are staring at our own reflections, or the face of a stranger.

From my briefcase I take out the lecture I have written, nervous about how it will be received by an audience more interested in knowledge than storytelling. I scribble a few marginal notes before turning back to the window, watching the railway lines unreeling, running in parallel, merging and diverging again. The racked cables and overhead wires repeat the same mesmerizing movement. I think of the labyrinth. Dead ends reached in darkness. The vain groping for a light.

Hardly a week passes that I do not hear of another group of young West African migrants dying in the Libyan Desert or in trying to cross the Mediterranean Sea. Their tragic stories bring home to me that journeys, like stories, often begin with a situation that has become unsupportable—a poverty-stricken village, a country at war, a family feud, the death of a loved one, a sense of intolerable limits or radical disenchantment. To speak of a crisis is to invoke a moment when old attachments fall into abeyance and new ones are presaged, often in the imagination, inchoate and diffuse. At such times, ties to a specific place or a specific person give way to a passionate embrace of some high ideal—a pristine wilderness, the benevolent deity, a perfect love, a promised land.

They come from all over West Africa, crossing one border then another, moving north, hitching rides, eking out their meager stash, walking for days on end, sleeping rough. In Niamey, in Niger, they loiter outside the Western Union office, waiting for remittances from home that will pay for food and water and transport across the Sahara.

They hear rumors of what they will encounter. Armed robbers stealing your money and leaving you to die. Guides abandoning you. They hear of a group of Sierra Leoneans, stranded in the middle of the desert when their lorry driver drove off one night. When their water ran out they collected their own urine in bottles, added sugar cubes and drank it to slake their thirst. They hallucinated, and walked off into the wastes, thinking they had seen palms or the roofs of houses. Only two survived. But you have reached the point of no return. You think of home. There is nothing there. And so you push on, traveling by day, resting at night. You eat bread and tinned sardines. You carry water in the inner tube of a car tire because these hold more than bottles. You suffer amoebic dysentery from polluted water. You huddle under a tarpaulin with your traveling companions, or under a lorry, but cannot sleep for the cold. But you make it to Tripoli. The journey took eight days. In all this time you have not washed. Your body is covered in insect bites. You look at the others and see disheveled madmen, but know you look the same to them. But this is only the beginning of your tribulations. You pay your way to a safe house along the coast where you wait for ten days. Everyone fears the Libyan police who are on the lookout for black Africans. One night, after paying an Egyptian middleman, you embark on a fishing boat, heading to Italy. The boat breaks down many miles from its destination. The boatman tries to restart it many times. It is no use. Women begin screaming that they are doomed. Some of the men begin to pray. You drift for ten days. When a ship appears on the horizon, the Egyptian boatman dives overboard and starts swimming toward it. Within minutes the sea has swallowed him up. People are losing consciousness. There is no water, no food. Several people drink seawater and lose their minds. They flail about, clutching their bellies, shouting the names of their loved ones. One man steps over the side, thinking he is stepping onto a wharf. You wither under the sun, and freeze at night. You prepare to die. Your boat is found the following morning, your eleventh day at sea. Thirteen are dead in the boat. You helped dump others overboard, perhaps as many as forty. Some drowned. You and nine others survive. You are taken to Lampadusa. Italian medics give you intravenous drips and medicines. You don't know what lies next in store, but it cannot be as harrowing as what you have just been through.

The so-called Age of Discovery that began in the fifteenth century with Prince Henry of Portugal's global quest for material wealth, fertile lands, and a religious coalition with the mythical Prester John, is often regarded as a uniquely European phenomenon: a product of the Renaissance, of the development of science, and of the rise of capitalism. But we would do well to recognize that in every society and at every period in human history there are individuals who journey far from the safety of their own homelands, hazarding their lives in a wilderness or on wild seas in search of some bounty that they consider to be as essential to their own well-being as to the existential viability of their world. Indeed, the personal quest is typically identified with a *collective* endeavor in which individual ambition finds its justification and to which it is complementary.

This quest is one with which we can all readily identify. It is the quest to realize our own individual capacity to act upon a world that acts upon us, to make and unmake in some small measure the wider world that in large measure makes and unmakes us. But the personal struggle for being-in-the-world is also *socially* imperative, for the world to which we belong and without which we would have no life worth living does not come into being by itself or continue under its own inertia. On the contrary, it requires for its existence and continuity the consent, the creative power, and the vital energy of all who belong to it. Without exemplary acts of individual courage, cunning, and sacrifice, the social world would quickly fall into decay.

For the Greeks, the exemplary voyager was Odysseus. Among the Kuranko, countless folktales tell of a questing hero who braves the wilderness and overcomes all manner of obstacles to bring back to his community a musical instrument, such as a drum or xylophone, that will play a vital role in the initiation of children — and thereby bring a new generation into being. In Polynesian legends, the heroic quest is driven by the need for living space and plentiful food, and involves arduous sea voyages, remote landfalls, and new beginnings. For the Vikings and Mongols a man's worth depended on his prowess in battle, the plunder he brought home, and his brave death. In Renaissance Europe, we find all these time-honored themes. Gold is the shining symbol of the lust for wealth, while the religious quest involves a search for some lost paradise, eternal youth, or closeness to God. What is new, however, is the idea of manifest destiny. Europeans not only conquer or plunder new lands; they settle them and subject their indigenous peoples to enslavement, forced relocation, or forms of improvement and conversion that effectively spell their demise. The assumption of European superiority therefore entails a fundamental and nonnegotiable division of humankind into those who are destined to govern and those whose fate it is to be governed. It is this chauvinism, this notion of a civilizing mission, this assumption of "natural" inequality—modeled on distinctions between parents and children, gods and men, reason and unreason—that informs our way of thinking about non-European peoples to this day.

Thankfully, not everyone is a voyager, or a conqueror. For some of us, the heroic journey is not across deserts and oceans but through the working day, or the long night, struggling against the adversities of age or illness, rather than tropical fevers and the assaults of savages. At the same time, many people are never happier than when they are within the four familiar walls of their own homes, or keeping to well-worn paths and strict routines. Others, however, will find confirmed in the words of great explorers the exhilaration they feel when the ground is moving beneath their feet and they wake every day to new vistas and surprises. "Of the gladdest moments in human life," wrote Richard Burton, "methinks, is the departure upon a distant journey into unknown lands. Shaking off with one mighty effort the fetters of Habit, the leaden weight of Routine, the cloak of many Cares and the slavery of Home, man feels once more happy."[21] Herman Melville's Ishmael echoes this sentiment. "Whenever I find myself growing grim about the mouth; whenever it is a damp, drizzly November in my soul; whenever I find myself involuntarily pausing before coffin warehouses, and bringing up the rear of every funeral I meet . . . then, I account it high time to get to sea as soon as I can."[22]

Although European exploration between the fifteenth and late nineteenth centuries has shaped the world in which we now live, with its north-south divide, its racial and religious prejudices, its contested borders, and its gnawing memories of old wrongs that daily threaten us with new injustices, the mystery of the exploratory imperative remains, and with it the question as to how this impulse might be guided

21. Richard F. Burton, *Zanzibar: City, Island, and Coast*, 2 vols. (London: Tinsley Bros., 1872), 1:16–17.

22. Herman Melville, *Moby-Dick; or, The Whale* (Harmondsworth: Penguin, 1986), 93.

into actions less ruinous in their repercussions than those I have alluded to above.

Consider the case of the Scots explorer, Alexander Gordon Laing, whose burning ambition, shared by many others in the early years of the nineteenth century, was to be the first European to trace the Niger River to its source and show for certain whence it flowed.

The mystery of how and why our hearts become set on some imagined goal is directly analogous to the mystery of how and why we fall in love. Moreover, the object of our unrequited love, like a goal we dreamed of but failed to attain, can fascinate and enthrall us more than any other image. Familiarity may not always breed contempt, but it is fertile ground for mimetic desire. The person who returns our love, in whom our love is consummated, can never compete with the person we desired but whose heart we never won. That person nourishes our dreams forever, a figure of boundless promise and eternal youth, to whom we obsessively return, and whom we cannot let go. Such, I suspect, was the case with Alexander Gordon Laing.

In 1821, Laing was a twenty-five-year-old lieutenant serving with the 2nd West India Regiment in Freetown, Sierra Leone.[23] Slavery had been abolished eight years before, and the British governor of Sierra Leone was keen "to ascertain the state of the country, the disposition of the inhabitants to trade and industry; and to know their sentiments and conduct as to the abolition of the Slave Trade." Laing's expedition took him two hundred miles inland to the northern town of Falaba where he learned that he was within three days' journey of the Niger headwaters.

The Niger source had been the subject of speculation from at least the fifth century BC. Arab geographers speculated that it flowed from east to west; Pliny the Elder, Herodotus, and Ptolemy believed that it flowed from west to east. Pliny claimed that it flowed into the Nile. Several late-nineteenth-century explorers attempted to locate the Niger by traveling south from North Africa, but it was not until 1795

---

23. For details of Laing's life and career I have drawn extensively on Laing's letters and journals, as well as E. W. Bovill's commentaries, in *Missions to the Niger*, vol. 1, ed. E. W. Bovill (Cambridge: Cambridge University Press, 1964), 124–394. It should be noted, however, that I have occasionally elaborated the facts to flesh out my narrative.

that Mungo Park established that the Niger flowed east, and not until the 1830s that Richard and John Lander showed that it flowed into the Gulf of Guinea. In 1821, however, the source had still not been located and uncertainty still surrounded the connections between the Niger, the Nile, and the Congo.

Laing reached Falaba in June, the first white man to visit the Sulima capital. Though given a royal welcome by the Sulima king, Laing was suffering from a tropical illness that laid him low for several weeks. But sickness was not the worst of his woes. Though now within reach of the Niger, Laing found himself detained by a host who, while expressing sympathy for the white man's desire to travel to the "great river," threw obstacle after obstacle in his path. The Sulima king was at war with the Kissi to the east, and it would not be safe for Laing to venture into that country. Laing explained that it was his own life he was risking, no one else's. But when the king finally relented, and Laing set off, he was soon waylaid by messengers from Falaba, summoning him back. The king had had second thoughts about Laing proceeding without enough trade goods to ensure his safe passage. It was now the middle of August, and the exasperated explorer was growing desperate. After acquiring tobacco and salt to use in bartering his way east, Laing told the king he was determined to depart.

"How will you cross the large rivers without a canoe?" asked the king, whose name was Assana Yira.

"I suppose I must swim across them upon gourds."

"*Allah akhba!* There are deep swamps on the way, in which you will sink to the neck; how will you pass over them?"

"I must do as the people of the country do; if that will not answer, I must fell trees, and laying them across, scramble over their branches, but I tell you, once and for all, Assana Yira, that even a river of fire shall not deter me, if you are kind enough to give me your passport."

"*Alhamdulillah,*" exclaimed the old king. "God is powerful. Go!"

But Laing had not reckoned with augury. A day after leaving Falaba, a messenger caught up with him and relayed an ominous dream that Assana Yira had dreamed. The king had no option but to order Laing back to Falaba.

Laing made no attempt to hide his disappointment.

The king was baffled. "These white men are extraordinary people," he said to Laing's interpeter. "Here is one leaves me disappointed because

I save his life, by preventing him from going to a set of savages among whom I would not venture with half of Falaba at my heels."

Though it was considered a diplomatic and potentially commercial success, Laing's mission to Falaba only increased the explorer's ambition to reach the Niger. Back in Freetown, he was plagued by the memory of his aborted journey and determined to complete Mungo Park's work by discovering the main course of the river and, above all, its source.

Promoted to command a native company in the Royal African Colonial Corps, Laing saw twelve months' service in the Ashanti campaign of 1823 and was commended in the field for his skill and bravery. "Surely now," he wrote in his diary when dispatched to London to report on the state of the campaign, "my experience will entitle me to some advancement and qualify me for further expeditions."

In 1825, his prayers were answered. After months of petitioning his peers and superiors, Laing was promoted to the rank of major and given command of an expedition "for scientific researches in the interior of Africa." His brief was to follow the ancient Roman trade route from Tripoli to Timbuktu, locate the Niger, and follow it to its end.

The port of Tripoli was surrounded by irrigated fields of corn, barley and watermelons. Date, fig, olive, and mulberry trees dotted the outlying plain. Beyond them the embrasured walls of old forts and the domes and minarets of mosques crowded the seaward promontory. Within the city, decaying walls enclosed squalid courtyards and labyrinthine streets. The shadows of consular flags fell on shuttered windows.

Laing lodged with Colonel Hanmer Warrington, the British consul general, whose magnificent private villa, The Garden, lay two miles from the city in the oasis of Menchia. The dilapidated consulate bore such a contrast to The Garden that local gossip never tired of conjecturing how the plump Englishman, whose diplomatic blunders so often earned rebukes from Whitehall, could afford to maintain himself in such luxury. The truth was that Warrington had married an illegitimate daughter of the prince regent, Jeanne-Eliza Price, and it was to this connection that he owed his munificence.

At the time of Laing's arrival in Tripoli, English influence was low and French influence high along the Barbary Coast. Warrington resented the French consul, Baron Rousseau, and scoffed at his intimacy with the Moorish *bashaw* (ruler) and his scholarly devotion to Arabic.

Laing, however, regarded these as good reasons for meeting Rousseau, and he managed to do so without Warrington's knowledge.

Sitting in the French consul's study, Laing sipped Turkish coffee and ate apricots and grapes from a silver platter while the baron expounded his views.

"Timbuktu has become for us what the enchanted city of Iram Dhat al-'Imad was for the ancient Arabs. The sultan Hadramawt built a pleasure city to rival the deity, and we French and you English, to rival each other, have built in our imaginations a similar city. But do you not agree that it may be a chimera which will evaporate as soon as the many obstacles that block its access have been surmounted?"

"With respect, Sir, I do not," Laing replied. "My compatriot, Mungo Park, received reports of great splendor and wealth, and it is said that the king has a great treasure of minted coins and gold ingots."

"The ingots weigh more with every telling. Al-Bakri, Al-Idrisi, Ibn Khaldun, and finally Al-Hasan ibn Muhammad al-Wazzan al-Zayyati, who you will know as Leo Africanus, all described this gold and it grows bigger as the centuries pass. There is a mystery to Timbuktu, to be sure, but the mystery may be like the fountain of youth."

Suspicious of the baron's skepticism, Laing began to share the English consul's blighted opinion of Rousseau. In any event, when Warrington embarked on a clumsy plan to humiliate his rival, Laing did not demur about his part in it. For some time the French consul's son, Timoleon, had been courting Emma, the delicate and sentimental daughter of the English consul. Now Warrington encouraged her to entertain the major and show him the city.

The young couple strolled through streets filled with stalls of dried fruit gum, carob, watermelons, ostrich feathers, senna, madder, root barilla, and saffron. On Laing's urging, Emma took him to see the Roman triumphal arch, erected in AD 164 near the sea gate. It now enclosed a storehouse.

"There are some Roman ruins near The Garden too," she explained. "Father is a fossicker in his leisure time and has unearthed pieces of glass from Roman sepulchral urns."

In the evenings they sat in the garden. The air was fragrant with jasmine and violets. Laing spoke of the white desert to the south and of elusive fame. As the light faded they went indoors for supper, and afterward played vingt-et-un. When the first copies of his book (an account of his travels in Sierra Leone in 1822) arrived from England, Laing in-scribed one for Emma, "with deep affection."

The consul had not intended this convenient friendship to develop into a romantic infatuation. Watching Laing and Emma trot out their Arab horses through the wrought-iron gates of The Garden, he would turn with exasperation to his bureau, racking his brains for some way of dissuading his daughter from her growing attachment. Every morning he would accost her on the verandah with some new argument.

"I am aware that Major Laing is a very gentlemanly, honorable, and good man. But my dear Emma, I must insist that this attachment is reckless. The major is about to embark on a journey whose dangers must be perfectly apparent. Under these circumstances how can you consider an engagement? And have you taken into account the opinion, the feelings, of your poor mother?"

"My attachment," Emma responded, "was fostered and approved by you, father. And as for Major Laing's expedition, it is for us both a seal upon our love and an affirmation of our steadfastness that we should be wed before he leaves."

Though aghast at his daughter's resolution, the consul relented, and six weeks after their first meeting, Laing and Emma were married in a civil ceremony performed by Warrington himself. But the consul re-served the final say in the matter. On the afternoon of the wedding, he wrote to Lord Bathurst outlining the terms that his son-in-law had sworn to abide by:

> After a Voluminous correspondence, I found my wishes, exertions, Entreaties, and displeasure, quite futile & of no avail. & under all cir-cumstances, both for the Public good, as well as their Mutual happiness, I was obliged to consent to Perform the Ceremony, under the most Sacred & most Solemn obligation that they are not to cohabit till the Marriage is duly performed by a Clergyman of the established Church of England, and as my honor is so much involved, that I shall take due care they never be one second from under the observation of myself or Mrs. War-rington.

Two days later, Laing set off into the Sahara. He faced two thousand miles of desert and the ambiguous renown of reaching a city founded on hearsay and dreams. Plundered by Tuareg raiders, cheated by cara-vaneers, exhausted by the heat and oppressed by illness and malfunctioning equipment, Laing remembered a virgin bride sitting delicately among the geraniums of a cool, white villa, and the sea glimpsed through palms. Each night he diligently recorded the day's events in his journal or dutifully drafted a letter to Warrington summarizing his slow progress.

Warrington read Laing's unpredictable letters warily, for he still supposed that the explorer's heart might turn his head and rashly bring him back to Emma. Selecting those of Laing's letters that Emma might peruse the consul justified this censorship by arguing that romantic passion could still jeopardize the expedition on which British prestige in Tripoli depended. As for Emma, she was distressed that Laing's messages to her were so brief and formal. She at once commissioned a family friend, Josef Gomez Herrador, the Spanish consul general, to paint her portrait in miniature to send to Laing.

By the time the portrait arrived at Ghadames, the heat had stopped Laing's chronometers and evaporated the ether in his hygroscopes. In the minimal shade of his tent the explorer contemplated the pallid cameo of his beloved. It was the first time he had felt any misgivings about his venture. He promptly wrote to Warrington urging the consul to let him know if Emma was in poor health.

> Tell me, has Mr Herrador, or has he not, made a faithful likeness? If he has, my Emma is ill, is melancholy, is unhappy — her sunken eyes, her pale cheeks, and colourless lip haunt my imagination, and adieu to resolution — Was I within a days march of Tombuctoo, & to hear My Emma was ill — I wou'd turn about, and retrace my steps to Tripoli — What is Tombuctoo? What is the Niger? what the world to me? without my Emma —

When Laing had finished the letter he placed the cameo in his tunic pocket with great tenderness, then strode out to attend to the fractious camels. That night he strolled to the edge of the oasis and saw a comet crossing the sky toward the southwest. He took it as a "happy omen" that his wife's illness had passed, and he imagined the star marking the source of the Niger — indications, one might surmise, that Laing's desire for fame and love for Emma were now competing for his undivided attention.

Emma's sentimentality also embraced augury, and when she was awakened months later to a storm wind off the sea lashing the palms outside the open windows she was convinced her husband was dead. Throwing herself into her father's arms, she made him swear that he truly wished to see his son-in-law return safely. Warrington saw that the servants fastened a slamming louver before assuring his daughter that such storms were common at that time of year. "Yet we experience no more calamities than usual."

As for Laing, he lay bunched in the sand at Wadi Ahnet, left for dead by a band of Tuaregs from the Ahaggar Mountains who had joined the caravan uninvited some days before. No one had wanted to invite trouble by ordering them to leave.

One night they cut the tent ropes and plunged their swords into the collapsed canvas around Laing until he ceased to move: they then murdered whoever had not escaped into the darkness, and plundered the stores.

For months Laing was barely able to travel or write. He had received ten saber cuts to the head, a musket bullet in the hip, both legs had been badly injured, and his hands had been mangled as he tried to fend off the swords and free himself from the tent.

It was five months before Emma's interpretation of the storm was corroborated. One morning in November she chanced to see a letter from Laing dated July 1 lying open on her father's bureau. It was suddenly clear that her father had been keeping her in ignorance of much of what Laing wrote in his letters. Although the consul was embarrassed, he chided his daughter for tampering in official matters.

"But much of the letter is addressed to me," she protested.

"That is so, that is so. But when such news as this contains is so out-of-date when it reaches us, I thought it best to save you from the suffering it would surely cause."

Emma flung herself from the room, and when that evening Warrington brought her the letter containing Laing's reticent account of the attack at Wadi Ahnet, she took it from him without a word and sat in the darkness of the verandah for hours before she read it.

When she put it down, she felt as if a stone were lodged against her ribs.

The consul found her staring at the stars. "Emma, you must come inside. You are unwell."

Only when her father placed his arm around her shoulder was she able to speak. "Can any man endure such suffering without losing his reason?"

"I cannot tell," replied the consul. "But of one thing I am certain. Your Major Laing is no ordinary man."

That night Emma did not sleep. Between bouts of sobbing she wrote a letter to her husband, to be included with other messages being taken by caravan to Ghadames the next day. "Oh my beloved dearest Laing," she wrote,

> alas, alas what have you been exposed to, what danger, what suffering, to have saved you one pang I would with joy have shed every drop of blood that warms this heart—Had I been with you in that fearful moment my arms which would have encircled you might for some time have shielded you from the swords of those Daemons—and at last we might have fallen, pierced by the same weapon, our souls might have taken their flight together to that land sorrow can never come to—My beloved Laing sorrow has laid a heavy hand on your Emma's head & so it has on yours—Alas Laing how cruel, how sad, has been our fate—Are we destined to endure more misery, or will a kind providence at length pity our unhappiness and restore us to each other—Will you my own idolised husband return to your Emma's kind arms, will you come & repose on her faithful bosom—Will you restore happiness to her torn heart?

Warrington had not told Emma that Laing had announced his intention of returning to Tripoli from Timbuktu rather than continuing down the Niger. Nor had he allowed her to see a note from Laing, marked "Very Private," which had been enclosed with the July letter. In the note Laing asked the consul: "Will you still consider it necessary to keep me to the promise which you have from me *in writing*? (and which wou'd be sacred was it merely verbal) or will you absolve me from it?"

The consul did not regard correspondence as a suitable place to discuss such a delicate matter, and left Laing's question unanswered.

The survivors of the attack at Wadi Ahnet spent three months recuperating in the camp of a friendly Arab chief before yellow fever broke out and Laing's last European companions succumbed and died. Against the advice of the Arab chief, Laing pushed on to Timbuktu, arriving there on August 13, 1826. The city, which had become for Europeans a metaphor for ancient learning and exotic wealth, turned out to be an arid warren of mud-brick dwellings in a desert of smudged lilac sand. The roofs were flat, and decayed beams jutted from eaves and squat turrets. Laing was met everywhere by an air of appalling desertion. The city was disputed territory and many of its Songhai inhabitants had fled when war broke out between the Tuareg and Fulani. The leader of the Fulani regarded Christians as children of Satan and had vowed to prevent Laing's entry into Timbuktu.

Laing delayed in the city for two days, studying fragments of Arabic manuscripts in a vain endeavor to know how Timbuktu's power and wealth had vanished. He felt sick in his stomach as he remembered Baron Rousseau's opinion of the place. Yet he could not believe that his suffering had brought him to a mirage. When he quit the city for Segou in the west, bypassing the nearby Niger because its banks were occupied by the Fulani, he told himself that time would reveal the wealth he had missed. And in a letter to Warrington he referred to another consolation:

> I sometimes give the river a left-handed blessing, when I think it is the cause of my separation from my Emma; at other times I am more charitable towards it, when I consider that had it not been for the Niger, I might never have been blessed with a sight of the dear object, which I prize more than life.

Laing was with Bungola, an African servant whom he had freed, and an Arab boy. They had walked thirty miles from Timbuktu when four horsemen rode up, led by Muhammad ben Abayd, a sheikh of the Berabich tribe who controlled the route as far as Arawan. Laing had already sought and obtained his permission in Timbuktu to go that way.

The sheikh and his men dismounted by an atil tree. Bungola looked at Laing in terror. The carriers bolted.

"Follow them!" Laing yelled to Bungola.

The sheikh's men approached, casting their eyes over the boxes, papers, and instruments the carriers had thrown down. Laing addressed the sheikh by his more familiar name, Ahmadu Labeida, and asked what had brought him thither.

Labeida launched into a tirade against Laing's faith, and demanded that he embrace Islam. Laing refused with an obstinacy that enraged the sheikh. Labeida's men pinioned the explorer's arms and Labeida drew his sword. A second later, Laing was dead.

The Arab boy, who had interpreted Laing's final defiant words, had fallen onto his knees whimpering. Labeida ordered him killed.

They severed the explorer's head and broke open the boxes. The sheikh made a souvenir of Emma's portrait. Laing's papers were burned for fear they possessed magical properties. It was September 24, 1826.

It was not until almost two years later—when Bungola returned to Tripoli—that Laing's death was confirmed. Emma's grief was greater for having read Laing's last letter, in which he excused himself from writing to her personally despite her being uppermost in his thoughts. Laing's parents piously ignored her, and Warrington was too obsessed with the political implications of the ill-fated expedition to pay much heed to his daughter's distress.

The consul had become convinced that his son-in-law's death was the result of a French plot. He even believed that the explorer's journals were in the hands of Baron Rousseau. The ensuing accusations and counteraccusations caused an international scandal, and the French consul was forced to return to France to defend his good name. Tripoli passed once more into the hands of the Turks. Warrington took his pension and retired to Patras to live with his eldest daughter and her husband, who was consul there.

Three years after Laing's death, in April 1829, Emma married again, according to her father's wishes. Warrington himself again performed the ceremony. Her new husband was the British vice-consul in Benghazi. But the frail girl whom the explorer had imagined waiting for him in the cool, white arbor of The Garden died of consumption at Pisa less than six months after her wedding. Since Laing's death she had suffered from insomnia and a dread of summer storms. Her father duly reported to Bathurst on the circumstances that had brought his "adored daughter to an untimely Grave":

Thus has that Monster of Iniquity the Baron Rousseau sacrificed two Victims to His Diabolical Intrigue—for to my last, shall I conscientiously believe He was concerned in that sad History.

In the same year that Emma died, a twenty-year-old poet won the chancellor's medal at Trinity College, Cambridge, for a poem entitled "Timbuctoo." In his poem, Alfred Tennyson asks if the rumor of the city of "argent streets imaging the soft inversion of tremulous domes" might not be a dream "as frail as those of ancient Time," and he answers:

the time is well-nigh come
When I must render up this glorious home

to keen discovery: soon yon brilliant towers
Shall darken with the waving of her wand:
Darken, and shrink and shiver into huts.
Black specks amid a waste of dreary sand,
Low-built. mud-wall'd, Barbarian settlements.
How chang'd from this fair City!

In these images of disappointment, in the personal tragedies of Laing and Emma Warrington, and in the political repercussions of Laing's failed search for the Niger, we are brought to a question that may, for all I know, be unanswerable. Yet it is a question that refuses to go away. Given that we need to go out into the world, to discover it for ourselves, to make sense of it, to live in it on our own terms, how can we prevent this necessary ambition hurting those we love and bringing ruin upon the world? How can we judge whether what seems best or even necessary for us is going to be wrong for others? These are questions that colonial discourse refused to broach. Yet Laing, in his last days, was brought to ponder them, and in his journal jottings we may discern how grand ambitions for fame or fortune may be transfigured by love for one person, "the dear object" he came to prize "more than life itself."

The Nature of Things

That spring I taught a course on community and alterity in Africa. Every Tuesday at one o'clock, I walked the short distance from my office to Divinity Hall, climbed the stairs to the third floor, and with my students explored variations on the theme of bush and town—the ubiquitous African metaphor for the relationship between the moral order of human community and the antinomian forces of the wild without which, paradoxically, the human world falls into decay. A few doors away from the room where my class met was a small chapel and one day, with ten minutes to kill before my class began, I wandered in and took a look around. My eyes soon lit upon a commemorative plaque on the back wall, and I read that this was where Ralph Waldo Emerson gave his famous address to the senior class in Divinity College on Sunday evening, July 15, 1838, encouraging his audience to "dare to love God without mediator or veil" and oppose rites and forms with "soul . . . soul, and evermore, soul."[24] I read the full text of Emerson's address that weekend, before driving to Walden Pond, which happened to be close to where I lived, in order to enjoy the spring sunshine and a walk through the woods. I was pondering the curiously nondialectical tenor of the thinking of the New England transcendentalists. Not only did Emerson feel that formalized and ritualized religion tended to be "cold, barren & odious";[25] he felt that modern society was inimical to spirituality, beauty, and natural being. As for the scholar, he becomes a mere functionary, a "parrot of other men's thinking" and a "victim of society" unless he opens himself up to the flux of the natural world — the measure of all ultimate value.[26] But my years among the Kuranko had given me to understand that fulfillment comes from our ability to draw upon the resources of both culture *and* nature, town and bush, and I could not help thinking that in reifying antithetical terms like poetry and science, faith and reason, materiality and spirituality, civilization and wilderness, we create illusory choices for ourselves, convinced we cannot have it both ways and that to make gains in one domain it is necessarily to expunge or suffer losses in the other.

In the 1970s I taught anthropology at a university in a provincial New Zealand city. My closest friends were not academics, and I spent more time in pool halls and public bars than university common rooms. For a couple of years, my regular weekend haunt was the Workingmen's Club at Fielding where Allan Campbell (a local panel beater), Dave Irving (a landscape architect), Bill Maughan (a writer), and I drank beer and played snooker. Looking back on those lost weekends, I regret that I kept no record of the badinage that went on around us as we played, for the vernacular idioms gave remarkable insights into the preoccupations of that exclusively male world — insights I could have turned to good use when years later I did fieldwork in a Warlpiri initiation camp, also separated from the world of women and children, and heard the same chauvinist raillery.

24. A week before delivering the address, Emerson noted in his journal, "We shun to say that which shocks the religious ear." In *Foundations for a Learned Ministry: Catalogue of an Exhibition on the Occasion of the One Hundred Seventy-Fifth Anniversary of the Divinity School of Harvard University* (Cambridge, Mass.: Harvard University Press, 1992), 95.

25. Ibid.

26. "The American Scholar," in *Selected Writings of Ralph Waldo Emerson* (New York: Signet, 2003), 226, 227.

When someone miscued or failed to pot his ball, his mate would ask, "Didn't the missus turn over for you last night?" And amid the declarations of feeling "fucked," "shagged," or "buggered," I sometimes wondered whether the game we were playing had some oblique connection with conjugal life and the perpetual struggle in which men seemed to be engaged to sustain their manhood and sexual vigor in the face of debilitating female influence. Or were women simply the scapegoats for anxieties that were not sexual at all?

One weekend in the winter of 1978, Allan asked me if I would accompany him on a deer-shooting trip to the Kaimanawa Forest Park north of Waiouru—the military base where he had spent his army years and learned his trade. When I said that I had no interest in shooting deer, Allan said that this wasn't the only reason he was going. During the past six months he had rebuilt a 4x4 Land Rover from scratch, and he needed to see how it would perform off-road. Besides, he wanted my company.

A few hours before our departure, Allan phoned to say that Bruce had got wind of our trip and wanted to come along. Would that be OK with me? Bruce was a local jeweler and a sometime mate of Allan's. I had met him a few times, and neither liked nor disliked him. Why should I object to his company?

We left in the late afternoon, with the darkness already falling. Allan and Bruce drove ahead in the Land Rover, towing the caravan in which we would sleep and cook our meals. I followed in my DS Citroën.

It was just past eleven at night when we turned off Highway One and lurched down a track of gritty black volcanic sand toward the dimly silhouetted range. When we reached our campsite on level ground above the Waipakihi Stream, Allan unhooked the caravan and announced his intention of reconnoitering a little. He had hunted deer in the Kaimanawa Mountains during his years in the army and couldn't wait to see if the area was the same as he remembered it. So the three of us piled into the Land Rover and roared off into the night. After descending steeply into the valley, Allan turned down a deeply rutted and boulder-strewn track running parallel to the river. He said he was looking for the ford.

The moon was still down, and the valley filled with mist. Even so, I could see that the river was broad and fast-flowing, with dark swellings and turbulence that suggested underwater boulders and deep holes.

When Allan turned the Land Rover toward the river and we plunged in, I asked if he knew what he was doing. He assured me he did. He recognized the ford. We could cross here, no worries.

Gunning the engine and wrenching the gear lever, Allan bullied the Land Rover into surmounting sunken stones and getting a grip on the riverbed. But we were sinking deeper and deeper into the dark torrent, and soon came to a standstill in midstream, the engine stalled, ice-cold water surging around our feet. "The Rover can't swim," Bruce said facetiously. Allan's response was to change gears, gun the engine, and force the flooded vehicle over the boulders that were hard up against the front axle. When this move was unavailing, he threw the vehicle into reverse gear. With an ominous lurch that had Bruce and me flailing for handholds, the vehicle now bellied on a huge submerged stone, heeled over, and sputtered into silence. The water that now flowed through the cab was slicked with engine oil, and I felt like pronouncing the Rover not only incapable of swimming but dead. But despite the fact that we now had only two-wheel drive and no clutch, Allan appeared unfazed. "I'll get the bugger out if I have to pick it up and throw it out!" He then shoved open his door and dropped into the tar-black river. His first efforts to free the vehicle made me think of those B-grade movies where trapped submariners and other heroes dive fully clothed into murky and rising water to shore up a breached bulkhead or open a vital valve. But as Allan went under time and time again, coming up with stones that he hurled into the darkness, I saw that life was refusing to imitate even bad art, and was relieved when Allan finally took the shouted advice from Bruce and me that he was attempting the impossible. He now began to work his way around to the front-mounted winch, from which he took the hook and hawser and began wading to the far bank, where I could make out the bulky shape of a dragline — which at once explained why the ford was now deep water and how we might yet rescue the Rover from a watery grave. It took Allan fifteen minutes to wade the rapid and waist-high river, attach the hook to the dragline, and return shivering and cussing to the Land Rover. He tried the ignition. The engine was swamped, the winch dead. He had no option now but to go for help. He would drive my Citroën to Waiouru, locate one of his old army buddies, and come back and winch the Rover — which had been renamed "the fucker" or simply "the cunt" — out of the river.

I chose to stay with the vehicle. After giving Allan my car keys and watching him and Bruce disappear into the darkness, I clambered over the back of the seat into the small canopied area behind it. Removing my sodden boots and socks, I wrapped my feet in a Swanndri bush shirt, and settled back to enjoy my liberation from the mayhem and machismo of the last hour.

My eyes quickly became accustomed to the darkness. I could smell the sour dankness of the beech forest. Then the moon came up, and for a moment I thought I saw the carcass of an animal borne downstream, the surface of the river shaken like foil on a bed of indigo. The moon floated across torn spaces between the clouds. On the far riverbank, the toittoi caught the moonlight. Occasionally I heard a louder plop or splash of water, as if an animal were fording the river, but I told myself it was only the swift current encountering a hidden snag. Before long I had fallen into a kind of reverie, drinking in the cold night air, inhaling the clean decaying smell of the beech trees, and watching the clouds flow overhead as swiftly as the river coursed blackly beneath the stranded vehicle. When I heard the sound of a truck descending the hill in low gear I rued the interruption. And when Allan began shouting from the riverbank, I was loath to answer, not wanting to be drawn once more into the mock heroics, the loud and willful barging about, and the endless cursing.

Allan's mate lost no time in hauling the 4x4 from the river and towing it back to our campsite, and though it was now two in the morning and we were all dog tired we drank beer and bragged our way out of the ignominious situation in which we had found ourselves. There was irony, for Allan, in the fact that he had once owned the truck with which his mate had come to our rescue. This helped save face. There was humor, too, in stories recalled of vaguely similar incidents in the past. So that the picture of Allan plunging fully clothed into the river brought to mind an anecdote about a Maori guy who used to be in search and rescue. When Allan's mate Wayne got lost in the Kaimanawas one time, the Maori guy turned up at the base camp wearing flip-flops. Someone asked him, "You're not going into the fuckin' bush with those things on?" "No," the Maori said, "I'm going to take them off first." And finally, there was solace in the fact that I had written a poem while waiting in the middle of the river. So all in all, it had been a good night, and would, in time, make a good story.

In the morning, we ate a breakfast of bacon and eggs, drank black coffee, and prepared to head into the bush. Allan and Bruce shouldered their rifles. But unimpressed by the clumsy way Bruce handled his firearm, I made sure that I brought up the rear when we set off.

Seeing the river in the light of day made it obvious how foolhardy we had been to attempt to cross it. The huge dragline had scoured the riverbed, piling up moraines of graywacke boulders and gravel along the banks, and destroying the ford that Allan remembered and now could not forget. As we moved upriver, he kept cursing the way in which "they" had "fucked over" the place, and asking what the fuck they were thinking of anyway, deepening the river. When we left the river and headed up the track into the beech forest, the noise of coursing water suddenly ceased and we were surrounded by fantails, riflemen, bellbirds, and waxeyes darting among the horopito and koromiko. Later, as the beech forest became more stunted, weather-beaten, and sparse, there were fewer birds, and matagauri and bush-lawyer snared our jackets. "We'll never get through this shithouse stuff," Bruce complained. But it wasn't the barbed vines and entangled undergrowth that was slowing him down. It was his blistered feet. Before we had reached the tussock above the tree line, Bruce had had enough. Despite the fact that I was now carrying his rifle and rucksack, he could not walk another step.

The place where we stopped was dripping with cold water. The trees were rotten. The track squelched underfoot. Everything was damp and decayed. After a quick conference it was agreed that I would stay with Bruce while Allan went on to the tops and spent a couple of hours stalking deer. We had heard a stag only minutes before, its roar reminding Bruce of a boy whose voice is breaking. He had tried to imitate it, only to declare that he could not do "the falsetto bit."

When Allan had gone, Bruce decided to light a fire. I thought it was futile to try, given the wetness of everything, but Bruce was convinced he could use the powder in his cartridges to get a fire going. I watched his pathetic efforts, and listened to his life story. The father who discouraged his early interest in archaeology, his wife who was always on his case, pushing him to expand his business, and make a better go of it. "Do you have children?" I asked. No, Bruce said, "and that's another thing . . ."

I must have become deaf to Bruce at that moment, because when I later made surreptitious notes of our conversation I could remember nothing else he told me, even though his complaints were legion. Nor did they stop when we were back in camp that evening and I was lighting a fire in the open. "Why don't you stop being so bloody energetic," Bruce said, as my fire began to show more flame than smoke. But he was already drunk, having got stuck into his hoard of Dominion Bitter as soon as we got back, and pressing bottles on his reluctant companions.

That night I lay in my bunk, half-listening to Bruce ear-bashing Allan, first with a story I now wish I could remember, concerning a guy who "fucked his way into a fortune" and then with his blighted opinions about women "who aren't physically up to it." I heard Allan politely dissent from this view, saying, "I'd like Ngaere to come on one of these trips if we could both get away from the kids for a few days," but Bruce wasn't listening and I was on the verge of sleep.

A few months after our trip, I learned that Bruce had got drunk one night, beaten his wife with his rifle butt, and threatened to shoot her in the knees. According to his wife's testimony in court, he had also threatened to blow his own brains out "so that she would be sorry." The reason he assaulted her (and it was apparently not the first time) was that she failed to do the housework, which he deemed to be a "woman's job." Bruce was sentenced to three months in jail, and a court order barred him from making any kind of contact with his wife, who had filed for divorce. I was researching Oedipal myths at the time and had been struck by the recurrent association of heroes with difficulties in walking. In Roman and Greek thought, suppleness in the legs connoted potency and strength, and the Indo-European words for the knees, generation, narrative, and knowledge are all cognate, suggesting that the knees are a kind of "male womb" connected with "second birth."[27] Did Bruce feel that his manhood was impugned by a wife who would not accept a subservient role? And were his anxieties in any way typical of New Zealand men, who often expressed an aversion to marriage because it would allegedly sap their creative power and compromise their freedom? Domesticity diminished a man, and even sexuality

27. H. A. Bunker and B. D. Lewis, "A Psychoanalytic Notation on the Root GN, KN, CN," in Psychoanalysis and Culture, ed. G. B. Wilbur and W. Muensterberger (New York: International Universities Press, 1965), 364.

was dangerous since women connived at trapping men and tying them down. I recalled an incident at a party not long after our trip to the Kaimanawas when Bruce, again drunk, was stroking his beer gut and boasting that he was pregnant. But it was only many years later, when I read Gilbert Herdt's *Guardians of the Flutes*, that I made the connection between the male fear of women and ritualized homosexuality.

Sambia men are preoccupied by the need not only to resist the baleful effects of female influence but to actually arrogate women's reproductive power to themselves. This they accomplish symbolically by taking seven- to ten-year-old boys from their mothers and initiating them into a male cult where for many years they engage in ritualized homosexual fellatio. By ingesting semen (which is equated with women's breast milk), the initiates acquire strength and masculinity, just as an infant grows by drinking from its mother's breast.[28] Sambia are, of course, not the only human beings to associate whiteness with generative power, health, and life. For the Ndembu of Zambia, "white is, inter alia, the symbol of nurture," a quality that is "made visible," Ndembu say, "in such material forms as breast milk, semen, and cassava meal. It represents smooth continuity from generation to generation, and is associated with the pleasures of eating, begetting, and suckling."[29]

Is it too far-fetched to interpret the froth on a glass of beer as semen or breast milk, to associate the male bonding that takes place in a Kiwi pub or hunting trip with the ritual cultivation of masculinity in a Sambia cult house or Warlpiri initiation camp, and to ask why men the world over feel compelled to assert their manhood through the disparagement of women, the extirpation of the feminine in themselves, and, often, physical violence against the allegedly "weaker" sex? Is it perhaps true that men feel inferior because they cannot bear children and create life, and compensate for this by asserting their power *over* life, and through baroque imitations of women's generative capacity?

Certainly, the wherewithal of life is always scarce. There is never enough to go around. And so it must be subject to continual ritual

28. Gilbert Herdt, *Guardians of the Flutes: Idioms of Masculinity* (Chicago: University of Chicago Press, 1994).

29. Victor Turner, "Color Classification in Ndembu Ritual: A Problem in Primitive Classification," in *The Forest of Symbols: Aspects of Ndembu Ritual* (Ithaca, N.Y.: Cornell University Press, 1967), 75.

redistribution, and symbolically brought from where it is abundant to where it is wanting.

Allan shot no deer. And though he got his Land Rover running again, it was clear to me that he was looking for a way out of an impasse, looking for a new lease of life. It came to him by way of tragedy. That spring, a close friend from his army days was killed in a car wreck. For several weeks after Mac's funeral, Allan moved in a daze. He would get through the day at his body shop, hoping that hard work would stop him thinking too much about Mac. At the end of the day he would slam the metal doors shut, shoot home the bolt and snap the padlock. Then the smell of engine oil and acetone was gone. He would walk down the alley and into the main street, still in his overalls, still wearing his steel-capped boots. His footsteps would echo vapidly under the iron verandahs. It occurred to him often that he could walk down that street blindfold, the asphalt familiar underfoot, the smells of Cooper's Pharmacy, the Para Rubber Company, Hairport, Moncrieff's Carpets . . .

Then one night everything changed.

It began like any other night. Allan reached the Denbigh Hotel. His drinking mates greeted him with the usual abusive banter, he bought a round of beers, shot some pool, listened to Harry complain about his bankrupt sex life, shot some more pool. He remembers going out for a piss. He remembers the press of bodies when he walked back into the bar, the smoke and shouting. He saw Harry and the others waiting for him at the pool table. But he could not bring himself to push through the crowd. He stood there in a kind of stupor, rooted to the spot. It wasn't that he had drunk too much, he told me later, but he had the unnerving sensation of being suddenly remote from everything that was going on around him, that he was seeing everything clearly but was himself unseen. He felt for a moment that he was actually leaving his own body, drifting away from himself. This sensation lasted only a few seconds: the froth slipping slowly down the inside of a drained glass, the bent minute hand of the wall clock quavering, two men mouthing incoherent curses into each other's faces. But when the moment passed he was saying to himself, "Hell, is this the rest of your life?"

A couple of days later he said to Ngaere, "I want out. I'm going to sell the business." He was sick of chasing up customers who wouldn't cough up what they owed him. He wanted to clear out of town, buy a few acres of land on the coast, build a house, grow their own vegetables, live without overheads. He had done a muffler replacement for a Maori guy who'd told him how shoals of kahawai came along the Coromandel coast in early summer. The waves dumped fish in their thousands on the beach. "We could survive on what we got from the sea," Allan said.

Not long after Allan and Ngaere moved, with their five children, to Coromandel, I also moved on, and nine years passed before we saw each other again. I was now teaching in Indiana in the United States but was back in New Zealand to begin researching my book on home. After phoning Ngaere and Allan from Auckland and getting instructions on how to find them, I headed south in a rental car and arrived at Karuna Falls at the end of a hot summer day.

The house was built on poles, with creosoted weatherboarding and windows from a demolished schoolhouse. The chimney was of hammered tin. Tree ferns and manuka surrounded it, and the air was shrill with cicadas.

As I climbed up some steps of river stones to the deck, Ngaere came out of the house. I felt as though I had returned from the dead. Nine years had been a long time. But Ngaere's effusiveness quickly dispelled my suspicion that we had become strangers. She made a pot of tea and invited me outside, where we sat on the deck and she talked of how she and Allan had made a life here, schooled their kids, and found fulfillment.

"Don't you feel cut off from the outside world?" I asked.

"Never, for all the isolation," Ngaere said, and she told me how the *Guardian Weekly* ran a column in which subscribers to the newspaper living in far-flung corners of the world wrote about their situations and sent photos of where they lived. Ngaere sent the *Guardian* a photo of herself immersed in the old bathtub down in the manuka, reading the *Guardian Weekly*. It had been published.

Suddenly, several dogs were scampering up the stone steps with Allan close behind.

He had grown a black beard. His hair was matted and filthy. In one hand he held a sawn-off shotgun, in the other a blood-flecked haunch of wild pork. He set the meat down on the deck, wiped his hand on his shorts, and we shook hands. Allan began to unstrap the sheath of his bone-handled hunting knife that was laced around his thigh. His bare legs were cut and smeared with blood and dirt.

"Let me just take care of the dogs," he said.

Pickle, Flo, and Maxwell were bull terriers. They'd been gored by a big boar that Allan had run to ground, then lost track of. Maxwell had suffered the worst mauling. Allan called him over to a patch of paspalum grass beside the deck. He gently pushed the dog onto its side, lanced its ear with his knife, and injected penicillin into the wound. The dog did not even whimper.

"Doesn't he feel anything?" I asked.

"Not these buggers," Allan said. "They don't feel pain."

Ngaere announced that her daughter Kate was doing some tie-dying in the studio, and promptly disappeared into the manuka with a bolt of muslin that had been propped against the deck rail. I figured she must have been on her way to the studio when I turned up.

Allan now hung his haunch of pork from a verandah post and told me how easy they had it there: vegetables from the garden, fruit and olives from the orchard, pheasant, quail, venison, and wild pork.

I admitted it seemed like a good life.

"You still drink?" Allan asked.

He fetched a jug of feijoa wine from inside the house, and we drank and talked about old times. I got the impression that for all his passion for the bush, the Allan I was listening to was a very different man from the Allan I had accompanied into the Kaimanawas ten years earlier. He was a man who had come home to himself, and was at home with where he lived, a man who had nothing to prove.

A couple of years ago, Allan said, he had shot a 140-pound boar. It took him four hours to drag it home through the bush. By the time he had finished butchering it, darkness had fallen. He filled the outside bathtub with water and lit a fire under it. A full moon was rising over Takapari. He poured himself a gin and tonic and rolled a joint. Then he climbed into the bath and lay there, sipping his drink, blowing the joint, looking up through the manuka at the stars. "That's when I got to thinking I should start a diary," Allan said. "A pig hunter's diary. Some kind of record of my life here."

That night, writing in my own diary, I thought again of the penumbral regions where we lose sight of ourselves—the bush, the wilderness, the other—and how natural it seems to understand this experience in sexual terms, since it is in making love that our ordinary sense of boundedness and being is overwhelmed and momentarily lost before we return to ourselves once more, renewed.

The Road of Excess

This happened in 2002, when I was a guest professor at Copenhagen University's Institute of Anthropology. One day, a tall young man with a gaunt but sensitive face, shy manner, and intelligent eyes entered my office and asked if I would supervise his M.A. fieldwork in India. He wanted to embark on a phenomenological study of Tibetan Buddhist meditation, a field of which I knew next to nothing. After talking for about half an hour, Sebastien thanked me for my encouragement and interest and assured me he would let me know how things turned out. Over the next few months, Sebastien tried without success to find funding for his project. Disheartened, he returned to me for advice. My suggestion was that he consider yogic techniques for disciplining breath, body, and discursive consciousness as analogous to other techniques for playing with consciousness, including alcohol and drug use, vertigo and trance, music and dance. I spoke a little about my own experiences of Hatha Yoga over many years, and referred Sebastien to books on altered states of consciousness that explored this fascinating field without assuming Dionysian intoxication and self-abandonment to be *necessarily* irrational, archaic, dysfunctional, or immoral.[30] Indeed, as Walter Benjamin observed in one of his essays on his experiments with hashish and opium, "a moralizing attitude . . . gets in the way of essential insights" into drug use, for "the principal motive" for taking a drug is the universal human search for ways of augmenting inner resources "in the struggle for existence."[31]

This Nietzschean theme struck a chord in Sebastien,[32] whose reading of Georges Bataille and Michel Maffesoli had already persuaded him

30. Just as play comes naturally to human beings and is a vital part of the experimentation essential to personal and social development, so too does the impulse to play with consciousness. Andrew Weil observes that "we seem to be born with a drive to experience episodes of altered consciousness"—a drive not unique to adolescence or to any one human society—and drugs are only one means of achieving this end. *The Natural Mind: A Revolutionary Approach to the Drug Problem* (New York: Houghton Mifflin, 2004), 19.

31. Walter Benjamin, "Crock Notes," in *On Hashish*, trans. Howard Eiland et al. (Cambridge, Mass.: Belknap Press of Harvard University Press, 2006), 83–84.

32. Friedrich Nietzsche, *The Birth of Tragedy*, trans. Douglas Smith (Oxford: Oxford University Press, 2000).

that human beings are driven not only by a rational desire to improve or consolidate their situations in life but by a transgressive drive to throw caution to the winds, expend surplus energy, interrupt routine, and experiment with consciousness, even at the risk of losing their reason or their lives. It also transpired that Sebastien had spent the fall of 2001 working as a student assistant on a research project in the Danish town of Ringsted, studying alcohol and drug use among the young. Thus was conceived a fieldwork project involving further fieldwork in Ringsted, with additional, comparative work in Toulouse, France.

Sebastien's fieldwork culminated in 2004 in a brilliant thesis, in which he argued against the widespread view that the youth of today are increasingly nihilistic, asocial, and self-centered, and that drug and alcohol abuse are symptoms of this pathological condition, this social problem, this moral decadence. Building on the insights of the young people among whom he lived and worked, Sebastien showed that the intoxication that inspired wildness, degradation, excess, and transgression also enabled youth to escape the stresses and routines of their workaday worlds. But one did drugs for the hell of it, and not just to find refuge from the hellish conditions under which one lived. In bars and clubs, the young entered intimate havens, curtained against the outside world and without clocks. "Intoxicants put the ordinary order of things in limbo," Sebastien wrote.[33] One passed from a world of strict schedules and time constraints into a timeless state of being spaced-out. In some cases, people compared the club to a church, a place for forging an intimate sense of connectedness. But this transfiguration seldom comes naturally, and the violent images with which the break from normalcy is described suggest how desperately difficult it is—even with the aid of intoxicants, music, and the close-packed, supportive, bodily presence of like-minded others—to blow one's mind. Hence the aggressive metaphors in which partying is said to set the roof on fire, to give it gas, to blow it off, to run amok, and being high makes you fucked up, short-circuited, smashed, wasted, bombed, or stoned.[34] In this nightlife, intense feelings of solidarity, belonging, and fusion seem to produce the same results that, in other societies

33. Sebastien Tutenges, "The Accursed Share of Nightlife," thesis submitted to the Institute of Anthropology, Copenhagen University, 2004, 29.
    34. Ibid., 32.

or social contexts, are achieved through whirling, swinging, dancing, and trance. One is thus led to question the discursive conventions that define different modes of transgressive behavior as religious or secular, social or antisocial, positive or negative. That the impulse to run wild, violate norms, degrade oneself, squander money, take risks, lose one's reason, reverse roles, and break habits has no obvious social value does not mean that it has no existential value, since it is by magically deconstructing the order that is imposed on us in our everyday lives that we discover our capacity for creating order for ourselves. In other words, *the excising or rupture of mundane connections is a necessary prelude to the forging of extraordinary bonds.*

In its most deeply existential sense, religious experience has its origins in this impulse to destroy, renounce, or abandon the quotidian world in order to be reborn within wider fields of cosmic connectedness, natural being, or human community. And nowhere is the link between limit experience and the creation of communitas more evident that in initiation ritual, where the painful passage from childhood to adulthood, with its sleepless nights, physical ordeals, genital mutilations, and inculcated terrors, paradoxically forges the interpersonal loyalties, binding ties, and mutual recognition on which the generation and regeneration of a community depends. Among the Kuranko, for example, initiations take place in the dry season, after harvest, when people have returned to their villages from scattered wet season farmsteads. The ritualized creation of a new generation of men or women therefore goes hand in hand with a celebration of communal life. Whether we decipher the word "religion" as referring to binding ties or relationships, to submission or transcendence, initiation encapsulates and condenses all these definitions while reminding us that our original ties with parents are never entirely eclipsed but simply disguised in adult fantasies of benevolent or punitive divinities. At the same time, the modernist emphasis on education over initiation makes one wonder whether our vital connections with our ancestors, our past, and with successive generations, as well as our sense of belonging to a common world, have also passed away. As Hannah Arendt observes, "Through many ages before us—but now not any more—men entered the public realm because they wanted something of their own or something they had in common with others to be more permanent than their earthly lives . . . There is perhaps no clearer testimony to the loss of the public realm in the modern age than the almost complete loss of authentic concern with immortality, a loss somewhat overshadowed by the simultaneous loss of the metaphysical concern with eternity."[35]

The Eternal Ones of the Dream

In 1994, my wife and I, with our small son Joshua, lived with an Aboriginal family in a rainforest camp on southeast Cape York Peninsular. After several months in the field I became friendly with Harry Shipton, a man roughly my own age, who lived in the nearby settlement of Wujal Wujal on the Bloomfield River. Harry had proved eager to talk with me about his life, and he took Francine and me on excursions to various places associated with his childhood, his youth, and with Kuku-Yalanji creation myths. One April day, Harry, his wife Ina, Francine, Joshua, and I drove into the hills that rose steeply from the coast. Our journey would take us to a "story-place" called Buru, or China Camp, named for the Chinese, Javanese, and Malay "wages men" who mined alluvial tin in the area from the mid-1890s to the period around the First World War; we would then drive on into the forested watersheds of the Daintree and Bloomfield rivers.

The road was little more than a rain-gouged track. It took us through partly cleared grazing land, past the site of China Camp near Roaring Meg Falls, and across boulder-obstructed streams—with Harry regaling us with stories about where certain old-timers were buried and where the old tin workings lay hidden in the near-impenetrable rainforest. At last we came to a grassy clearing, cropped by a couple of untethered horses. "This is it," Harry announced. "We're here." I parked our Toyota near a barbed wire fence and gate, beyond which was a garden filled with citrus and pawpaw trees and banana palms. Harry got out and began shouting Peter Fisher's name.

The old man, stiff in the hips, came hobbling through the pawpaws to the gate, and it was apparent from the relaxed and open expression on his face that he was happy to receive visitors.

After Harry had made the introductions, we sat in the small open-sided shed with a dirt floor where Peter slept and cooked. I noticed

35. Arendt, *The Human Condition*, 55.

some onions, chili peppers, salt, and plates on a makeshift counter. "I don't eat much," Peter said. "Tea and damper mostly, like when I was a boy." And he said he felt guilty that he had no *maiyi* (food) to offer us.

Francine said no apologies were needed; we had brought something to eat

Peter had been living in the wilderness for fifteen months. It was the site of the old Collins homestead, he explained. He had had to clear the lantana and scrub before making his garden. The river ran nearby, so he had plenty of water. And the horses kept the grass down. I expressed amazement that he had accomplished so much in a little over a year.

Harry explained to Peter that we had visited the falls on our way up. "Kijanka," Peter said, using the *bama* (Aboriginal) word for the locality (literally 'moon place'). "You have to be careful when you approach the falls," Peter warned. The falls had the power to draw a person over the edge. He also mentioned a rock at the top of the falls that could move to the bottom of the falls of its own accord, and back to the top. But when white miners began blasting with gelignite at China Camp, they killed the stone, which now lies immobile at the foot of the walls, bereft of life. "Same thing happened at Daintree," Peter said. "There was a stone. No matter how many times *bama* rolled it to the bottom of the waterfall, it would find its way back to the top. But you know how pig-headed Europeans can be? Well, some policemen wanted to roll the stone down to the bottom. *Bama* said, 'No, don't touch it, don't go near it.' But they rolled it anyway. After that it stayed there at the bottom, dead."

"I can tell you some terrible stories about this place in the early days," Peter said. "Europeans were very bad to Aboriginal people. *Bama* would try to help them, but they were always repaid with unkindness."

Peter's biological father was a part-Aboriginal man called Dick Fisher, the son of a German immigrant, who mined tin for a while at China Camp. Peter never met his father because when his mother became pregnant she was sent away. When Peter was a very small boy, the police came to his mother's camp looking for "half-castes." He hid in the bush, but his friend and agemate Oglevie was caught and taken to the mission station at Yarrabah, south of Cairns, where he died two months later, Peter said, "of homesickness and a broken heart." As for Peter, his mother disappeared when he was seven, leaving him in the care of his maternal grandmother. "My granny was very good to me.

She looked after me better than my own mother. When I was starving, she fed me wild yams. She is buried near here. That is why I came here to live and to die. I have had this place in mind all my life. I wanted to be close to her."

Peter made us mugs of tea, and we shared the food we had brought with us, even though Peter's garden contained enough food to feed a small community.

After eating, we strolled along the grassy paths, Peter showing us his yams and taro, string beans, cabbage, tomatoes, cassava, and tropical fruit, while Francine plied him with questions about the changes he had witnessed in his seventy-six years of tin-mining, of working on pearl luggers and in the cane fields of northern Queensland, of living in places like Daintree, Mossman, Wujal Wujal, and Wonga Beach.

Peter wryly observed that if you visited another camp in the old days, as we had visited his today, you would sit and wait beyond the perimeter with eyes downcast, saying nothing, until the hosts approached you with food. But the worst infractions of traditional protocol centered, in Peter's view, on marriage. "These days, everything is mixed up. People marry just anyone, like dogs. Cousins, even in-laws. I can tell you about one man, he married his mother-in-law. When he had a daughter, that means he was supposed to marry her. The old people had it the right way. Just like with cattle. You keep a bull in the pen. You don't let it in with the cows just anytime, anyhow. The breeding would be too close."

Peter also spoke of young people's disrespect toward elders, their shameful indifference to the rules of in-law avoidance, and the various taboos that helped control the exploitation of natural resources. His twenty-something grandson had come and spent a few weeks with him. Peter had tried to teach him the names and uses of various trees—the *wumburru* (bull oak) that was good for making furniture, the *gujiguji* that was good for fence posts, the *galkanji* (spiky bark) that burned easily and cleanly—but the young man was uninterested and did not want to learn.

I asked Peter if he ever felt isolated and alone up there in the middle of nowhere.

"I am never afraid or alone," he said. "I have seen God with my own eyes. He is with me. I pride myself in owning nothing. A storm could blow away this camp. It's nothing. I wouldn't worry. Not like those houses people build. I'm nothing. I was never cut out to be a boss over anyone. I'm just a storyteller."

When it was time for us to return to the coast, Peter said: "I wouldn't want to live at Wujal. All that drinking, smoking dope, that confusion. I worked all my life. I couldn't just sit around like the people at the mission. I don't need money. I never smoked. I never drank. I can buy my flour and tea at Mareeba every three or four months. If my family come and visit, that's all right. But I never feel the need to leave here. Never."

Strange Lights

I felt drawn to Peter Fisher for reasons I could not, at first, fully fathom. He reminded me a little of my mother, someone who had made her peace with the world under circumstances that would ordinarily, in Emily's favorite phrase, "try the patience of a saint." Peter's life in his rainforest clearing, midway between a tragic past and an uncertain future, came as close as any life I had ever known to absolute acceptance, to the peace that passes all understanding. At once anchorite and sage, he seemed more than reconciled to his lot; he appeared entirely at one with it. Here was a man whose freedom was defined by the confines of his clearing—a clearing I could not help but see metaphorically, not as an Eden recreated on earth but as a form of enlightenment. Here was a man who was avowedly "nothing," yet whose story was the story of "everyman."

One might also say that Peter Fisher lived in a penumbral zone between the living and the dead, a place of ghosts. In ongoing conversations with Peter, and in the course of everyday life in our camp, Francine and I were constantly made aware of the ways that Queensland's violent past impinges on the consciousness of Aboriginal people in the here and now, perpetuating fears of further injustices, clouding the possibility of a future. During one of his reminiscences, Peter described what happened after the death of an old man known as Sandy.

When Peter was a small boy, Sandy would carry him everywhere and, at night, allow him to sleep close by for protection. When Sandy died in his sleep one night, the small boy was unaware that his protector had passed away.

"I'll tell you something that'll be hard for you to believe," Peter said, "but I saw it with my own eyes when I was a child. People had come from Wujal, Daintree, Mossman, from everywhere, for Sandy's funeral. We all sat in a line so the spirit in the body could get out. It came out like a firefly. It stopped at the doorway. Then people spoke to him. It then brightened up, so we could see our shadows. They said, 'All right now. You leavin' us now. You gotta go see father. Before you go, you see our people at Banabila [a large Aboriginal camp near the mouth of the Bloomfield River].' There was a big mob there. It was a bright light. He flew down that way. And they said, 'Oh, he came down and visit us now.' I don't know if anyone else still remembers. You might ask."

It was impossible to ignore this numberless and nebulous community of lost souls. They were like the afterimages of loved ones lost. Semi-embodied memories. And like the past they were ever-present, hovering in the penumbra of consciousness, shadowy and repining.

Dubu, or ghosts, most often appear to the living as strange lights—a trail of fireflies moving in the darkness, a torch that mysteriously switches itself on in the middle of the night, a bright light that for several hours uncannily follows the car in which one is driving home after a funeral in another settlement, a blue light hovering in the sky like a UFO, or lights flitting among the trees. In almost every case, ghosts are spirits of the dead made manifest—unquiet shades that torment and haunt the living who have abandoned them, or spirits that are reluctantly making their way to the land of the dead. But ghosts are not only external phenomena, haunting the living. They are also projections of the inner distress of those of who have lost loved ones. Ghosts are, to use Winnicott's term, "transitional phenomena." They make their appearance in the "potential space" between intrapsychic and external worlds and are important means whereby people undertake the difficult passage from attachment to separation. It is in this "potential space" that people disclose their fears and feelings, review the troubling phenomena they have just witnessed, and reach agreement as to its cause, its possible consequences, and what course of action may best deal with it. In other words, standardized cultural notions about the spirits of the dead and subjective feelings toward an individual who has recently passed away come together to produce a provisional understanding that then serves as the basis for dealing with one's confusion and dismay. Among the Kuku Yalanji this involves sticking together (since ghosts don't trouble people in company), ensuring that proper mortuary rites are performed (notably "smoking" the deceased's possessions by passing them over a fire, and thereby decontaminating them), and reinforcing an avoidance relationship with the dead by not speaking their name or otherwise remembering them in public. Often, Francine and I would be enjoined not to leave water standing around our tent when we were away; it might attract some errant ghost.

Kuku Yalanji responses to strange lights and inner grief demonstrate the healing power of shared experience. To be witness to unusual phenomena, or subject to disorienting thoughts and feelings, is to risk feeling different, isolated, and even crazy. But as soon as an experience is brought from the private into the public realm and shared, its character is instantly changed. Assimilated to the collective wisdom of the tribe, and subject to conventional actions, it is literally made common; it is brought within the familiar bounds of what is recognized and within reason. It is like bringing an outsider back within the social pale, or releasing a prisoner from solitary confinement—restorations of the sociality that alone provides security and sanity.

There are, however, places where people resist translating outlandish experiences into familiar terms, preferring to see strange lights as essentially inexplicable and beyond our grasp. Such was Robert "Bruiser" Coomb's response to the strange fuzzy circle of light that is sometimes seen near the small town of Boulia in Western Queensland. Known locally as the Min Min light, and reminiscent for Bruiser Coombs of "an emu running around with a torch up its arse," the phenomenon has attracted so many tourists to Boulia that a two million dollar tourist center has been built to accommodate their fascination with what is advertised as an "unsolved modern mystery."[36] Recently, however, a neuroscientist from the University of Queensland cleared up the apparent mystery of this Australia fata morgana, or inverted mirage, by showing how the light is caused when a pocket of cold air is trapped below warm air close to the ground. Bruiser Coombs was not impressed. "They should leave it alone," he said. "It's one of the great mysteries of the world."

What we call a mystery is the result of a refusal to translate phe-

36. Ashleigh Wilson, "Making Light of a Mystery," *The Australian*, December 26, 1994, 3.

nomena, either external or intrapsychic, into shared meanings. Accordingly, the phenomenon remains in extrasocial space, and as such is labeled either a natural phenomenon or a purely subjective experience. I think it is as easy to understand why Bruiser Coombs, a self-styled loner and maverick, should prefer not to translate strange natural phenomena or inner feelings into words as it is to understand why Kuku Yalangi so assiduously subject all natural phenomena to orthodox understandings.[37] People who regard themselves as marginal or different, or want to be recognized as such, will be attracted to the idea of mysteries to the same extent that people whose priority is belonging to a collectivity will tend to assimilate the meaning of all phenomena to the conventional wisdom of the group. This explains the lack of espoused skepticism in tribal societies, and the fact that people so readily pay lip service to views they do not necessarily "believe." Thus Kuranko accept received ideas about bush spirits, even when they have no personal evidence of their existence, and go along with Islam, now that it has taken hold in Sierra Leone, despite having been *suniké*—or free-thinkers—for centuries, and resisting Islamic jihads. In the telling words of Fore Kande, an elderly Firawa man, who had been a *suniké* all his life but embraced Islam in the late 1980s: *Be minto i le to i ban wo ma*—Where everyone is, would you not be there too? And he added, "If you refuse you will become the subject of ill-feeling."

Yet, for all this, there always remains something that cannot be explained away—something residual, irreducible, and fugitive; like a stranger outside the pale, fireflies among the trees, an inexplicable shadow.

Recognitions

One Sunday morning in the late fall, my friend and colleague Davíd Carrasco drove out to Lexington to have lunch with me. It was cold but sunny after several days of wind and rain, and dead leaves and pine straw

37. Among the Aboriginal people of the Daly region in northwest Australia, the Min Min light figures in several *wangga* songs as a wandering ghost. One such song was received in a dream from two song-giving agents—the ghost of a deceased songman and a small bird. Allan Marrett, *Songs, Dreamings and Ghosts: The Wangga of North Australia* (Middletown, Conn.: Wesleyan University Press, 2005), 39–40.

covered the asphalt. I suggested to Davíd that we go for a walk around West Farm and through the woods before sitting down to lunch.

Walking always loosens the mind and aids conversation, and before long we were talking about the affinities and connections that bring the most unlikely people together and cannot be explained in terms of age, gender, ethnicity, or even common interests. When Davíd asked if this was something I was writing about, I sketched some of the themes I was struggling to bring together—my attempt to show the historical depth of every biography and the biographical dimensions of every history, and the significance of those critical situations in which we die to one life and are sometimes reborn to another.

Davíd said that I might be interested in the interviews he and a colleague had conducted with the great Mexican archaeologist Eduardo Matos Moctezuma, since every critical juncture in this man's life had been connected in some way with his explorations of Aztec prehistory and had, moreover, powerful resonances with Aztec myth. In his sixties, Moctezuma saw that his life had been marked by five momentous breaks (*rompimientos*), each of which combined "powerful separations with uniquely new opportunities." Each, indeed, had involved a death and a rebirth. The first was his break, at age fifteen, with religion. The second was his repudiation of the bureaucratic world of Mexican archaeology and his return to full-time research. The third break coincided with the discovery of Coyolxauhqui, a hefty sculpture of a sacrificed, naked, and mutilated woman in the heart of Mexico City. This was the break-up of his first marriage and the beginning of a new and passionate relationship. The fourth breaking point came with the realization that what mattered in life was not fame or fortune but the small pleasures and fleeting illuminations of life that carry one deeper and deeper into the heart of the world. The fifth break will be the hour of his death, when life itself is left behind.

The Aztecs had five epochs in their cosmology, Davíd said, and space had five dimensions, the fifth being the center of the world. There was therefore a correspondence between Moctezuma's life course and Aztec cosmology.

"What about you?" I asked. "Have you discovered parallels between your cultural history and your own life?"

Davíd said he would send me something he had written on the subject. He would be interested in my reactions.

A few days later I read Davíd's paper, in which he describes how, when he was a fifteen-year-old boy living in Mexico City with his parents, his aunt Milena had taken him to the Museum of Anthropology on Moneda Street.

Wandering through the halls, I found myself wide-eyed and astonished at my first encounter with actual Maya jade, Maya writing, the treasures of Monte Albán, the Aztec Calendar Stone, the giant statue of Coatlicue, the imitation *penacho* of Moctezuma, and the many ritual objects in the Salón de Monolitos. Among the latter were monumental serpents and eagles, faces of gods, and images of cosmic time. Strong sensations welled up in me. In a kind of stupor, I wandered out into the street and over to the grand Zócalo. My feelings continued to grow, and I could not stand still but walked intensely in a winding path in the great open space. As the feelings took shape in my mind, I became aware of a deep emotional self undergoing an agitation, revealing a division in my heart. I was feeling both intense pride and cutting shame at my Mexican ancestry.

Davíd refers to his epiphany as an "Aztec moment," and goes on, in his essay, to describe the images of inferiority and bloodthirstiness with which Old World discourse has depicted Mesoamerican culture, and how the "authentic" Aztec heritage that archaeology and scholarship have brought to light enables Chicanos to reconnect with a shared heritage and thereby restore their human dignity and pride.

I was moved by Davíd's essay, and envious of his knowledge of Mesoamerican civilization. For in my case, I had never experienced this kind of connection with a period of history, a culture, or an ethnic group. In fact, I had never wanted to, wary of the dangers of seeking personal empowerment through an identification with an ideology or polity, past or present. But was this repudiation of cultural identity simply an expression of the privileged position I occupied as a white middle-class male? Even though I rejected the identification, had I not taken advantage of it? Had I been Maori, would my path have been as smooth?

Mostly, however, I found myself wondering what connections and recognitions in my own life resembled the "Aztec moment" in Davíd's youth. For me, perhaps, such illuminations have been typically associated with the discovery of an artist with whom I felt a deep affinity. Seeing Colin McCahon's *Gate Series* when I was nineteen, for example, or discovering Thomas Wolfe that same year. But falling in love, or forming a friendship that will last a lifetime, have meant as much, which is why the kinds of connectedness that Davíd describes come very close to the experience of agape—that overwhelming sense that one's hitherto isolated ego is merged with a wider world, even, some- times, it would seem, with the cosmos. It is in this sense that Davíd's image of "borderlands," drawn from his direct experience of the his- torically contested and socially vexed space of the American-Mexican border becomes a metaphor for all those existential situations in which we lose our way, reach the limits of our endurance, place our lives at risk, or discover something new about ourselves through an encounter with a text from outside our own tradition, a person whose story bears no obvious relationship with our own, or a defining experience for which nothing could have prepared us.

During our walk in the woods, Davíd told me another story that seemed to me to belong to this mosaic. Some years ago, Davíd had taught at the University of Colorado at Boulder. Driving to work, he would often notice a man waiting at a bus stop about ten minutes from the campus. Since he knew from newspaper accounts that this man also taught at the university, Davíd stopped one day and asked him if he would like a lift. This happened several times over the next few weeks, and Davíd got to hear Eugene Salomé's extraordinary story. Sa- lomé was Lou Andreas Salomé's nephew and a citizen of Finland. In the early stages of the Second World War he served in the Luftwaffe, but upon realizing the full implications of the Nazi plan for Europe, he deserted and joined the Resistance. Arrested as a conspirator in a plot to assassinate Hitler, Salomé was sent to Dachau concentration camp, where he was subject to brutal interrogations. One of the aims of the Gestapo appeared to be to get him to declare that Jews were subhuman and that he, as a member of the master race, felt no identification with them. Salomé, who was a chess grandmaster, imagined during these interrogations that he was playing a game of chess, and that if he could outthink and outwit his opponents he would defeat them, even though they murdered him. One day, as he was being dragged to yet another interrogation, his guards stopped and pointed out to him a group of naked Jewish men and women, about to go to their deaths. The pris- oners were making love outside a barracks. The Gestapo guards asked Salomé if he could ever bring himself to behave in such a way, to which he responded without thinking, "No, I could not." And then, as the

Gestapo threw back at him the implication of his confession—that he could not identify with these Jews because they were mere animals, he realized he had been tricked, that he had been checkmated. This weighed upon his mind for the rest of his life, Davíd said, and though Salomé published many pamphlets on chess problems, including "The Two Knights Defense with 5 e5," "The Polugayevskyy Variation of the Najdorf Defense," and "The Advance Variation of the French Defense," he never came to terms with the moral dilemma from which he had failed to escape. I mentioned to Davíd that many of the stories in my book touched upon the same question as to whether a person who has suffered terrible wrongs and brutalizing experiences can ever escape their effects. Whether, when one's life is stripped away, stolen, or degraded, one can salvage and recover it, drawing a line between now and then so that one gives oneself a second life, a life that is no longer in thrall to the past.

It was then that Davíd recalled Salomé's remark on the day news broke of Primo Levi's suicide in Turin. "The camp got him. The camp got him." For it was always there, waiting to claim you, waiting to drag you back.

That evening, after Davíd had gone, I turned on the television, wanting respite from the terrible implications of Eugene Salomé's story. I found myself watching the 1987 movie *84 Charing Cross Road*. Toward the end of the movie, which is a fictionalized account of the writer Helene Hanff's correspondence with the staff of a famous London bookstore of Marks & Co., Helene is in her New York apartment, writing a letter of complaint about the Modern Library edition of selections from John Donne and William Blake that she has just received in the mail. Not only does she fail to see what these two writers have in common that should justify their sharing a single volume, she is miffed that only a selection of Donne's sermons are included in the book. She then reads from the well-known Meditation XVII:

> All *mankinde* is of one *Author*, and is one *volume*; when one Man dies, one *Chapter* is not *torne* out of the *booke*, but *translated* into a better *language*; and every *Chapter* must be so *translated*; *God* emploies several *translators*; some peeces are translated by *age*, some by *sicknesse*, some by *warre*, some by *justice*; but *Gods* hand is in every *translation*; and his hand shall binde up all our scattered leaves againe, for that *Librarie* where every *booke* shall lie open to one another.

In my journal, I asked myself: for we who cannot believe in any day of reckoning when justice is finally dispensed, is it possible in some small measure and, perhaps, in how we write, to make good the losses we bear witness to, and if not bind up the scattered leaves at least lay open to one another the various lives we have been a part of, and show that while crisis transforms a life utterly that same crisis may translate it into something richer and redemptive because is enables another life to begin?

I then copied out a passage from Axel Munthe's memoir in which he struggles to come to terms with his impulsively erotic act of kissing a beautiful young nun, Suora Ursula, with whom he was keeping vigil as the abbess of her convent lay dying of cholera during the Neapolitan plague. Despite the randomness and pandemonium that appear to prevail whenever life and death do battle on a grand scale, as in pestilence, war, or earthquake, Munthe observes, "The battle is regulated in its minutest details by an immutable law of equilibrium."

> Nature sets to work at once to readjust the balance, to call forth new beings to take the place of the fallen. Compelled by the irresistible force of a Natural Law, men and women fall in each other's arms, blindfolded by lust, unaware that it is Death who presides over their mating, his aphrodisiac in one hand, his narcotic in the other. Death, the giver of Life, the slayer of Life, the beginning and the end.[38]

The Other Portion

I find it fascinating that when people tell the story of their lives, they often tell of some memorable coincidence, some moment of truth or life-altering event that defies explanation. Consider, for example, the following story that Carl Jung recounts in his autobiography, *Memories, Dreams, Reflections*:

> It was at a wedding of a friend of my wife's; the bride and her family were all entirely unknown to me. During the meal I was sitting opposite a middle-aged gentleman with a long, handsome beard, who had been

38. Axel Munthe, *The Story of San Michele* (London: Hodder Headline, 2004), 125–26.

introduced to me as a barrister. We were having an animated conversation about criminal psychology. In order to answer a particular question of his, I made up a story to illustrate it, embellishing it with all sorts of details. While I was telling my story, I noticed that a quite different expression came over the man's face, and a silence fell on the table. Very much abashed, I stopped speaking. Thank heavens we were already at the dessert, so I soon stood up and went into the lounge of the hotel. There I withdrew into a corner, lit a cigar, and tried to think over the situation. At this moment one of the other guests who had been sitting at my table came over and asked reproachfully, "How did you ever come to commit such a frightful indiscretion?" "Indiscretion?" "Why yes, that story you told." "But I made it all up!"

To my amazement and horror it turned out that I had told the story of the man opposite me, exactly and in all its details. I also discovered, at this moment, that I could no longer remember a single word of the story—even to this day I have been unable to recall it.[39]

There are people who will seize on such uncanny coincidences as proof that we possess an archaic faculty, enabling us to divine what another person is thinking or about to say. These are the people who, when you phone them, tell you how incredible that you should have called at that precise moment; they were just about to call you. Of such people, for whom the world abounds with symbols and portents crying out to be read, and who will draw your attention, say, to seven rooks in a fallow field and wonder why you can't see what they can see, Umberto Eco coined the term "cogito interruptus."[40] Such people are comforted by the thought of a hidden hand guiding if not governing our lives. They like to think that fate works darkly in our favor. Of happily married couples they will exclaim, "they were meant for each other"; of an accident or catastrophe, "it was bound to happen." The writing is always on the wall. For them, our lives are storied—with well-marked beginnings, middles, and ends. Wrongs are righted, mysteries solved, and miracles happen, not through our own actions but because of the inscrutable workings of fate.

39. Carl G. Jung, *Memories, Dreams, Reflections*, trans. Richard and Clara Winston (London: Fontana, 1967), 68–69.

40. Umberto Eco, *Travels in Hyperreality*, trans. William Weaver (London: Picador, 1987), 222.

Myself, I think only of the miracles that do not happen. The lives that lack all rhyme or reason, the people who get away with murder, and the millions of unremembered coincidences that involve no transfiguring moment, no meeting with destiny, no path that makes all the difference. When I think of the stones left unturned, the tears unshed, the deeds undone, the doors that were never opened, and the sheer contingency of existence, I find it impossible to hear the word "synchrony" without recoiling. And yet, for all my skepticism I am drawn to such stories, perhaps because a story would not be a story without coincidence, and since there is no inherent order in the world, the order we artificially give to life through art must have recourse to such artifice.

I've always loved the kind of stories that Paul Auster tells in *The Red Notebook*—stories about uncanny coincidences and epiphanies that reshape the way a person sees his or her world. So when *True Tales from American Life* was published in 2001 I began reading avidly—though in a bookshop, since I did not have the money to purchase a copy at that time.[41] The first story I read, though only two pages long, stunned me, and I returned to the bookshop every other day for about two weeks to read more.

True though these stories were—in the sense that they set down exactly what an individual remembered about a critical episode in his or her life—it was clear that what made an event both memorable and narratable was the extent to which it disclosed synchronicities, coincidences, or insights that transfigured the humdrum reality of everyday existence. Despite the fickleness of fate and the contingency of events, and the fact that human lives lack natural symmetry or narrative coherence, most people crave evidence of an implicit order, a latent design, or some natural justice.

Although I could not afford a copy of the book for myself, I shared my enthusiasm for it in e-mails to friends, and when Christmas came around I made a gift of it to my daughter's partner—exactly the sort of book I knew he would like—placing it among the other presents under our Christmas tree.

Next day there was a package in my mailbox from Amazon.co.uk. Inside was a copy of *True Tales from American Life*. I inspected the in-

41. Paul Auster, *True Tales of American Life*, ed. and introd. Paul Auster (London: Faber, 2001).

voice for clues as to who had sent me the book. It had been ordered on December 14. "This delivery represents part of your gift," said the invoice. "The other portion is being sent separately."

Who could have sent this gift, and what was "the other portion?"

I had told my wife how affected I had been by this book, so assumed she must have ordered it for me. The kids in my son's class at school send one another small, anonymous gifts at Christmas. Perhaps she was my "Secret Santa."

"No," she said, as mystified as I was, "it wasn't me."

I look forward to finding out, sooner or later, who my Secret Santa is, and thanking her or him or them not only for the gift of this book but for the gift of this story that would not be out of place among Paul Auster's *True Tales*. I'd also like to tell them that on the same day they sent this gift, the German writer W. G. Sebald died in a car crash in East Anglia. Max Sebald would, I think, also have liked Paul Auster's collection, if only for its lack of literary pretension. For so deeply did he abhor our habit of transforming terrible events into literature that he dedicated his life to creating a way of writing that did justice to experience. If he was reluctant to call his books "novels," it was because he believed that meaning lies less in who we think we are than in the mysterious concatenation of events that embroil us and the curious outcome of our relationships with others. Rather than the loquacity, introspection, and "grinding noises" that we associate with the modern novel, Sebald sought something closer to the "chaste compactness," as Walter Benjamin put it, of the oral tale.

It Happens

On my flight from Indianapolis to LaGuardia I was sitting next to a man in his late fifties. He fidgeted a lot, adjusting his overhead ventilator, stowing his bag under the seat, straightening his jacket. And his talk at first was fidgety too. Asking me if the temperature outside would mean ice on the wings. Talking about the American Airlines crash in northern Indiana last year. Wondering why we weren't being served orange juice before takeoff. Then we got talking. He said he had always thought of himself as a bit of a nomad, but this would be his first time in New York City. "There's always got to be a first time," I said helpfully. "You married?" he asked. "Yes," I said, though I suppose I could have just as accurately said "no." "How about you?" "Like you said," he said, "there's always a first time for everything." "You mean you're going to New York to get married?" I asked. "You got it," he said. "First time in New York. First time married." I was moved by his story. At fifty-six he had never been kissed. He put it down to always being a wanderer. Never long enough in any one place to meet anyone, to form any attachment. He said, "One day I had to go down to Brown County to pick up a re-conditioned gear box for my Chevy truck. It wasn't far, wasn't a short trip neither. Well, I asked Muriel if she'd like to come along. You know, for the ride. Maybe have a coffee at Nashville. I knew she liked those dried flower arrangements they sell there. And knew she didn't get out too much. She didn't say yes right away. But that evening she called me up. Yes, she said, she'd be happy to come. To keep me company. To see those dried flowers in Nashville. Anyway, we got the gearbox and drove back to Nashville. I mustta driven up and down that main street for twenty minutes. I was pretending to be looking for a parking space, but the truth was I was trying to pluck up courage to say something to Muriel, and I knew that if I stopped, if I wasn't behind the wheel of the truck, with my eyes on the road, I wouldn't get to say it. So we was driving up and down the street, not saying anything much. And then it was like something outside myself, like someone or something prompted me. And I kinda turned to Muriel and said those words that were coming into my head, just like that. I said: 'You're someone that it would be very easy to love.' I surprised myself. I guess I surprised her too. She'd never married. She'd been engaged to a guy when war broke out. When he came back from the war four years later she found out that he had been unfaithful. She couldn't reconcile infidelity with love, and so had given him back his ring. That's the way Muriel is. Never does anything by halves. But now she was hearing this word 'love' from me, a word I'd never used before, that she'd probably never heard much neither. It was the same for her she told me later—like a voice outside herself, outside of us, was speaking. 'You're someone that it would be very easy to love, too,' she said. My very words. 'It,' she said. 'Not I.' Isn't it strange. That at the most intimate moment between two people, that moment of love, everything comes down to that totally impersonal word 'It.' As though It, whatever it is, is doing all the talking for us, calling all the shots."

"That's what love is," I said. "It's more than us. It always is." And I thought of Georg Groddeck's essays on the It, and back to when my wife and I first met and I had this overwhelming sense that it was not so much a meeting of two separate human beings but of a mutual recognition, which came upon me with the force of a revelation or conversion, that our relationship had a life quite independent of us, a life of its own, and that we were part of It, expressions of It, and that It had existed before us, and would in all likelihood outlive us both.

Ships That Pass in the Night

For three successive summers (2003–2005) we stayed in Zurich, where my wife Francine attended seminars at the C. G. Jung Institute as part of her analytical training. Every morning, after Francine left our apartment for her day's session at the Institute, I would pack a lunch and take Joshua and Freya down through the beech forest to Küsnacht, where the children would buy breakfast croissants and hot chocolate while I would order an espresso and read the *Herald Tribune*. Our first summer, we spent almost every day at the lakeside, where Joshua and Freya swam and gamboled in the shallows while I read my paper, struggled with the crossword puzzle, or scribbled idle thoughts in my journal. Every few days, we ventured into the city to buy something to read at the Orell Fuessli Bookshop on Bahnhofstrasse. Joshua and Freya would sit for hours on the sofas downstairs, giggling at *Garfield*, while I would sometimes wait for them in a nearby café, watching the passers-by, sipping a citron pressé, or dipping into the novel I had just bought. Toward the end of the afternoon, we would return to Küsnacht by train, trudge up the steep streets of the town into the beech forest, climb the one hundred and forty nine steps that led from the valley to the heights, and walk on through the long grass that fringed the Schubelweiher pond to our apartment. There, the children would write another chapter of their "novels" and illustrate them while I prepared dinner.

Our second summer was cold and wet, and Joshua and Freya were often at a loose end, unable to summon the effort for a trip into Zurich and at odds over almost every proposal I made (Freya eager to go down to the lake and feed the ducks, Joshua insisting on a game of football; Joshua desperate to see *Batman: The Movie*, Freya indifferent). One of my last attempts to come up with something that might interest them both was a suggestion that we visit the Children's Museum. Though Joshua, in the throes of distancing himself from childish things, understandably rejected the idea, Freya enthusiastically embraced it. The three of us set off for the city anyway, only to fail to find any children's museum on Paradeplatz—the address I had been given by a neighbor. After asking several people for help, I made one last effort to locate the museum, leading my now peeved and weary children down a narrow cobbled street off Bahnhofstrasse where we came to a building with a blue commemorative plaque on the wall that read "James Joyce Corner." I was instantly intrigued, but the children were not, and I wound up taking them to *Shrek 2* at the Metropole and afterward to McDonald's. "The day that never was," I wrote selfishly in my journal that evening.

On our third and final visit to Zurich the following summer I was determined to satisfy my curiosity about the Joyce connection. It was June, already very hot, and Freya was happy to remain in our hotel room watching TV while Josh and I explored the city. To my pleasant surprise, Joshua was fascinated by the history of Zurich, and after taking in the Romanesque Grossmünster cathedral, famous for its associations with the Reformation in German-speaking Switzerland under Huldrych Zwingli (1484-1531), we strolled together along the Limmatquai to Marktgasse with me endeavoring to spell out the implications of Zwingli's exhortation that people return to the study of holy writ and the preaching of the gospels, and explaining why the reformers stripped the cathedral of everything that gave it a worldly appearance—its pictures, images, sculptures, and musical instruments.

We now turned up one of the narrow cobbled streets to our left and came upon the Cabaret Voltaire at Spiegelgasse 1 where Dadaism was born in February 1916—with its anarchic soirées, its sound and simultaneous poetry, its song and dance, and its transgressive élan. Passing the house of the casuist, poet, and mystic Johann Kaspar Lavater, where Goethe stayed in the 1770s, Joshua and I stopped for a while outside the house in the same street where Lenin lived in exile between 1914 and 1916. I was struck by the incongruities of that period—the Russian exiles working side by side with Swiss workers in the local factories (with the exception of Vladimir Ilyich, who was studying in the local library and writing pamphlets against imperialism!), while the Dadaists played their "noise music," donned their bizarre masks, and recited their abstruse poems. This sense of arbitrary juxtapositions was only increased when, next day, after leaving Josh and Freya to their own devices at the hotel, I made my way downtown to search for the house where James Joyce completed drafts of the early chapters of *Ulysses* in 1916.

It took me some time to locate Seefeldstrasse 54, which was down an alley off the main street. As I approached the dirty gray stucco, two-storied building, I was no longer conscious of the noise of the trams on Seefeldstrasse or of the ninety years that separated me from the Irish writer's period of exile in Zurich. I looked up at the windows on the second floor, the window boxes planted with impatiens, as if Joyce were still in residence. It was close to the middle of the day, the heat intense, the sunlight blinding. When I saw that the front door was open, presumably so that air could circulate in the stuffy wooden building, I crossed the lane and stepped into the shadows of a narrow hallway, its floor covered with broken linoleum, its lower walls paneled in wood that had been painted cream. Everything about the place was consistent with what I had read of the penury and shabbiness of the Joyce family's life in their damp, two-bedroom flat at this address, and it was easy to understand why Joyce spent long evenings in cafés and restaurants, including the nearby Club des Étrangers on Seefeldstrasse.

After leaving Zurich, I found myself wondering whether these famous exiles, Joyce, Lenin, Jung, and the Dadaists, ever met and, if they had, what they had thought of one another. Apparently, Joyce and Lenin had both been regular customers at the Café Odeon in Spiegelgasse, and on the one recorded occasion that their paths had crossed, the Russian opined that the Irishman was "a great personality." As for Joyce and Jung, they never met face to face until, a decade later, desperate to find help for his mentally ill daughter Lucia, Joyce briefly entrusted "his 'yung' daughter so 'easily freudened' to the ministrations of the 'grisly old Sykos.'"[42] But his attitude toward Jung was negative from the start, and he described Jung as "the Swiss Tweedledum" and Freud as "the Viennese Tweedledee," amusing themselves "at the expense (in every sense of the word) of ladies and gentlemen who are troubled with bees in their bonnets."[43] As for Jung, he would dismiss *Ulysses* as boring, and

---

42. Deirdre Bair, *Jung: A Biography* (Boston: Little, Brown, 2003), 303.
43. Ibid., 302.

wonder how anyone could "go through the book from page 1 to page 735 .. without fatal attacks of drowsiness." After his one meeting with Joyce, in the course of treating Lucia, he concluded that both father and daughter were doomed, "like two people going to the bottom of a river, one falling and the other diving."[44] Joyce's reaction was to ask himself how a person who misconstrued *Ulysses* could possibly understand Lucia, and he rejected Jung's suggestion that Lucia was his *anima inspiratrix*, the implication being that he was exploiting as grist for his literary mill an existential tragedy.

One of the lines of research I pursued concerned the month of February 1917, when news of the revolution reached the Russian exiles in Spiegelgasse. What, I wondered were Jung, Joyce, and the Dadaists doing as Lenin and his comrades packed their bags and tried to figure out how best to return to Russia? That month, Tristan Tzara published one of the first issues of the periodical *Dada*. As for James Joyce, he contracted glaucoma, his *Portrait of an Artist as a Young Man* came out in England, and his first significant patroness, Harriet Shaw Weaver, began her financial support of the penurious writer. Jung was writing *Psychological Types*.

I suppose one could classify all these figures as "introverted thinking" types, but such discursive summarizing obscures the great differences between their various commitments, to revolution, to art, and to understanding. And any attempt to find some "acausal connecting principle" of synchronicity, revealing some pattern beneath the temporal and spatial coincidences that all of us, now and then, are momentarily struck by, seems somehow beside the point when the overwhelming evidence is not only of contingency and disconnectedness but of the miraculous appearance of something new in every encounter that makes it impossible to precisely predict the future or reduce the present to the past, yet offers us the perennial possibility of redemption.[45]

44. Richard Ellmann, *James Joyce*, new and rev. ed. (New York: Oxford University Press, 1982), 679.

45. I am echoing Hannah Arendt's notion of "natality" here, the "character of startling unexpectedness [that] is inherent in all beginnings and all origins" and occurs "against the overwhelming odds of statistical laws and their probability, which for all practical, everyday purposes amounts to certainty." *The Human Condition*, 178.

Café Stelling

During my last year in Copenhagen I would break off work in the middle of the morning and walk from the Institute of Anthropology on Frederiksholms Kanal to the Café Stelling on Gammeltorv where I would order an espresso, find a table near the window, and either leaf through one of the English-language magazines to which the café subscribed or idly watch people passing up and down the street. Famous for many years, the Café Stelling had closed its doors in the late 1990s but reopened in late 2004, completely refurbished, on its former corner site. Hoping to attract new customers, the new owner advertised several special offers, including a double espresso for twelve kroner, which was enough to persuade me to take my patronage from my old haunt, the Europa on Amagertorv, and become a habitué of the Stelling. Even after the special offer sign was removed from the window, I continued to pay only twelve kroner for my espresso, thanks to Antoine, the French waiter with whom I exchanged small talk every morning about the Danish weather, the inferior quality of Danish chocolate and cheese, and the pleasures of Paris.

One morning I walked into the Stelling and Antoine wasn't there. When I asked casually where he was, the girl at the counter said he had been sacked for turning up late for work. A couple of days later, I ran into him on Norregade and he told me that the owner had never liked him and had been looking for a pretext to lay him off. But he had already landed a better-paying job in the Brasserie Bleue at the five-star Hotel Skt. Petri. I should come there for my morning coffee. It was the best espresso in town, guaranteed. I said I would drop in sometime, but since the Hotel Skt. Petri was so far from my office, I would probably continue going to the Stelling.

After ordering my double espresso from the Danish girl who had replaced Antoine, I placed a ten and a two kroner coin on the counter. The girl picked up the coins, took a long hard look at them, and told me that a double espresso cost twenty kroner, not twelve. Embarrassed, I explained that I had been a regular custom at the Stelling from the day it reopened and that I had always paid twelve kroner for my morning coffee. It was an understanding I had had with Antoine. The waitress seemed to accept my explanation and dropped my coins into the cash drawer without further ado.

The following morning there was a different server, a young Danish guy with silver rings in his ear lobes and lower lip. I ordered my coffee and, to avoid ambiguity, explained the deal I had struck with his colleague the day before.

"We don't really have a special rate for coffee," he said, "but since you're a regular I guess it's OK."

For a week or so, the servers gave no indication that I was asking for special treatment, but because new staff were coming and going all the time, I had to repeatedly make my case, and soon began to feel deeply uncomfortable with the arrangement. Since no special deal was being offered to others, apart from the occasional pensioner or drifter who came into the café for an early morning coffee, what right did I have to receive special treatment? Indeed, rather than a privilege, it felt like a degradation. As if I was a bum, begging a favor. And the more I thought of this, the more uneasy I felt asking for my twelve kroner espresso, and the less right I felt I had to sit in the coffee shop, reading the English magazines and enjoying the view of the square. My value as a person seemed to have fallen with the value of the coffee. And so I reasoned that if I paid the regular rate perhaps I could restore my honor, and become a valued customer rather than a mere "regular" or, worse, a "bludger." But on the day I insisted on paying the full amount for my coffee, the server refused to accept it. I was a regular, she said. There was an arrangement. It was all right. I didn't have to pay so much. I insisted. I said I didn't want to be a freeloader, getting something for nothing. No question of that, I was assured. The café was happy to continue with the understanding that had been reached last year.

Unable to renegotiate the terms of my "arrangement," I gave up going to the Stelling for several months, hoping that my absence would help the servers forget me, and that I could become anonymous again before one day returning to the café where I would be treated like any other client.

When I told my story to my friend Hans Lucht, who was teaching a course on reciprocity at the Institute of Anthropology, he wanted to know if I intended my tale to be a fable about Danish egalitarianism. And was the problem akin to the problem of being a guest who overstays his welcome, degraded by the generosity he receives because he is not in a position to repay it?

I was grateful for Hans's insights, but told him that I had something else in mind. I wanted my story to frame a conversation about values, "those invisible chains that link relations between things to relations between people,"[1] and I wanted to show how contrasted modalities of value — material and social, quantitative and qualitative — are entangled in almost every human encounter. In particular, I was fascinated by the way that life crises precipitate a radical rethinking of values, sickness transforming a concern for material well-being into a concern for health, divorce replacing the desire for love with demands for recompense.

Value Judgments

Three months after the death of my wife Pauline in 1983, I went to North Canterbury with my daughter Heidi, to spend some time with Pauline's parents. It was high summer. The peak of Te Rako in the inland Kaikoura Range was already bereft of snow, and the hills around Waiau had been singed by the nor'westers and the sun. Walking alone on back-country roads, or sitting under the willows at the confluence of the snow-fed Mason and Waiau rivers where my daughter and I had scattered Pauline's ashes, I felt that my life now amounted to nothing. A gust of wind or rain could sweep me away, and the world would go on, nothing altered, a dog barking on a distant farm, clouds sailing across the sky, the borage blue along the roadside, birds lisping in the willows. I thought: *I am free for as long as I think this way, thinking I am noth-*

1. C. A. Gregory, *Savage Money: The Anthropology and Politics of Commodity Exchange* (Amsterdam: Harwood Academic Publishers, 1997), 12.

ing, that I am going nowhere. Yet, in the midst of my grief, I experienced a curious sense of liberation as my love for Pauline metamorphosed into an intense feeling for the landscape, a greater sensitivity toward my friends, and a sense that my suffering had somehow immunized me from further hurt.

Returning to the house of my parents'-in-law after these long and aimless walks, I would find Jack watering his vegetable garden, the trellis festooned with runner beans, potatoes, radishes, carrots, spring onions, iceberg lettuces growing in neat, carefully weeded rows.

So often was I in tears that I felt self-conscious and would dash cold water over my face before seeing anyone. But Jack seemed not to notice. And he certainly did not want to talk about his own grief. Perhaps it was better this way, returning to the common ground we had always shared, and of which we could still be certain.

"Getting back to what I was saying this morning, Michael, there's one thing you can't legislate for, and that's human nature."

Jack had been a socialist all his life. But he had learned that trying to create a society in which power and wealth were evenly distributed was a profound challenge to our "human nature."

"What I mean to say," Jack said, "you give a man a couple of bob and he's a capitalist."

But Jack was not going to name names, even if we both knew he was speaking about his other son-in-law, for whom the only thing more important than making money was squirreling it away where it could return the highest dividend. So Jack talked about some cheapskate he had known years ago, who would join a drinking school in the pub toward closing time so that when his turn came to buy a round the bar would be shutting down. As if this calculated avoidance of reciprocity were not enough, this joker would, seemingly without thinking, scoop up the small change that had been allowed to accumulate on the bar and walk off as if this was his due.

"A bit on the nose," I said.

But Jack wasn't going to pass judgment too directly. This was not his style.

"Put it this way, Michael," he said, "he never spent more than he had to."

We stood in silence for a while, Jack hosing the scarlet runners, shadows lengthening across the summer lawn.

"You know," Jack said, "Pauline was generous to a fault, even as a little girl. If she was going down to Christchurch with Noellie, I'd give her a pound note to buy something at Ballantines, but she'd come back with presents for everyone. Never spent a penny on herself."

It wasn't that money was the root of all evil for Jack; rather that you had to be constantly on your guard against its baleful influence.

During the depression Jack and a mate were panning for gold. They were camped in a remote part of Central Marlborough, living rough and working hard. Months would pass without them seeing another living soul. And though their pickings were meager, their needs were few. When they made trips to town to sell their takings and buy provisions, they refreshed their memories of how tough it was in the outside world and were glad to get back to their camp.

For a long time, Jack's mate seemed to accept the isolation and hardship, but deep down he was getting increasingly frustrated. For him, the hard labor could only be redeemed by the discovery of a nugget, a small bonanza that would buy their way out of the wilderness. At the end of a long day's work in the river gravels, Jack's mate bemoaned the miserable amount of gold they'd found. "It's not worth a tinker's shit," he complained, "it's not worth the effort."

"If it's not worth anything, let's give it back to the river," Jack said. And he took the pan and emptied the flakes of gold into the swift-flowing, ice-cold water. His mate was furious, though not for long.

"We lost the gold," Jack told me, "but we salvaged our friendship."

Bringing things down to earth. Restoring a sense of proportion. Getting things back into perspective. I suppose these clichés capture something of what Jack was about.

In his youth, he worked as a linesman on the West Coast. It was during this time that he broke his ankle. Because the gang was remote from any doctor or hospital, Jack set the fracture himself and struggled on. Now he walked with a limp, and the old wound caused him considerable pain. But pain was to be borne, not bemoaned, and Jack would cite an old friend whose favorite adage was "This too will pass."

"Everything changes," Jack said. "For the better or for the worse, you never can tell. But nothing stays the same, you can count on that."

Pauline must have picked up this phrase quite early on. A couple of years after we married and I went to Cambridge while she remained in New Zealand, finishing her studies before joining me, I found the separation difficult. Pauline sent me a photograph of herself on which she had written, "Courage, my darling, this too will pass."

One evening, Jack recounted another story. I had heard it before, but I listened to it now for its consoling familiarity, and for the way Jack would laugh when he came to the end of it.

"One bitterly cold day in the dead of winter," Jack said, "a new chum joined our gang." The man was a braggart, so full of himself and so preoccupied by his own exploits that no one wanted to work with him, especially in a situation of danger. At smoko [a smoking break], the men feigned interest in his tall stories about sexual conquests, his accounts of fortunes made and lost in Christchurch, his ability to go without sleep for days at a time. But all were racking their brains for a way of taking the braggart down a peg or two, or simply getting him to shut up. One day the boaster went into the bushes for a shit. No sooner had he settled into a squat, one of the gangers crept up behind him, slipped a long-handled shovel under his butt, only to withdraw it noiselessly when the boaster rose to wipe his arse. The ganger knew his mark would look down to inspect his doings, Jack said, "you know, the way you do when you're outdoors. You can imagine his surprise when he found that his handiwork had disappeared!"

Back on the road, everyone in the gang was quickly made aware of what had happened and they watched without a word as the nonplussed boaster struggled within himself to explain the disappearance of his "doings."

I soaked up Jack's stories. They were glimpses into an egalitarian world that no longer existed, the kind of world in which socialism had a natural purchase, even though, as Jack constantly reminded me, it was probably impossible to implement on a universal scale the kind of ethos that might sometimes be achieved in a particular workplace, a small community.

And I loved Jack's indirectness. The sidelong, nonconfrontational skill with which he realigned relationships, corrected course, created the kind of humility without which human beings cannot live in harmony.

During the years that Jack described as the best in his life, he worked every summer as a shearer on the big North Canterbury stations. One shearing season, he found himself again in a gang with a loudmouth. Jack listened as the younger man bragged about the records he had set in New Zealand and Australia, all the while challenging the other shearers to keep up with him. Jack was biding his time, keeping pace with the boaster, yet slowly putting pressure on him, subtly pushing him into a faster turnaround. It quickly became clear to everyone in the shed what was happening, and as the day wore on it also became clear that Jack was not only going to best the younger man but set a New Zealand record for shearing Romneys. But it was not the record that Jack walked away with at the end of that day but the unspoken satisfaction that he had reined in an unruly and disturbing presence and restored moral order to the shed.

Jack dreamed of not only socialism but a world free from domestic strife, which is why, when he and his wife had a falling out in the years when Pauline was not yet in her teens, he betook himself into the hills where he had a piece of land and spent months in a shack on his own—a period Pauline would remember as an abandonment, and even a betrayal. Perhaps retreat into the wilderness is the only option we have when the world disappoints us. A place of escape and silence, where the hardships of winter snow and summer drought put the pain of human relationships in perspective, and offer the illusion of restoration. Yet only once did Jack confide to me any experience that took him beyond any social or moral order known to him, or touched on the ecstatic.

This must have happened sometime in the 1940s. Jack and a couple of mates had headed up the Maitai River from Bruce Bay in South Westland. There was no track, and they followed the river for two or three days until they came to the Morse Valley. The Strachan glacier was at one end, and elsewhere high bluffs. Jack felt certain that he and his companions were the first people ever to set foot in the valley. That first night, the sky was clear and filled with stars, but the moon was rising. Suddenly, as Jack was looking up at the dark sides of the mountain and at the rising moon, a stag appeared, silhouetted against the milky sky, the moon perfectly captured in the spread of its antlers.

I now think that the mystery of this conjunction between the stag and the moon is connected to the river stones he carried out of the wilderness and later cemented together as the foundations of the "Jack House" where Pauline and I slept when we visited Waiau, as well as the hunks of wood he salvaged from the sawmill he built and managed for several years—wood that he turned on a lathe, dressed with raw linseed oil, labeled and placed in a glass cabinet in the living room . . . "Kowhai from log skids at the mill"; "Matai, South Westland"; "Walnut burr, Cloudy Range"; "Gorse: Emu Plains" . . . an oblique poem, perhaps, pointing to an ethic that I tend to associate with societies far from my own, where it is perfectly natural to devote one's life and labor not so much to oneself but to God, to one's children, to the perpetuation of one's lineage, or to a transcendent ideal. To lose one's sense of connectedness or belonging to something greater than oneself is to risk abandoning one of humanity's most proven strategies for surviving tragedy, for it is, paradoxically, only by yielding one's own life to the larger life of the world that one is able to find one's way back to oneself, and endure.

After Noellie's and Jack's deaths I visited Waiau only once. Their house had been sold. A young family now occupied it, no memory of the faces and events I remembered so vividly, the life I had known there. I went up to the sports field on the river terrace where Jack had planted a kowhai tree for Pauline almost twenty years before. The tree was now lost among other trees, all fighting for the light. Below me, on the outskirts of the town, the Mason ran clear and cold. In the south, Te Rako was covered in snow.

The Bottle Imp

In 1890, Robert Louis Stevenson and his wife settled in Samoa. Stevenson thought of the place as a promised land where he might recover his health and make a new beginning.

Within a year of moving into his new house at Vailima, and despite ill health, Stevenson wrote, among other things, his fable of the bottle imp.[2] The germ of the story was a German folktale, adapted by a minor playwright, Richard Brinsley Peake, for a performance at Covent Garden in 1828, but the leitmotifs—the spiritual price paid for material gain, the trade-off between one's own happiness and the happiness of others—have universal appeal. For Stevenson, the tale was, perhaps, an allegory of his own search for renewal—for the wellspring of life that always lies beyond the confines of one's own particular life, and from which one imagines one might recover what one has lost.

2. In one corner of Stevenson's house at Vailima was built a large safe that rarely contained much money "but was supposed by the natives to be the prison of the Bottle Imp, the source of all Stevenson's fortune." Graham Balfour, *The Life of Robert Louis Stevenson*, vol. 2 (New York: Scribner's, 1912), 130.

In Stevenson's fable, a poor but adventurous Hawaiian called Keawe travels to San Francisco to seek his fortune. Seeing this modern city for the first time, he is overcome with admiration and envy, and is baffled when he meets an elderly man who has everything money can buy but is oppressed with sorrow.

The American explains to Keawe that he owes his wealth to a djinn, and should he die with this djinn in his possession he will suffer eternal damnation. The American goes on to explain that long long ago the bottle imp was worth a great deal, but whenever it changed hands it had to be sold for less than was paid for it or it would find its way back to the seller. The bottle was now worth so little that the American feared he would die with it still in his hands, and go straight to hell.

Keawe dreams of one day returning home and building a fine house where he will live without care among his kinsmen and friends. Yet he is mindful that whatever gains he makes in the course of his travels will cost him dearly. So it is no surprise when, having bought the bottle imp and set sail for his native land, he receives news that an uncle and cousin have died. Arriving home, he learns that he has inherited his uncle's lands, and that his uncle had become exceedingly rich in his final days. This confirms Keawe's suspicion that his improved situation is a sordid boon, and as soon as he has built his fine house on his newly acquired land he vows never to ask another favor of the djinn.

Keawe now sells the bottle imp to his friend Lopaka, whose dream is to own a schooner, and he settles to a life of perfect happiness in his mountain home. But shortly before his marriage to the beautiful Kokua, he discovers that he has leprosy. Desperate not to lose the happiness he has found, he sets out to retrieve the bottle imp from Lopaka. But by now the bottle has changed hands so many times that its value has dropped to two cents, meaning that the next buyer will be unable to sell it and will be damned. Keawe does not hesitate. He buys the bottle imp, is instantly cured of leprosy, marries Kokua, and determines to live with the evil that comes with the good. Yet his mind is haunted by images of hell, and his terrible fate casts a pall over his new life.

Inevitably, Kokua wrests the story from her husband. So deeply moved is she that Keawe had been willing to sacrifice his soul out of love for her that she vows to save him. She points out that in French Tahiti and in England there are coins whose value is less than an American cent, which means that they may yet be able to sell the accursed djinn. They travel to Tahiti where their search for a buyer proves fruitless and Keawe becomes increasingly depressed. But mindful of her duty to the man who, because of his love for her, has taken the curse upon himself, Kokua finds a sick old man with whom she strikes a bargain—that he will buy the bottle imp and immediately resell it to her so that she, not Keawe, will be damned. Unexpectedly, the old man, who feels that happiness has passed him by and that death holds no terrors, wants to keep the imp, and it takes some time for Kokua to hold him to their bargain.

When she returns home, she does not tell Keawe that she now owns the bottle imp, and is distressed at his callousness toward the old man, now doomed to suffer the fires of hell. Keawe and Kokua have a falling out, but when Keawe accidentally discovers that his wife has sacrificed her soul that he might live, he is determined to set things right and arranges for an intermediary, a boatswain, to buy back the bottle from his wife.

Once the boatswain has made the purchase and realizes what the djinn can do, he refuses to allow Keawe to take it off his hands. Keawe reminds the boatswain that he will go to hell if he dies with it in his possession, but the boatswain explains that his profligate life dooms him to hell anyway, and he keeps the bottle, leaving Keawe and Kokua to live happily ever after.

Henry James observed that for any writer "there is the story of one's hero, and then, thanks to the intimate connection of things, the story of one's story itself." In the case of Robert Louis Stevenson's tale of the bottle imp the connection is fairly clear, for the hero of the story is traveling the South Seas to save his soul and his marriage, while the author is traveling the length and breadth of the Pacific in an attempt to recapture a time when he was fit and healthy, without TB. This translation of time into space is crucial, and holds good for the migrant who journeys to another place, not so much in search of the past but in order to gain a future.

There are, moreover, plenty of examples of romantics who travel to places where time has supposedly "stood still," their fantasy of personal regeneration reinforced by the fact that as they move further and further afield, exchanging their traveler's checks or currency as they go, the value of what they have increases. Since material value can be increased, so, one imagines, one's life may be renewed, augmented, or redeemed. Indeed, in such myths of "fantastic reparation,"[3] images of material and spiritual value mirror each other, for to redeem means to buy back something one has temporarily given up *and* to make amends or compensate for some moral fault. In both cases, sacrifice is required—either in the form of what one owns or who one is.

It sometimes happens that as life overtakes us, or gets the better of us, we begin to think that the best is behind us—our youth, a halcyon year, a moment in the limelight, a place where we were completely happy—and that everything since has paled in comparison. To retrieve what has been lost in time we imagine making a journey to another place, as though the past were not gone forever but simply transposed to somewhere else in the present, just out of reach.

When the writer and media critic George Trow died in Naples on November 24, 2007, I discovered that the author of the provocative indictment of the emptiness of modern discourse, "the context of no context," had resigned from the *New Yorker* in 1994 and roamed North America from Texas to Alaska to Newfoundland, living frugally but increasingly overwhelmed by nostalgia for the glory days of the *New Yorker*, when William Shawn was editor and his "Talk of the Town" articles conjured and celebrated a Manhattan of scintillating conversation, dinner jackets, and champagne evenings. Engulfed in despair, Trow sought psychiatric help, then expatriated himself to Italy, unable to reconcile himself, in the words of his friend Rory Nugent, to the fact that "the rest of the world was onto something new."

Perhaps repairing to the Old World, or the discovery of places where one's capital still has currency, are increasingly unlikely avenues of self-revitalization. Yet the fact remains that it is not only gold and silver that rise and fall in value but our own sense of self-worth, our own well-being. Not only wealth but love, happiness, and care are unequally distributed in this world. In *The Philosophy of Money*, Georg Simmel observes of money that it is the most "striking symbol" of the flux and inconstancy of human life. Money taken out of circulation resembles a person who refuses to participate in the life of the world. Like the miserly Silas Marner, it is no good to anyone. But Simmel also points

3. Joan Riviere, "Hate, Greed and Aggression," in Melanie Klein and Joan Riviere, *Love, Hate and Reparation* (London: Hogarth Press, 1953), 23.

out that despite its ephemeral character in a world of exchange, money resembles God, love, culture, or natural law; it appears to transcend the trade and traffic of our everyday world as "a measure of things" that cannot themselves be measured, and thus serves as a symbolic constant.[4] Is it then true that we cling to possessions because they help us believe that life itself may be secured and held, safe from the ravages of time, and that the market has displaced nature and God as our most potent symbol of constancy and ultimate value?

Marginal Notes

Graham Greene begins the chronicle of his journey in the late 1930s into the lawless provinces of Mexico with reminiscences of the "two countries" of his childhood. These "countries" were not on any map; they were the contrasted lives he led as a boy. Each weekday, he would suffer the torments of school; each weekend, he was free to roam the open fields beyond the school, where rabbits munched the grass, the distant sounds of a choir reached his ears, and he became aware of God. Where the world of school was hateful and "lawless," the world outside it was a world of order and of love.

> And so faith came to me—shapelessly, without dogma, a presence above a croquet lawn, something associated with violence, cruelty, evil across the way. One began to believe in heaven because one believed in hell, but for a long while it was only hell one could picture with a certain intimacy—the pitchpine partitions of dormitories where everybody was never quiet at the same time; the lavatories without locks: "There, by reason of the great number of the damned, the prisoners are heaped together in their awful prison . . ."; walks in pairs up the suburban roads; no solitude anywhere, at any time.[5]

In due course, this symbolic contrast underwent a series of metamorphoses. But always, for Greene, there remained this fascination with the border, for "the border means more than a customs house, a passport

4. Georg Simmel, *The Philosophy of Money*, trans. Tom Bottomore and David Frisby (London: Routledge, 2004), 510–12.
5. Graham Greene, *The Lawless Roads* (Harmondsworth: Penguin, 1971), 14.

officer, a man with a gun. Over there everything is going to be different; life is never going to be quite the same again."

The man seeking scenery imagines strange woods and unheard-of mountains; the romantic believes that the women over the border will be more beautiful and complaisant than those at home; the unhappy man imagines at least a different hell; the suicidal traveler expects the death he never finds. The atmosphere of the border—it is like starting over again; there is something about it like a good confession: poised for a few happy moments between sin and sin. When people die on the border they call it "a happy death."[6]

So deeply did Graham Greene's reflections resonate with my own childhood experiences—the aversion to school, the sounds of a girls' choir reaching my ears as I marched up and down a schoolyard for ten consecutive days practicing military drills, the fantasy of a world beyond in which I would find satisfaction—that I wondered what metamorphoses of that early contrast between the hell of school and the Wordsworthian bliss I found in nature unfolded for me. Rather than find in the experience or idea of God the consummation of all that redeemed the hardship and unfairness I felt around me, I stumbled upon books, or more precisely pure thought—the power to make things up, to connect poetic images, to pursue an idea, to speculate on some entirely imaginary proposition. Thought gave me a way of distancing myself from the turmoil of the mundane world, almost of immunizing myself against it. Thought gave me a sense that I had a place in the world, a place apart yet from which I could see the world in my own time, on my own terms, in my own way. This may suggest that I found escape and salvation in the intellectual life. But by "thought" I mean something more than pure reason or mere cognition, for thinking, in my case, involved dreaming up new modes of connectedness, both narrative and poetic, and exploring the margins of the world where the ordinary is interrupted and unhinged, where unconscious, occult, or normally invisible forces impinge, inundate, sweep away, and reshape our sense of who we are. In *The Scarlet Letter*, Nathaniel Hawthorne captures this disposition perfectly when he speaks of a "tendency to roam, at will, in that broad and quiet field where all mankind may meet,

6. Ibid., 23.

rather than confine [oneself] to those narrow paths where brethren of the same household must diverge from one another."[7]

A Storyteller's Story

To think critically and see clearly, one needs to distance oneself, if only momentarily, from the overwhelming weight of the world. This is true of all societies, not just those with traditions of speculative reason, for thought is born of the borderlands between custom, which inclines us to take life for granted, and crisis, which unsettles everything. Nonetheless, it is never a straightforward matter to take up this view from afar, which is why the vocation of seer, diviner, and storyteller often has its origins in borderline experiences that bring a person close to madness and despair.

Such was the case with Keti Ferenke Koroma.

I have already recounted my friend Sewa's story of the Magbas' struggle to retain the right to rule in the Kuranko chiefdom of Diang. Now it is time to tell the story from the Ferenkes' side—a story of what it means to be on the margins of secular power, and how this marginality opens one up to the sacerdotal power associated, in Kuranko thought, with the bush.

Unlike most of my Kuranko informants, Keti Ferenke would never explain things away with the stock phrases "that is how it happened" (*maiya ta ra nya na*), "that is how our ancestors let it happen" (*ma bimban' ya ta rya na*), or "that is what we encountered" (*maiya min ta ra*); he would address every situation as a moral quandary demanding discussion and, hopefully, resolution. The folktale (*tilei*) was the perfect vehicle for this pedagogy. Since this narrative genre was ostensibly make-believe, a form of entertainment, Keti Ferenke could cunningly conceal his serious and often provocative opinions in it. Moreover, he could create his own stories and pass them off as part of the traditional corpus. In Keti Ferenke I found a man with an ironic and critical sense of his own culture, someone who respected conventional wisdom but saw that events in the real world constantly called that wisdom into question.

7. Nathaniel Hawthorne, *The Scarlet Letter* (Harmondsworth: Penguin, 2005), 41.

But can one confidently identify the events that set a person apart from the world into which he or she is born, creating a kind of displaced consciousness that cannot help but question the things that others take for granted?

In Keti Ferenke's case, the troubled chieftaincy of Diang suggests one way of exploring this question.

When Keti Ferenke's grandfather, Sewa Magba Koroma, died, the chief's son Samaran Bala Koroma succeeded him. As I explained earlier, it was Bala's brother Mamadu Sandi who wielded the real power, a power that he abused by assaulting people, stealing other men's wives, and generally throwing his weight around. In this insufferable situation, a certain Alhaji Magba Kamara, whose mother hailed from Diang, decided to intervene. Having had a few years of schooling, Magba wrote a letter to the British district commissioner that purported to be from an exasperated and weary chief Bala, asking that he be allowed to resign the chieftaincy. Magba took the letter to Bala and explained it was from the government, and required his signature before development work in Diang could be approved. The illiterate Bala thus signed away his chieftaincy, and the staff of office was taken from him.

Elections for a new chief were now called, and candidates presented themselves from the two ruling lineages of the Koroma clan — "the Magbas" and "the Ferenkes."

At this time rumors had spread that the new Paramount chief would be a Muslim. But since none of the candidates were Muslims, people were mystified. Fearing the worst, Mamadu Sandi and his followers drove the Muslim Mandingos from Kondembaia, the main town in Diang. But some of the old men knew of whom the diviners had been speaking, and they traveled to Kono in search of Sheku Magba. As I have already recounted, Sheku returned home to find himself at the center of arguments among the Magbas, many of whom felt he was too young to be chief, and attacked by the Ferenkes, who did not want power to devolve to the junior line, or to a Muslim.

Not only political misfortunes cast their shadows over Keti Ferenke's early life. His sister and brother both died when they were young, and in his tenth or eleventh year, tragedy struck again.

When his maternal grandmother died in Kamadugu Sukurela (a ten-mile walk away from Kondembaia), Keti Ferenke's mother asked him to go at once to Tongoma in Kono to inform his classificatory sister of the death and bring her back to Kondembaia for the funeral. But his mother was suffering from a severe headache and Keti Ferenke was reluctant to leave her.

When she insisted, he left. It was the twenty-ninth of the month before Ramadan. Two days later he reached Tongoma and informed his sister that their grandmother had died. But it was now Ramadan, and Keti Ferenke's brother-in-law would not allow his wife to travel until the fast month had ended.

While he was away in Tongoma, Keti Ferenke's mother died. People were wailing, "Ferenke has not come yet, Ferenke has not come yet, Ferenke has not come yet." Although the tragic news had reached towns throughout the chiefdom, people kept the news from Keti Ferenke, and he learned of what had come to pass in his absence only when he returned to Kondembaia and found himself in the middle of the funeral rites. It was now the middle of the month of Ramadan.

On the last day of the month Keti Ferenke's father went to the mosque. It was a Friday. But as Kona Sumban joined the others to pray, he began trembling and could not stand without support. People urged him to go home and rest, but he insisted he would be all right. As prayers ended, it was clear to everyone that Kona Sumban was seriously ill. They helped him to his house, but he died later that day. "It was a terrible thing," Keti Ferenke remembered. "From Friday, through Saturday, until Sunday, no one could bury him because his death had been so sudden and so strange."

In explaining these distant events to me, Keti Ferenke spoke fatalistically. "What Allah had destined had happened." But he also spoke of how he was received into his father's elder brother's household, and cared for as a son. "My father had gone, but chief Bala was still alive. So I was not heartbroken. I found no fault with my elder father, who provided bridewealth for me to marry and cared for me as a father. Indeed, I feel that my own father never died. So my heart is at peace."

What I could not ask, and did not know how to ask, was whether his skill in composing thought-provoking stories had helped him make a virtue of his marginality.

In Keti Ferenke's frequent comments on the value of intelligence, one glimpses an answer to this question.

Consider the following exposition on the power of social nous or intelligence (*hankili*):

To start with, my great-great-grandfather was a chief. Down to my grandfather, they were all chiefs. Until my father, they were chiefs. Now, when you are born into a ruling house you will be told many things. If you are a fool you'll be none the wiser, but if you are clever you will inspect everything carefully. And when you lie down, you will think over certain things. If you do this, it is good. That is how I think of things.

We say *kina wo* and *kina wo* [near homophones]. They are not one [the first means "beehive," the second means "elder"]. If you hear *kina* [elder], he knows almost everything. But if you hear *kina* [beehive], it does not know anything. The elder could be found in the younger and the younger could be found in the elder.

Even if a person is a child, but behaves like an elder, then he is an elder. If he thinks like an elder, then he is an elder. Even if a person is old and senior, if he behaves like a child then he is a child. Therefore, this matter of seniority comes not only from the fact that one is born first, or from the fact that one is big and strong; it also concerns the manner in which one behaves and does things. For example, you will see some old men who have nothing; they are not called "big men" [*morgo ba*, elders]. But some young men have wealth; because of that they are called *morgo ba*. Therefore, whatever Allah has put in your head, that is what will make you what you are. I am speaking now, but some of these words of wisdom [*kuma kore*] that I am explaining to you are not known by everyone. You may ask a man and he may know them. But I have explained them to you. Therefore, am I not the elder? Therefore, if you hear the word *kina* you should know that it is intelligence [*hankili*] that really defines it.

Where Keti Ferenke and I differed was in the way we explained intellectual giftedness. Where he saw it as innate — a divine gift — I saw it as partly genetic, but mostly acquired. Yet our *experience* of creative apperception was identical, for creative ideas and "divine" inspiration were seen to arise on the thresholds between sleep and wakefulness, night and day, confusion and clarity.

"It is Allah who endows a person with the ability to think and tell stories," Keti Ferenke told me. This was consonant with the Kuranko idea that a storyteller simply "sets down" or "lays out" something that has been given to him or put into his mind; he is, therefore, a *til'sale* — one who sets down *tileinu* (stories). In this sense a storyteller is like a diviner. The diviner is "one who lays out pebbles," though it is God or a bush spirit who implants the idea of how to interpret the patterns in the diviner's mind.

"When you are told something," Keti Ferenke said, "it is good if it stays in your mind. Ideas come into my head, just like that. I am not asleep. I am not in a dream. But when I think on them, I put them together as a story. I could never stop thinking of stories, though I could stop myself telling them." And he went on to describe how, as he worked on his farm or lounged in his hammock at home, he would try to develop a plot and scenario that did justice to the idea that had been seeded in his mind, so that it came to life in an entertaining and edifying way.

Not only did ideas come to him when he was relaxed and susceptible to "divine" (we might say unconscious) inspiration; it soon became clear to me that his stories themselves were plotted, like folktales throughout the world, as a series of critical episodes or encounters, usually three in number, that interrupt the narrative flow, creating moments of impasse and heightened suspense that are preludes to a breakthrough, a surprising intervention, a novel perspective. In Kuranko stories, these moments of hiatus and tension usually occur at a sociospatial threshold—a river's edge, a ford, a crossroads, a bridge, the perimeter of a village or chiefdom—or at the temporal borderland between the rainy and dry seasons, or night and day. Spatial and seasonal boundaries thus provide Kuranko with concrete images of existential limits in the same way that images of the no-man's land between *ius humanum* and *ius divinum* or of a censoring ego that regulates traffic across the threshold between the unconscious and conscious provide the European social imaginary with its metaphors of border situations.[8] But in both life-worlds, it is quasi-human figures—from djinn and fetish to scapegoats and homo sacer[9]—that demarcate and embody the ambiguous zone where we cease to be recognizable to ourselves yet may see ourselves more completely than at any other time.

In Kuranko stories, these moments of maximum suspense are not only signified spatially by images of borders; they are viscerally experi-

8. These foregoing points are fully explored and amply illustrated in my study of Kuranko storytelling: Michael Jackson, *Allegories of the Wilderness: Ethics and Ambiguity in Kuranko Narratives* (Bloomington: Indiana University Press, 1982).

9. Giorgio Agamben, *Homo Sacer: Sovereign Power and Bare Life*, trans. Daniel Heller-Roazen (Stanford, Calif.: Stanford University Press, 1998).

enced as a shift from narrative to song. At such moments of narrative hiatus, the storyteller's voice is joined with a chorus of voices, adults and children alike all chiming in. Signaling a transition from one critical episode to another, songs not only increase the intensity of audience participation; they enable everyone to actively share in the telling of the tale rather than remain spellbound as passive listeners. Not only does the song mediate an individual listener's close identification with the protagonist, who is stuck in a quandary and sings in sorrow or for supernatural help; the song helps break the impasse or spell, allowing the story to proceed toward its denouement.

Structurally, therefore, every Kuranko story encapsulates the interrupted rhythm of life itself—its periods of unreflective routine, its unpredicted moments of adversity and bewilderment, its ritualized return to normalcy. Kuranko stories play out, as it were, the existential aporias of everyday life—the descent of order into chaos, the desolating losses that follow death or migration, the estrangement of kin, the brutality of power, the falling out of friends. Like other forms of play (*tolon*), Kuranko stories safely enact, in ways that admit of artificial resolution, the dilemmas of life. But the operative word is "artificial," for everyone knows that life can never be cajoled into conforming to the scenarios he or she wishes upon it, and it is not for nothing that stories are told in the twilight zone between day and night, between waking and sleeping, when people can for a moment accept the illusion that what they can imagine or think is also a measure of what they can actually do.

Big Thing and Small Thing

It was in a crowded and fetid room in the village of Kondembaia, lit by a single hurricane lantern, that I recorded, in the dry season of 1970, Keti Ferenke's story about the value of small things.

Big Thing and Small Thing had a quarrel. Small Thing said that he was the elder. Big Thing said this was nonsense. "I am the elder. Haven't you heard people saying that I am big?" They went to the Big Men [the chief and his council of elders]. The Big Men told Small Thing not to be so impudent. They said, "Everyone calls Big Thing 'big' and Small Thing 'small.'" Small Thing repeated that he was the elder. The people said, "No, Big Thing is the elder. Have you forgotten the meaning of the word 'big'?"

Small Thing asked Big Thing to accompany him on a journey around the chiefdom. Wherever they went they found people quarreling. Small Thing would say, "Let us sit down and listen." The Big Men would summon the people who had quarreled and ask them to explain themselves. When the explanations had been given, the Big Men would tell the troublemakers what a small thing it was that they had quarreled over. Small Thing would say to Big Thing, "Did you hear that?" And they would go on their way.

They came to a village where people were making palaver about a man who had beaten his wife badly. Small Thing said, "Let us sit down and listen." They listened, and heard the explanations from all sides. Again, people commented on how the quarrel had arisen over a small thing. Small Thing said to Big Thing, "Surely I am the elder, because people are always referring to me." Finally, Big Thing had to admit that Small Thing was indeed the elder.

Therefore, everything begins with small things.[10]

In Wim Wenders's film *Wings of Desire*, two angels are discussing the minor calamities and joys that have marked the lives of Berliners during the course of that day. One angel suddenly confesses that he is weary of his ethereal life, of being privy only to what is spiritual in peoples' minds. "Sometimes I'm fed up with my spiritual existence," Damiel says. "Instead of forever hovering above, I'd like to feel a weight grow in me, to end the infinity and to tie me to earth. I'd like, at each step, each gust of wind, to be able to say 'Now.' 'Now' and 'now' and no longer 'forever' and 'for eternity' . . .

"It would be nice, coming home after a long day, to feed the cat, like Philip Marlowe, to have a fever, and blackened fingers from the newspaper, to be excited not only by the mind but, at last, by a meal . . . by the line of a neck, by an ear. To lie! Through one's teeth . . . to feel what it is to take your shoes off under a table and to wiggle your toes barefoot."

Damiel contemplates rebirth as a mere mortal. Instead of invisibly attending tragic events, he will once more be a part of a world where tragedy may, at any moment, befall him, but also where he may fall in

10. Previously published in Jackson, *Allegories of the Wilderness*, 36–37.

love. The prospect of pain, uncertainty, and despair is offset by the possibility of again belonging to a world of simple pleasures.

His yearning is recognized by Peter Falk, a former angel who is aware of Damiel's presence and preoccupations. Outside a snack bar, in a wasteland left over from the war, he reaches out to Damiel. "I wish I could just look into your eyes and tell you how good it is to be here, just to touch something that's cold . . . to smoke, to have coffee, and if you do it together it's fantastic, or to draw . . . you know, you take a pencil and you make a dark line, then you make a light line, and together it's a good line. And when your hands are cold, you rub them together."

Not long after this encounter, Damiel tells his fellow angel Cassiel that he's going "to enter the river"; he is going to know what no angel knows; he is going to give up eternity for life on earth.

One does not need to conjure a God of Small Things to celebrate the value of homely events, homely objects, homely words.[11] In a world of ambitious schemes and dogmatic assertions, grandiloquence is often taken for wisdom and we are persuaded that there is no phenomenon that cannot be named. Under such conditions, it becomes less imperative to get "the big picture" than to recover a sense of the countless little things that give us a measure of the real, and remind ourselves that a life emerges from unremarked moments, just as the soil and climate of a region impart to a vintage its terroir. To become fixated on the abstract and the absolute is to become estranged from the everyday world in which our lives take shape, for the fact of our existence is always more than can be thought, more than can be said, and more than can be foreseen. It is in small things that we are redeemed as thinkers and renewed as persons. "It's the little things that count" is undoubtedly one of the most tedious platitudes, since it is usually cited by those who have fallen short of greatness. But in the paradoxical, contingent, and fugitive character of small things lies the perennial possibility that we may be surprised by life and dwell in the moment. In any event, it is only when thinking is set aside that we can fully live. As Hannah

11. As Hannah Arendt notes, referring to Hofmannsthal's famous farewell letter to Stefan George and Husserl's "to the things themselves," phenomenology consistently celebrates "'the little things' as against big words, since precisely in these small things the secret of reality lies hidden." "What Is Existenz Philosophy?" *Partisan Review* 13, no. 1 (1946): 36.

Arendt remarked, "Every thought is an afterthought, that is, a reflection on some matter or event."[12] Yet it is not the "thoughtlessness" of an Eichmann that we aspire to but the raptness of a poet who allows himself or herself to experience whatever presents itself to consciousness without immediately supplanting that experience with a verbal, conceptual, or moral response.

In the first poem in *Birthday Letters*, entitled "Fulbright Scholars," Ted Hughes recounts his first, half-remembered meeting with Sylvia Plath. But of only one detail is he absolutely sure—that on that same day he bought the first fresh peach he ever tasted, from a stall near Charing Cross Station. "At twenty-five," he writes, "I was dumbounded afresh / By my ignorance of the simplest things."[13]

At such moments there is no risk of becoming sealed off from the world; the danger, if any, lies in one's openness to it, with the possibility that one becomes the other or the object that has entered one's life. It is this absorption in the not-self that absorbs Walter Benjamin in his essays on Baudelaire, for it is not that the poet *thinks* of Paris in the mid-nineteenth century as the site of a burgeoning form of commodity capitalism; rather that he lives the spirit of his times through his senses as he wanders the crowded streets, explores the mercantile galleries, and hangs out in the cafés. Later, Benjamin himself, following in Baudelaire's footsteps, will also locate the spirit of that epoch in specific artifacts, in "little *métiers*," and in the miniaturized world of the arcades that he allows to affect him, to act upon him. Susceptibility, surrender, and a willingness to be shocked and surprised define both the method and madness of a poetics that makes present the character of the world.

Sacrifice

On Massachusetts Avenue, as I am heading to my bank, a woman with a Jamaican accent thrusts a green leaflet at me and chants, "Jesus died for you, Jesus died for you, he died for you." I take the leaflet, feeling the

12. Hannah Arendt, "'What Remains? The Language Remains': A Conversation with Günter Gaus," in *The Portable Hannah Arendt*, ed. Peter Baehr (Harmondsworth: Penguin, 2003), 19.

13. Ted Hughes, *Birthday Letters* (London: Faber and Faber, 1998), 3.

weight, the accusative nuance, given to the word "you," as she mouths on, "For God so loved the world, that he gave his only begotten son that whosoever believeth in him should not perish but have everlasting life."

A split second later I am remembering how I came to get my first teaching job. I had worked for a couple of months that summer as a steward on the inter-Island ferry and was on my way back to Auckland when someone suggested I meet Jan Pouwer, the newly appointed professor of anthropology at Victoria University of Wellington. I might get work as a tutor or lecturer. As it happened, Jan and I hit it off immediately, largely because of a shared enthusiasm for Lévi-Strauss's structuralism, but to his great regret Jan could not offer me a position; he had already agreed to hire a young Australian anthropology graduate whose husband was a Ph.D. student in the geography department. He did, however, invite me to leave him my name and address; if something came up he would get in touch.

A few weeks later I learned that the Ph.D. student in geography had walked out of a seminar on the seventh floor of the Easterfield Building and leaped to his death from an open window. His devastated widow returned to Australia, and Jan offered me her job. But for as long as I held that position, I could not shuck off the feeling that my destiny was now tied to hers and that I was somehow implicated in her loss. I even imagined that my good fortune had come at her expense, and that I had been, in some oblique and unfathomable way, complicit in her husband's suicide.

The idea of linked destinies has continued to haunt me. Sometimes it assumes the stoic form of thinking that one is wise to divest oneself of wealth and comfort lest possessing more than others invites some daemon to strip one clean and redistribute one's possessions to those in need. Sometimes it takes the form of the well-known superstition that warns one against parading one's good fortune in case it catches the eye of a vengeful spirit. And once, after Sewa and Ade lost their baby, it brought me to the horrible conclusion that Sewa's dutiful sacrifices to the ancestors had cost him nothing, and that the ancestors, insulted that he should ask so much and be prepared to give so little, took the life of his child as a reprimand. But mostly, this idea of connections feeds my abiding interest in the principle of reciprocity.

One of the most compelling paradoxes of human social existence is that we are often convinced that we stand to gain more from giving away or giving up the life we have than from retaining or clinging to it. Undoubtedly this reflects the peculiar ethical quandary of human existence—that life in the most expanded and generous sense of the word is gained when the individual defers his personal desire for immediate gratification, suppresses his individual needs, brackets out his particular point of view, and transcends his circumstances—yielding to an-other, recognizing her needs, her point of view, her humanity. It is in our evolved capacity for sharing and cooperating, for sinking our differences in a collective enterprise or common cause that we consummate our social humanity, indebted and bound to one another in ways that can never be counted or repaid. But there is a far more immediate and compelling sense in which sacrifice may be said to produce life by taking it, and this is exemplified by martyrdom. For to give one's own life for a greater good is the very condition of the possibility of life itself—not because martyrdom guarantees one personal immortality or even because one's family or community receive recognition and honor from one's self-sacrifice; value accrues to the *ideal* for which one ostensibly died, and it is ideology, not personal interest per se, that binds people together and makes social existence viable.

But precisely what is the logic whereby we renounce or risk the life we know for the possibility of a life more fulfilling, enduring, or abundant? And what of the dark side of this logic that leads male power holders in so many human societies to subjugate, scapegoat, or ritually sacrifice children, women, and "lesser" mortals in order to guarantee the continuity and vitality of *their* social order? Why should the prosperity, longevity, or potency of one class require the death of another?

Rather than see this class struggle, as Marx did, as a function of scarcity, I see it as an inevitable product of human intersubjectivity—of the fact that our sense of self is so profoundly contingent on the recognition and responsiveness of significant others. So uncertain and unstable are our relations with others, even those we trust, that our ontological security is continually being called into question. Thus, human beings everywhere bemoan their lot, convinced that what they have, who they are, and what they can do falls short of what is necessary for their complete fulfillment. The missing element is variously imagined to be health wealth, potency, strength, clout, mobility, voice, luck, love, or looks, and people will wager what they have on the promise of making good their felt loss, of gaining compensation for what they have been unfairly deprived of, of augmenting, expanding, or revitalizing their lives. Sacrifice, gambling, and trading are all expressions of the same endless existential search for increase in a world where the affordances of the external environment, the affirmations of others, and one's inner resources are never sufficient.

As for the ritual expression of the fantasy that the sacrifice of an actual life may somehow secure "life" in the abstract, this may have its origins in the bereavement reaction. The injunction not to speak ill of the dead reflects a universal tendency to replace an actual life that has been lost with an artificial image of life itself. This abstract idealization, that is recovered and celebrated after every death, gradually eclipses idiosyncratic memories of the deceased while bringing into relief the moral principles on which the continuity of *social* being or *natural* life depend.

The evanescent and fugitive nature of individual life is thus "sacrificed," one might say, to the contemplation of what is eternal and abiding. Symbolic deaths involve the same process. The transcending of childhood ties in initiation ritual, the renunciation of earthly ties among ascetics, the sacrificial killing of a consecrated victim, and the sharing of life-giving resources with others in dire need, all facilitate the focusing of a reified image of the social, the eternal, the divine, the natural, or the human to which particular lives are simply contributory.

But it would be difficult for human beings to express the ultimate value they place on *collective or transcendent* forms of being, sustained over time, without images of sacrifice that are drawn from interpersonal life.

Among the Kuranko, the concept of personhood (*morgoye*) connotes generosity and care—a mindfulness of the needs of others, and a readiness to share with them the wherewithal of life. A selfish or stingy individual is simply "not a person," or is dismissed as "a bush person" and compared to a broken vessel or dilapidated house. But in Kuranko myth, the spirit of *morgoye* is exemplified by an altruistic stranger *who is under no obligation* to show concern, give succor, or provide help.

This may reflect a universal logic, since no human being can exemplify absolute virtue. Accordingly, someone from beyond the pale of one's familiar world—a totemic animal, a Messiah, a passing stranger—embodies the ethical essence of humanity. In Kuranko myths such as the following, the outsider is a magnanimous animal, and the crucial encounter with a human ancestor occurs in the bush.

The Kuyaté [clan] do not eat the monitor lizard. Their ancestor went to a faraway place. There was no water there. He became thirsty. He was near death. Then he found a huge tree, and in the bole of the tree was some water left from the rains. The monitor lizard was also there. The ancestor of the Kuyaté sat under the tree. The monitor lizard climbed into the bole of the tree, then climbed out and shook its tail. The water splashed the man. The ancestor of the Kuyaté realized there was water there. He climbed up and drank. He then declared: "Ah, the monitor lizard has saved my life!" When he returned to his hometown he told his clansmen about the incident. He said: "You see me here now because of that monitor lizard." Since that time the monitor lizard has been the Kuyaté totem. Should any Kuyaté eat it, his body will become marked and disfigured like the body of the monitor lizard. His joking partners will have to find medicines to cure him.

That sociality is founded on unconditional giving is even more powerfully expressed in the following myth that explains the origin of the joking partnership (*sanakuiye tolon*) between the Kargbo and Sisé clans.

Long ago, journeying together from the Mande heartland, the Kargbo ancestor, Mansa Kama, and the Sisé ancestor, Bakunko, came to the banks of a great river. There, Bakundo Sisé transformed himself into a crocodile [his clan totem] and ferried Mansa Kama across the river. But Mansa Kama was famished after the crossing, so Bakunko cut off the calf of his leg, roasted it, and gave it his companion to eat. To affirm their friendship in perpetuity, Mansa Kama declared that the crocodile should thenceforth be considered the Kargo totem as well, and given respect, never killed, never eaten.

In this story, the gift of life involves something more than magnanimity; it involves self-sacrifice, since Bakunko's gift of his own flesh prevents him from continuing his journey to a new homeland. But the *act* of self-sacrifice is predicated upon a *disposition*. One literally puts oneself in the place of an-other, seeing what is imperative for him, setting aside all consideration of what this eclipse of self-concern might mean for oneself.

Consider the story of the ruler Saramba and his low-ranked finaba, Musa Kule.

> Saramba was a ruler and warrior of great renown. But his half-brothers became jealous of his fame and decided to kill him. They plotted to ambush him along the road. Though the conspiracy was discovered, Saramba was unable to delay his journey. A *finaba* called Musa Kule decided to disguise Saramba in his clothes. He donned Saramba's clothes so that he would die and thus save Saramba's life.
>
> On the day of the journey, they left together. A little way along the road Musa Kule took off his hat, gown, and trousers and gave them to Saramba, his lord. Musa Kule then dressed in Saramba's clothes. They went on, riding on horseback. As usual, Saramba was riding ahead. When they reached the place where the ambush had been laid, Saramba, disguised, passed by. The men in hiding said, "Oh no, not that one, it is only his poor *finaba*." Musa Kule then came, dressed in Saramba's clothes. They shot him.
>
> Therefore, since the time of Saramba and Musa Kule, they have always been together. Therefore they say, "Musa Kule and Saramba," meaning that they "go together."

What "goes together" is secular power, embodied in the figure of a ruler, and human virtue, exemplified by the low-caste finaba. Human agency, we might say, is never simply a matter of exercising one's will and realizing one's own potential; it is also a matter of abnegating one's will and of giving up something of personal value so that the greater good may be realized.

Prince Vessantara

One of the most often recounted and ritually enacted stories in the Theravada Buddhist countries of Southeast Asia is the story of Prince Vessantara.

The story celebrates selfless generosity in the figure of someone who has a world to gain by succeeding his father, Sañjaya, king of the Sivis, but, from early childhood, wants only to give, even if this means giving his own heart, his own eyes, and cutting the flesh from his own body. As a young man, his great generosity leads him to give to a Brahmin emissary from another kingdom the white elephant that magically ensures adequate rainfall in his own land. Sent into exile by the enraged citizenry, Vessantara travels to Crooked Mountain, though not before giving away all his wealth and, in effect, renouncing the world. During his time in the wilderness, Vessantara is asked by another Brahmin, whose young wife has been hassling him to find servants for their home, to give up his sons. He does so without a second thought. Fearful that the generous prince will next give away his wife, the king of the gods disguises himself as a Brahmin and asks Vessantara to give Maddhi to him. Though Vessantara does not hesitate to accede to this request, he soon receives her back, as well as his sons and wealth, and returns home where he becomes king.

In exemplifying the Buddhist notion of *dana*, or giving, the story of Vessantara celebrates not only the karmic virtue of giving alms, making ritual offerings, and showing empathy and compassion to others; it illustrates the nirvanic ideal in which the ultimate gift is the giving up of all worldly attachments, including material possessions and family ties. But renunciation implies both a *metaphysical* affirmation of a mode of being that transcends mere being-in-the-world, and a *social* affirmation of the value of giving to others as the very precondition of a life itself.[14]

Perhaps the most universal human quandary lies in this proto-ethical reconciliation of what seems imperative for one's own well-being and

---

14. I am indebted to Sutopa Dasgupta and Donald Swearer for guiding my reading of the Jataka, and for referring me to works that elucidate the ethical quandaries and difficulties involved in exercising great generosity or seeking nirvana and, at the same time, fulfilling one's worldly obligations as a parent, a child, and a leader. And there is also the aporia of the gift whereby "self-interest" is part and parcel of even the most disinterested giving, and a gift is only "pure" when one forgets or ceases to recognize that it is a gift. See Jacques Derrida, *Given Time: 1. Counterfeit Money*, trans. Peggy Kamuf (Chicago: University of Chicago Press, 1992); Reiko Ohnuma, "Gift," in *Critical Terms for the Study of Buddhism*, ed. Donald S. Lopez Jr. (Chicago: University of Chicago Press, 2005), 103–23. Also Margaret Cone and Richard F. Gombrich, *The Perfect Generosity of Prince Vessantara* (Oxford: Clarendon Press, 1997); Steven Collins, *Nirvana and Other Buddhist Felicities: Utopias of the Pali Imaginaire* (Cambridge: Cambridge University Press, 1998).

what is imperative for the greater good. Many years ago, when I was living in the Manawatu, my wife and I were members of a small group of mainly expatriate men and women who spent a day each weekend tramping or camping together in the Tararua ranges. One evening, in front of a roaring fire in a tramping hut, Anton, a Dutch paramedic who had spent four years in a Japanese prisoner-of-war camp in Java, told us the story of how he survived. "When we were captured after the fall of Java," Anton said, "I pointed out to the other prisoners, with some urgency, that our survival would depend on a social pact in which, at any time or in any situation, the relatively healthy would undertake to help the relatively unhealthy, for everyone would get sick sooner or later, and many would die. Only by agreeing to this pact would anyone stand a chance of living."

"And this proved to be true," Anton said. "The ones who went it alone, confident in their own stamina or will, were those who died. The one's who were prepared to help others in need, were helped in their own hour of need, and lived. But even those who helped others and died, could be said to have lived," Anton told us, "because they had retained their humanity to the last."

The Girl Who Went Beneath the Water

Toward the end of the dry season in 1970, when I was six months into my fieldwork in northern Sierra Leone, I stepped outside my house one night to have a piss and was bitten by a night adder lying in wait for frogs from the nearby swamp. My wife drove me to the local clinic where I was given shots of antivenin. But for several days afterward, my leg was paralyzed, possibly from the snakebite, more likely from the serum that I had been injected with.

Unable to work, I became lethargic and bored. But instead of accepting my listlessness as a sign that I needed rest, I saw it as a challenge to my will, and when my research assistant Noah came by the house one morning and announced that he was going to make a trip to the Loma Mountains I asked if I could tag along.

We set off next day before first light. After driving the twenty-five miles to the Seli River, we parked the Land Rover, crossed a hammock bridge, and began our trek to Firawa.

In the grasslands, the pale light of the coming day showed us the path. Noah walked ahead, his sandals padding on the dusty ground. But I was dragging my right leg, already numb and useless, and struggling to keep up.

Noah was all for turning back, but I would not hear of it. I was still convinced I could will my leg back to life, and was determined to press on, at least as far as Firawa.

As the sun rose, we rested and shared the peppery venison and cassava that Noah's wives had prepared against our journey. But a couple of hours later, exhausted from limping, I accepted Noah's argument that we needed to rest and should spend a day and night at Firawa.

While Noah engaged in palaver with his agemates, sorting out domestic disputes and rehearsing the pros and cons of various ventures, I sat at the end of Abdul's porch in a state of trance. Yet I was not alone in succumbing to the lassitude of the season. Harvest was done. The men lounged in their hammocks, or held desultory conversations with neighbors. A young man patiently wove bamboo mats in Abdul's compound, threading the carefully split cane through a grid of raffia strings that were tied to small stakes in the ground. In the course of an aimless conversation with me, he said: "Many years ago, the white man came to Saralon and took us away to his country against our will; now when we want to go, he will not let us."

A second man, who spoke little, set up his weaving frame in the shade of the orange tree where Sanfan Fina had braided her hair before her initiation, and as others slept during the heat of the day, he added to his long narrow strip of white country cloth, winding it into a tight ball.

These were images, I thought, of Penelope's web, of the web of perpetual waiting.

That evening I took a stroll outside the village to test my leg, and passed the women as they came and went along the path that led to their section of the local stream. Momentarily captivated by the grace with which they carried pails of water on their heads, the coy smiles they threw me or their sudden gusts of laughter, I was also shamefully aware of their mocking comments, for once again the *tubabune* had invaded their space.

We pressed on next morning, leaving before first light. Soon we were in the bush. It was like entering a cage filled with cackling and hooting animals. Had our journey been dreamt, it would have been interpreted as a sign that a plot had been hatched against us. Neither of us spoke. Perhaps it was because we had been walking for so long in the hypnotic circlets of lantern light. Perhaps it was because we unconsciously deferred to the spirits of the forest who, according to Noah, could capture our names and use them to do us harm. The path led through swamps. The mist clung to us. The stench of decaying vegetation was overpowering. In the distance, the rapids of the Bagbe sounded like the wind.

At noon we entered a small farming hamlet—a circle of badly thatched huts around a compound of tamped earth and dead hearths. Noah introduced me to the town chief and explained to him where we were going, though not why. Then we plunged once more into the forest, stumbling over exposed roots and outcrops of stones, getting closer to the Bagbe River.

Overhanging trees and lianas threw shadows across the turbid water. Noah said that crocodiles lurked in the deep pools, but all I saw animate the sullen surfaces was the dappling sunlight and falling leaves. He also pointed out the trail that diamond smugglers used. "They make a dog swallow the stones," Noah said, "or they put them in a banana and eat it themselves. Sometimes the women put them in those cloths, the ones they use when they are bleeding."

We crossed the river on a hammock bridge and entered forest even more dense and overpowering than before. The narrow path was aswarm with ants. Myriads of butterflies illuminated the occasional shafts of sunlight. Green tree snakes slowly uncoiled along the trail, and the spoor of monkeys could be seen everywhere.

We reached Bandakarafaia in the heat of the day.

The chief explained that he was accustomed to having white men lodge in his village. They would make it their base before scaling the Loma Mountains. But I was the first white man to have passed that way in many years, which undoubtedly explained why the small children of the village, some stark naked, some in rags, fled in fear from my presence only to be dragged back by their older siblings and shoved before me, eyes wide with alarm.

The village was clustered beneath an immense granite escarpment. Blackened and eroded by rain, this intimidating wall of rock was like a materialization of the darkness. As Noah hastened away in search of his kith and kin, I attempted to make myself at home in the derelict house that had been allocated to me.

I lit a fire in the yard and boiled some water in the small country pot I found there. Then I sat on the front porch — or what remained of it — with a cup of tea clutched between my hands, hoping that Noah would soon return with something to eat.

Not far away, two mangy goats were nibbling at the grass. I picked up a stone and lobbed it toward them. One had a deformed hind hoof, and limped away to safety, bleating pitifully in protest. The other joined it, hovering and trembling, in the shadows of another ruined house.

It was dusk by the time Noah reappeared, bearing a calabash of parboiled rice, and a peanut and chili sauce. Having discharged his obligation, he left.

I could not sleep. I had scraped a hollow in the hard earth for my hip, and pummeled my rucksack into the shape of a pillow, but I could not rest. At first I was unnerved by the silence. Then, from the far end of the village, came the sound of wooden clappers, followed by a dull, hoarse muttering, as though someone were stuffing words into the mouth of a horn.

My fretfulness gave way to real fear as the sound came closer, but then silence fell again, and I heard only the unsteady thumping of my heart and the intermittent shrieking of a night bird in the bush.

As the night dragged on, I was plagued by a skin rash. Desperate for sleep, I scratched and clawed at my midriff, wondering what the hell I had touched or eaten that might have caused this reaction. I lost track of time. And when at last I dozed off, it was only to wake in a cold sweat from a dream of a clear blue sky suddenly darkened by smoke or cloud.

As dawn broke, I got up and paced about, shivering with cold and still tearing at my skin.

I passed the day in a stupor. The rash bothered me less, but still I could not sleep, and I was now besieged by fragments of long-forgotten poems, passages from novels I had read as a young man, and hallucinatory flashbacks to Cambridge.

As darkness fell and my second night in Bandakarafaia began, I struggled to get comfortable, and prayed for sleep. Noah appeared in the half-light for a moment, took one look at me, and left. Perhaps he was afraid of me, or bewildered by his inability to know what to do. Perhaps he had not been there at all, and I had imagined him.

I lay in a delirium, a sodden log drifting on the stream, the air warm and cloying, experiencing slight vertigo as the current rolled me this way and that. I thought: I am not lying on the earth; the earth is suffering my lying upon it. I am disembodied now watching myself lying on the ground, but I am not lying here. I have been placed here, to suffer the darkness, claustrophobic, hot, and the shrilling of a single cicada, but I am not feeling anything or hearing anything. These things are happening to me. I am having them happen to me.

Then I was looking down at my own supine body, my awareness drifting away from it like smoke, upward through the shattered roof, toward the stars, and I found myself looking back with a kind of calm pity at my abandoned body, thinking: *I am dying, is this dying?* Because I knew I could choose to go back into that prone form if only I made the effort.

In the lantern's dull penumbra, dark forms stir into life. I am aware of myself walking, of Noah's presence in the half-light ahead, but I am not so much moving as being moved, as in a dream. Out of the depths of the forest, howls and shouts give voice to scampering shadows.

Not a word passes between us. I walk in a daze. I think only of what I will do when we get back to Kabala.

At the farm hamlet, we rest for a few hours. I catch some sleep in the town chief's house, stretched out on a raffia prayer mat. My first sound sleep for two nights. I wake to an enamel plate of pineapple slices and bananas. Even Noah seems to feel relief now, nearing home. This strange white man, with his woes and silences, no longer a burden. And the forest already giving way to patches of open grassland, the mist lifting.

We stop again at the Bagbe, and I clamber down the riverbank, strip, and wade into the unmoving water. It is cold. It momentarily shakes the fever out of me, and brings me to my senses. On a boomerang-shaped beach, swallow-tailed butterflies quiver and flap in the early morning sunlight, before settling back on the dung. In the nearby shade lies the sloughed skin of a snake.

"Come," Noah said, as I regained the path. "There is something you might want to see."

He led me off the beaten track, to a small clearing in the bush. In the middle of the clearing, surrounded by fallen leaves and dappled by sunlight and shadow was an immense granite stone. Its surface was blackened by blood, and the ground immediately in front of it was covered in grains of cooked rice.

"Saraké," Noah said.

The word from the Arabic, *sadaq'a*, means sacrifice, but I was at a loss to understand the significance of the stone.

"What is it?" I asked Noah, who seemed pleased that he had succeeded in arousing my curiosity.

"It is a djinn."

"What kind of djinn?"

"Very powerful."

"And people give it food?"

"They ask the djinn to help them in their life."

"Have you ever asked it to help you?"

"It is very dangerous. You cannot get something for nothing. If the djinn gives you what you ask for, it will want something in return. You may have to give it one of your children. It may ask for the life of someone you love."

"Then I don't think I will ask anything of it!"

And yet, as we walked away, and as the sound of the river grew fainter and fainter, I felt that in some oblique way I *had*, despite myself, been granted a boon and thereby incurred a debt that I must now repay.

It took me years to realize that my trip to Bandakarafaia, to the limits of my endurance and sanity, was in many ways a reenactment of some of the Kuranko stories I was collecting at that time. One story in particular, that had many variations, bore an uncanny parallel to what I had been through.[15]

The story concerns an orphan girl, maltreated by her dead mother's co-wife. Ordered to fetch and carry, having to suffer the taunts of her half-siblings and to dress in rags, this Kuranko Cinderella one day drops a stirring spoon in the dirt and is sent by her mother's co-wife to wash the spoon clean in a distant river.

It so happened that when the mother died, she was transformed into a crocodile and was now living in the depths of this very river. Reunited with her daughter, the crocodile-mother takes the child beneath the water where for several years she receives affection and respect and is dressed in fine raiments.

When she comes of age she is sent back to her village with lavish gifts for her father, her mother's co-wife, and her siblings. Despite this gen-

15. "The Orphan Child and the Stirring Spoon," in Jackson, *Allegories of the Wilderness*, 242–46.

erosity, the child's mother's co-wife desires only that her own daughter come into possession of such riches, and she sends her to the distant river. This girl is also taken beneath the water, but instead of boxes of money and fine clothing, she receives boxes of scorpions and poisonous snakes. Unaware of what she has been given, she takes the boxes back to her village and gives them to her mother, who, determined not to share her windfall with anyone else, opens the boxes in the privacy of her own room and is killed by the deadly creatures they contain.

Kuranko stories do not conclude with any explicit moral message. But we might venture to say that they imply that it is necessary to lose one's life in order to find it, that to come into one's own one must go beyond the pale of what is known and brave the dangers of the wilderness, and that the spiritual resources that we need to find fulfillment in this world have to be found beneath the surface of consciousness or, to remain faithful to the Kuranko imagery, beyond the world of the everyday.

I carry a memory of that vast wall of eroded, rain-blackened granite, and the mountain in the mist I never climbed. It has become exemplary for me of the cybernetic truth that freedom is defined not by the absence of limits but by their presence, and by the obstacles one comes up against. There are, for many indigenous people, living in the shadow of mountains, remarkably similar prohibitions on venturing beyond the snowline, into the heights. The prohibition is supported by beliefs that demons, gods, or ancestors dwell in these places; these are their abode. But the prohibition applies equally to the depths, born of the wisdom that human beings do well to recognize limits to what they can bring under their control, influence, or comprehend, lest they fill the world with the debris of their vain endeavors and presumptuous understandings.

Ill-Gotten Gains

In his famous essay on the gift (1925), Marcel Mauss elucidates the threefold nature of reciprocity—the imperative to give, to receive, and to pass on or return that which is received. Gift-giving, Mauss argued, creates a sense of indebtedness or obligation between people. As such, it is the force behind the formation of social bonds and the basis of all morality. Mauss also points out that gifts are not only material things. We give respect in the way we listen to others, in the ways we recognize their humanity, and in the ways we show that their lives matter as much as our own. Gifts not only engender life; they bring home to us that life is a matter of living with others, of sharing what we have with them. Not to give, not to receive what is offered, or not to pass on to others what we have received goes against the grain of life.

What then of goods received that one gave nothing for? What of gifts that come into one's hands and cannot be said to be repayments for something one has given, to someone, somewhere, or at some time in the past? Is undeserved good fortune a sordid boon, and unearned rewards a curse rather than a blessing? If yes, then it would suggest that Mauss was right in assuming that the principle of reciprocity is innate, like the deep grammar of the languages we speak and the stories we tell, and that it informs the way we conceptualize and evaluate every interaction.

For many years, I have been collecting newspaper stories about individuals charged with fraud and embezzlement. Here's one from June 2004—a London secretary jailed for seven years for defrauding her bosses at the investment bank Goldman Sachs of nearly four and a half million pounds. What did Joyti DeLaurey do with her ill-gotten gains? She went on spending sprees, buying a £750,000 villa in Cyprus, several luxury cars, flying lessons, designer clothes, holidays, and £384,000 of Cartier jewelry.

It is as though wealth one has not earned has to be got rid of fast. It is squandered on things one does not really need, things one cannot possibly use, things that cannot compensate for what it is one truly wants—love or recognition. Material possessions are surrogates for the spiritual and emotional things one does not have. But they are poor compensations. They do not satisfy. And the kleptomaniac returns, time and time again, to his or her attempts to make wealth work the magic that only love can wreak.

I remember, too, the time my wife found a one hundred dollar bill on Oxford Street, Sydney. We were both unemployed at the time, and this was a huge windfall. But what did we do with the money? Within minutes of finding the banknote on the wet sidewalk we walked into a designer shoe store where Francine bought a pair of Italian shoes that proved to be too tight for her and which she never wore!

That the logic of the agora and the logic of the oikos are incommensurate is undoubtedly a reflection of the very different modes of reciprocity involved in each. While market relations are ruled by the principle of direct exchange, in which there is ideally no doubt as to the equivalence of what is given and what is given in return, intimate relationships are governed by a sense of indirect exchange, in which there is always ambiguity and deferral—so that what is given is never returned immediately or in kind.

Generally speaking, we try to keep these domains of love and money quite separate. We often feel there is something "wrong," though not necessarily in the moral sense of the term, when sexual favors are purchased, love is commodified, or a cash value placed on care. We try to prevent monetary worries coming between spouses, or competition over a legacy destroying the bonds among siblings. What matters most is the relationship itself, not the value of what is exchanged in the course of it. It is only when relationships fall apart, as in divorce, that we start calculating what we have gained or lost, balancing the books, settling scores, getting even.

When my parents died, and I received my share of the inheritance, I was astonished to find myself squandering it on a sports utility vehicle I did not really need. When I sold the vehicle at a significant loss one year later, I felt no qualms. It was as though the money had been tainted, and now I was cleansed. I would discover that my reaction was not unusual. It is not only that one has not merited such money (the fruit of one's parents' life of toil and hardship, not of one's own); it is as if money itself were antithetical to this relationship we think of in terms of consanguinity, of blood. The money sullies something whose value lies outside the monetary sphere. For a parent, one's relationship with one's children is one of care, not calculation. One does not exactly give with no thought to what might be returned, but the returns are "spiritual," we say, not material. They take the form of love, respect, and affection—values that are "incalculable" and "beyond price." To quantify this form of reciprocity, to translate kinship into capital, offends our sense of what family really means.

This sense that certain forms of income are incompatible with the value we place on kinship, friendship, and community is widespread. "Money" is symbolically inimical to love and, as Georg Simmel notes, "is never an adequate mediator of personal relationships . . . that are intended to be permanent and based on the sincerity of the binding forces." With the payment of money, a relationship ends "just as fundamentally as when one [pays] for satisfaction from a prostitute."[16]

Among the Luo of Western Kenya benefits received from unfair actions are thought to be "bitter blessings" (*gueth makech*). Money that is stolen or found, that is earned from the sale of land, cannabis, gold, or tobacco, that follows a windfall or lottery win, or that is received as a reward for killing (as a hired gun or mercenary soldier) is considered bitter (*makech*), and this bitterness brings misfortune to whoever gains wealth in these ways.[17]

As Parker Shipton shows, these are all in some sense unjust rewards, for they entail taking something from others with no thought of return, or doing deals that harm rather than benefit the other party. They are all examples of negative reciprocity. They diminish or take life rather than enhance or give it. The bitter irony of these ill-gotten gains is that sooner or later, one will have to pay for one's boon, usually by having something or someone precious taken from one. This justice is nothing if not poetic. A bride procured through tobacco sales can be expected to die in fire and smoke.

In traditional Maori thought, gifts not only convey goodwill and create social bonds; they carry something of the giver's personal being, something that longs to be returned ultimately to its source. "To give is to give a part of oneself," something that is "in reality a part of one's nature and substance," writes Mauss, "while to receive something is to receive a part of someone's spiritual essence."[18] To keep a gift to oneself and not hand it on is to interrupt the journey of the gift and prevent its return to whence it came. This "turning aside" of the spirit of the gift (*hau whitia*) transforms the blessing of the gift into a curse, and the possessor of the object—whether food or a valued greenstone heirloom—may sicken and die.

None of this needs be spelled out to take effect, since it is the imperative of reciprocity itself, haunting us, as it were, that pricks our

16. Simmel, *The Philosophy of Money*, 376.

17. Parker Shipton, *Bitter Money: Cultural Economy and Some African Meanings of Forbidden Commodities* (Washington: American Anthropological Association, 1989), 28–29.

18. Marcel Mauss, *The Gift*, trans. Ian Cunnison (London: Cohen and West, 1954), 10.

conscience when we keep what must be passed on, or come into the possession of something that is not rightfully ours.

Such questions assume that it is natural that certain domains of life be kept apart. While we in the West sometimes feel that blood and money are intrinsically incompatible, and that business or political life should not be corrupted by nepotism or croneyism, people in traditional societies are far more definite about the need to keep mutually inimical essences apart.

Among the Yurok, whose traditional homeland is centered on the Klamath River that borders Oregon and northern California, contrasted fluids such as salt water and fresh water, blood and water, semen and water, or urine and water should never meet in the same aperture or channel. Thus, salmon, which are water-born, must be kept away from the house of a menstruating woman; money, which originates in another "stream," must not be brought into association with sexual intercourse; a person must never urinate in the river; oral sex is banned because cunnilingus prevents money flowing and interferes with the salmon run on the Klamath River; and a saltwater creature like a whale swimming into the river mouth fills people with foreboding.

In Maori New Zealand similar taboos apply. A Maori friend once pointed out to me that there was something deeply amiss when one observes seagulls far inland, scavenging on human trash, for every species and every person has its own appointed place in the scheme of things, a place where it properly belongs. To transgress these boundaries is like mingling the water from different catchment areas or moving genetic material from one species into another—a disruption of their respective *whakapapa* and *mauri*, an infringement of *tapu*, and thus an invitation to disaster. While many Pakeha see biocontrol as a practical solution to an environmental problem, Maori argue that transferring genetic material across species boundaries constitutes a dangerous, unprecedented, and irreversible intervention in the natural order of things. Specifically, moving genetic material from one species (a virus or parasite) to another (the possum) outrages *tikanga Maori* (the Maori way of doing things), disrupts the *whakapapa* (genealogy) and *mauri* (life essence) of those species, destroys a primordial balance between Ranginui (sky/father) and Papatuanuku (earth/mother).

As for money, it is widely believed that it is sterile. The reason it is placed outside the pale of human community is that it cannot give birth to anything. Nowhere is this view more compellingly stated than among the pastoral Nuer, for whom cattle are the objects of ultimate value. Cattle, like people, are creatures of flesh and blood. They give birth. But money "has no blood." Yet blood is more than synonymous with life; it is "passed from person to person and from generation to generation, endowing social relations with a certain substance and fluidity."[19] While cattle, as gifts, bring life to people, creating and sustaining social bonds, money is seen as "an utterly depersonalized medium" and is therefore inimical to the generation of social bonds. Yet, as Sharon Hutchinson makes clear, it is not money per se that destroys the social weal, but "shit money"—the money earned from the degrading work of emptying latrines and of domestic service.

Is Nothing Sacred?

When I first traveled to Cape Tribulation on Australia's northeast coast in 1988, I stopped near a roadside sign that said "Bouncing Stones." The sign indicated that the nearby foreshore had "cultural significance for the Wujal Wujal people" and requested visitors not to remove stones from the beach.

Leaving my rental Suzuki in the shade of some trees, I walked down to the beach where several tourists were hurling stones at the face of a massive black outcrop of rock. Some were attempting to skip pebbles off the large plate-shaped stones on the beach. When the tourists decided it was time to go, they filled their pockets with bouncing stones as though the respect with which Aboriginals regarded this place was an invitation to desecrate it.

I walked down the beach until I was out of sight and earshot of the departing tourists, and for an hour or so I sat on the beach, looking out to sea and vaguely pondering the significance of what I had just witnessed.

When I returned to the black rocks there was no one in sight. I approached the rock carefully, mindfully. A mangrove egret flew from a niche on the seaward face, some kind of omen, I thought. Picking

19. Sharon Hutchinson, *Nuer Dilemmas: Coping with Money, War, and the State* (Berkeley: University of California Press, 1996), 75–76.

up two stones, I then began to knock them softly together, singing to the rock, announcing myself, letting it know my name, improvising couplets that conveyed to it my sense of what it had suffered, its body chipped and bruised with thoughtless stones. I circled it thrice, tapping my stones, singing, wishing it free from the vandals it attracted. The rhyming couplets came readily to mind. I did not have to think of what to say. Finally, I pressed the palms of my hands against the rock, and stashed my two stones in a cleft. I then withdrew slowly and circumspectly, sighing "ahh" as if to let it know my song was done, and that it would heal and endure.

It so happened that in 1993 my wife and I were living near Wujal Wujal, the Aboriginal community nearest the site of the bouncing stones, and one of the first things we learned when we introduced ourselves to the local council members was that they received several packages every month containing bouncing stones that tourists had pocketed without a second thought and subsequently rued taking.

I later learned that something similar occurred at the cultural center at Uluru in Central Australia, where there is a large ring-binder on a lectern that contains scores of letters (each sealed in a plastic sleeve) from visitors who removed rocks from around the great monolith only to suffer various misfortunes when they went home.

The letters were much the same, all beginning with words to the effect that "I visited Ayers Rock [in only a few instances was it called Uluru] in 1989 [the dates varied, of course, though some went back thirty years] and was at that time ignorant of the spiritual significance of the place. Since taking a rock as a souvenir my life [or 'our life' or 'my family's life'] has been cursed by misfortune, so I have felt the need to return the rock to where I took it in the hope that the curse will be lifted and my luck will change." In almost every case, the letter writer gave precise details of the location from where the rock had been taken, as if its exact restoration was required for the magical curse to be canceled.

These stones have not been returned to whence they came (the task is beyond the resources of the center's staff); they have been placed at the foot of the lectern—some egg-sized, some quite small, some as large as a loaf of bread.

Are there any clues here as to how one might understand the sacred? Is the sacred a synonym for our profound sense that we share our humanity with all other human beings despite entrenched views and primal fears to the contrary, so that in desecrating or vandalizing a "sacred" site we are haunted by the idea that we have denied the human in another and thereby brought disgrace upon ourselves? And is there any analogy to be drawn between Judeo-Christian notions of sacred space and Aboriginal notions of "sacred sites"?

My first visit to Uluru followed a night of rain. When Francine and I first saw the rock, it was sunk below the horizon, half-hidden in cloud. We thought of bypassing it and driving on to the Olgas. But then the cloud began to lift.

Approaching the monolith, I was staggered by its immensity. I had seen postcards of it, of course, glowing in the light of the setting sun, but now, with its rain-gouged, wind-pitted surfaces towering above us, I felt ill-prepared and was stunned into silence. It was not so much something you saw as a presence into which you came. Something you touched, as if through the palm of your hand.

It was Sunday and overcast. The climb was closed and there were few visitors. But even had we been at liberty to scale the rock, following the safety rope and the scuffed footprints of thousands of other tourists— two more "ants," as local Aboriginals were fond of saying, along the trail to the top—I would have demurred, for climbing this monolith whose massive presence so thoroughly put one in one's place seemed less an act of courage than of sacrilege.

Francine and I found the track that led from Mutitjulu around the base of the rock. We craned our necks to take in its stony features— fissures like scars from a spear fight, slabs of sandstone like butchered meat, eye sockets, and prognathous jaws, mouthlike caverns from which decayed teeth had tumbled out and become boulders, the petri- fied body of a blue-tongued lizard.

We played this guessing game for an hour or more, following the fence lines that marked off sacred sites, skirting the flattened outcrop of what was once a women's camp.

I would subsequently read that the origins of Uluru go back to the creation. Two boys heaped up a mound of mud after heavy rain. Baked in the sun, it became the monolith. Everywhere are places that show signs of the two boys' epochal journey. A rock hole in a dry creek bed at Wiputa is the remains of a ground oven at one of their campsites, a nearby crack in the earth is the euro wallaby tail the boys discarded, a fresh spring at Anari marks the place where the *tjuni* (wooden club) of one of the boys hit the ground instead of the hare wallaby at which it was aimed. The bodies of the two boys are preserved as boulders on the great table mountain of Atila.

Our trip to Uluru was the beginning of our first stint of fieldwork in Central Australia, and we would visit many other "sacred sites" in the company of Warlpiri friends and hear similar stories of ancestral events that shaped the landscape and left, seeded in the ground, the life-essence of those journeying heroes. We would also acquire a detailed understanding of how every individual was symbolically born, not of the union of man and woman but of a woman and the life-essence of a particular place. Accordingly, people belonged to the places where they were conceived, as well as to the lineages of their father and mother. Indeed, people spoke of their relation to significant sites as an umbilical connection to the "belly" or "womb" (*miyalu*) and used idioms of kinship to express their patrilineal or matrilineal connection to a place they called "father" or "mother."

To approach a place to which you had no such relationship was both wrong and dangerous. If the place, or the spirit guardians of the place, did not recognize your voice, your smell, your genealogical claim to connection, it could bring you harm. As I found in Africa, the curse was the inverse of respect. The curse was a kind of hubris that came as a consequence of presuming intimacy with a place that demanded one keep a respectful distance.

But was it accurate to refer to these places of existentially profound, ancestral significance as "sacred sites"? What did Warlpiri mean when they referred to such places as "proper dear ones" or as "sacred" (*tarruku*)?

These sites are places of great value. But this value is given to a place by the concerted ceremonial activity of those who call it "father" or are related to it through complementary matrilineal affiliation. From time immemorial, these primary custodians of the site have regularly and ritually reanimated and re-embodied its ancestral essence through narrative, song, painting, and dancing. The sacred may be understood, then, as the cumulative effect of this intense labor over time, and as a reflection of the depth and compression of human experience at moments of birth and death—for it is then that the original order of the world (the "law") is brought back into being, or lapses into potentiality again.

If the sacred is synonymous with the border situations where human experience is most intense, it is easy to understand why pain and suffering are so often associated with initiation into sacred mysteries. For nothing so concentrates the mind as pain, and ordeals both induce religious ecstasy and cement the deepest human bonds, particularly in the transitional spaces of initiation, birth, and death.

It wasn't until our second field trip that this connection between labor, limits, and value became clear to me. And it wasn't until I had spent many hours in conversation with older Warlpiri men that I began to understand where European and Aboriginal conceptions might share common ground.

In one such conversation, prompted by images of Christ suffering on the cross and of young Aboriginal initiates, pinioned by kinsmen as cicatrices are cut into their chests and their foreskins surgically removed, I asked what in the white man's world could be compared with a sacred site. "Would it be a church?"

Japaljarri said no; it was more like a memorial. Like the pioneer memorials that whites had erected along the Stuart Highway.

I asked Japangardi what he thought of the analogy between a sacred site and a memorial.

"The War Memorial in Canberra is like an Aboriginal sacred site," he said. And he recounted how he had visited it once—the Pool of Reflection, the Hall of Memory, the Roll of Honor.

But at that moment, my most vocal and self-confident informant, Zack Jakamarra, intervened.

There was no comparison, Zack said. "That monument bin made by people's hands. That tree [a reference to a specific site we had been discussing shortly before] bin born with the land."

"Our" notion of the sacred is thus a reification. The labor that goes into creating this value gets forgotten, and the value seems to be inherent in a place or object, and as such cannot be compared with the variable value that attaches to ordinary things, or even ordinary human beings. It is, as we say, "beyond" measure; it is "absolute." It suggests the point at which human being passes into the absolute ground of being, for which we have only limited access and inadequate descriptions, but in the face of which we are awestruck and overwhelmed.

While some people identify the sacred with the divine, others associate it with the ancestral order of things, or with nature (which may or may not be seen as divinely created and ordered). Thus, the "sacred" mountains of the Doi Suthep Doi Pui range in northern Thailand acquire their significance not only from legends of the Buddha's journeys through this region but from the shrines and landscapes that commemorate that pivotal period.

When the tourist authority of Thailand proposed to build a cable car from the foot of Doi Suthep to the monastery-temple, Wat Phra That, near the summit, "environmentalists, university professors, students, and ordinary citizens" joined Buddhist monks in protest, wanting "to preserve the Stupa Doi Suthep as it was given to them by Creation, as untouched as possible, as sacred."[20]

And so we return to Karl Jaspers's notion of extreme situations (*grenzsituationen*)[21]—the limits beyond which language and thought cannot go, the limits we nevertheless speculatively and imaginatively try to transcend, the limits against which we struggle, the limits that define human existence, the limits that "cannot be changed by us but merely clarified."[22]

A phenomenology of critical experience engages with those situations in which we find ourselves in despair, declaring I don't know what to do, I don't know what to say, I can't go on, I can't cope, I'm out of my depth. But, paradoxically, it is when stretched to breaking point and lost to the world that we come closer to what some call the nature of things, and others call the divine. The limit is therefore a threshold where we feel most constrained and yet, sometimes, most liberated—

20. Donald K. Swearer, Sommai Premchit, and Phaithoon Dokbuakaew, *Sacred Mountains of Northern Thailand and Their Legends* (Chiang Mai: Silkworm Books, 2004), 33–34.

21. Brache Lichtenberg Ettinger's concepts of "borderspace" and "borderlinking" and Michel Foucault's notion of "limit experience" bear comparison with Jaspers's notion of "border situation" since the possibility of seeing the world anew is inextricably linked to situations in which our habitual ways of thinking and speaking are stretched to the limits or radically disrupted. What is philosophical thought, Foucault asks, if not the "critical work that thought brings to bear on itself?" "In what does it consist, if not in the endeavor to know how and to what extent it might be possible to think differently, instead of legitimating what is already known?" *The Uses of Pleasure*, vol. 2 of *The History of Sexuality*, trans. R. Hurley (New York: Vintage, 1990), 8–9.

22. Jaspers, "Limit Situations," in *Karl Jaspers: Basic Philosophical Writings*, ed. and trans. Edith Ehrlich, Leonard H. Ehrlich, and George B. Pepper (New York: Humanity Books, 2000), 97.

released from the suffering of our being-in-the-world, open to the experience of ego-lessness, or samadhi. It is at this point that words escape us, though with words we strive to point at this experience that has taken us beyond language.

FULL MOON

When this bruised medallion, the moon
rose tonight
I thought how solitude allows
what human kind cannot–
openness to this hill whose eucalypts
are my hands,
the sky
that has seen me drown.

I float up
through these leaves, my skin,
breathing this blue again;
the moon
hangs round my neck,
under me men move to harvest
or lie against a golden stook
eating black bread
drinking red wine.

The moon is the pupil of my eye
I go as far as the blue hill goes
I flow like a river in the dark.[23]

The limits of logos are also a threshold or horizon, where we pass from understandings grounded in instrumental reason and ordinary language into a "wild" logos of distorted forms, dream images, carnality, and carnival Of this transitional space, that we variously call poetic, libidinal, oneiric, oracular, unconscious, or precognitive, Merleau-Ponty uses the term *logos endiathetos* (a meaning before logic).[24] Lying on the margins

23. Written a few months after my first wife's death, the poem appeared in my collection *Going On* (Dunedin: McIndoe, 1985), 57.
24. Maurice Merleau-Ponty, *The Visible and the Invisible (Followed by Working Notes)*, ed. Claude Lefort, trans. Alphonso Lingis (Evanston: Northwestern University Press, 1968), 12–13, 169.

of what can be assimilated to theological, normative, or philosophical systems, it is a domain where the mind is set free to wander or journey, where visions and hallucinations occur, and where we confront sides of ourselves that ordinarily do not see the light of day, yet from which new modes of consciousness may take shape. Being able to move to and fro between the worlds of received truth and oracular understanding is universally regarded as a talent without which life would be impoverished if not impossible. But such movement is always perilous. Insofar as it involves a suspension of normative knowledge, it threatens the social order. And insofar as it takes the boundary crosser to the limits of his strength, it brings him close to losing his reason.

Many of the Kuranko diviners with whom I worked received their gifts from djinn that appeared to them in dreams during a bout of life-threatening sickness, and both music and musical instruments are often said to have originally come from the bush. The great Malian musician Ali Farka Touré attributes his genius to the djinn. In his thirteenth year a series of visions and strange experiences transformed his playing, and he entered a new world that he compares with a prolonged sickness or epileptic seizure. "It's different from when you're in a normal state; you're not the person you know anymore."[25] Among the Dogon of Mali, the figure of Yourougou is associated with extravagance, disorder, and oracular truth, while its opposite, Nommo, represents reason and social order.[26] For the neighboring Bambara, a similar contrast is posited between Nyalé—who was created first and signifies "swarming life," exuberance, and uncontrolled power—and Faro, or Ndomadyiri, who was created next and signifies equilibrium and restraint.[27] For the Kuranko, the contrast between bush and town signifies the same extremes. Of these penumbral domains we may speak of a religiosity prior to Religion, of a language within languages, and of truths beyond Truth.

25. Ali Farka Touré, sleeve notes from *Radio Mali*, World Circuit CD WC8 044, 1996.

26. Geneviève Calame-Griaule, *Ethnologie et langage: La parole chez les Dogon* (Paris: Gallimard, 1965).

27. Dominique Zahan, *The Religion, Spirituality and Thought of Traditional Africa*, trans. Kate Ezra Martin and Lawrence M. Martin (Chicago: University of Chicago Press, 1974), 15.

Return to the Café Stelling

A year after leaving Denmark and coming to America, I returned to my old European haunts—in particular the Café Stelling in Copenhagen, where I had arranged to rendezvous with my friend Hans Lucht. We picked up our conversation from where we had left it, seemingly only a few days ago, with me describing to Hans my recent fieldwork among Sierra Leoneans in southeast London and Hans sharing with me stories of his seven months' fieldwork among Ghanaian migrants in Naples. We were both deeply preoccupied by the question of what a human being is prepared to give up in order to gain what he or she thinks of as a life worth living, and how the Mediterranean defines these days, for many Africans, a border situation that is not so much geographical as existential.

After his period of fieldwork in Naples, Hans returned to the coastal village in Ghana where he spent five months in 2001 and met the young men who had, since then, made their way to Italy. In Senya Beraku, he interviewed a woman whose eldest son, Charles, had died at sea, attempting to reach Italy. At first, Adjoa Kokor could not bring herself to speak of this tragedy, and Hans's interpreter, a close friend of Charles, who had not attended the funeral because he could not bear to see Adjoa Kokor's distress, was hesitant to proceed. But suddenly, Adjoa Kokor agreed to answer Hans's questions.

"We came to her house in the morning," Hans said. "Adjoa Kokor was sitting outside on a wooden bench, tending a small fire on which she was cooking some food. The house was below street level, so that when you looked up at the road it was like looking up at a stage with people going to and fro along it. Sitting outside Adjoa Kokor's house, however, you felt as if you were sitting in a dark hole.

Adjoa Kokor said her son had decided to emigrate after the death of his father. As the eldest son, Charles had felt duty-bound to take care of his mother, his younger siblings, and his own family—his wife and two children, ages six and three. Adjoa Kokor had not wanted her son to go. But he argued that there was no future in fishing.

Senya were fishermen. Hans had ventured out in their boats with them, observed their sacrifices to the gods, noted their skills and precautions, the daily gamble of netting enough fish to feed their families and having a small surplus to sell on the market for the petty cash needed for school fees and medicines. But the big industrial boats had come and taken the fish, leaving the locals with nothing. As a livelihood, fishing was now a dead end, and the young men had no choice but to migrate. What was Naples but another dangerous sea they had to learn to navigate, full of dangers they had to appease?

So, asking his mother to pray for him, Charles set out for Burkina Faso, and thence across the Sahara to Libya, where he made a single phone call home to recount details of the hardships of his desert journey and his misgivings about the journey that lay ahead.

"Every morning, I used to listen to the religious programs on the radio at dawn," Adjoa Kokor said. "One time there was an announcement on the radio that a number of illegal immigrants had washed ashore in Morocco. At that very moment a feeling engulfed me that something was amiss, even though I had heard no rumors yet about my son's fate. I just began to cry and couldn't stop.

"Three days later I had a dream that Charles had returned from Italy. But he was very quiet and was just standing at the gate. I asked him, 'Charles, what is the matter with you? Are you dead?' And he kneeled down and said, 'Mother, yes I am dead. I didn't listen to your advice, and have had to face it all.'"

As Adjoa Kokor went on to describe the stories that filtered back to her village, and then the official letter from Libya, returning Charles's passport and confirming his death, she broke down. As the tears streamed down her cheeks and fell onto her blue dress, she sought to avert her face from passers-by in the street by staring into the simmering pot on the fire.

Hans was loath to continue plying her with questions that so clearly rubbed salt into her wounds.

As Hans waited, his interpreter, Jonathan, tried to calm Adjoa Kokor.

Later, Hans asked Jonathan what he had told the distraught woman in the course of trying to calm her.

Jonathan said: "I was trying to give her some words of encouragement. I told her that life itself is a risk. There are no guarantees in life. Everyday we are risking loss in order to make some small gain, something that will give us and our children a better life. I told her that her son died in the course of this struggle for life. What could be more worthwhile? She had nothing to be ashamed of."

Hans told me that Jonathan, who had attended a Christian elementary school in Ghana, had gone on to draw a comparison with Abraham's preparedness to kill his beloved son Isaac, the child he and his wife Sarah had waited a lifetime for. "You do what is asked of you. You do what you must do. And you leave it to God to determine the meaning of what you do, the value of it, even though God does not appear to give a damn, or reveal his hand, or explain his actions."

Hans had been reading Sören Kierkegaard's *Fear and Trembling* as a way of deepening his understanding of what his Senya friend had told the grief-stricken mother of the young man who had lost his life trying to improve his lot in life.

For Kierkegaard, life requires of us repeated leaps of faith. We can never know whether our gambles will pay off, or if our actions will lead to the consequences we hope for. So we move continually and haphazardly into the unknown, our words and actions having repercussions we could not have foreseen, our hopes dashed one minute only to be revived the next—and it is this that makes faith or the absurd the measure of our humanity.

"By faith Abraham emigrated from the land of his fathers and became an alien in the promised land."[28] It was faith that sustained him in exile, faith that gave him the patience to endure so many years without a son, faith that preserved his eternal youth, and faith that enabled him to follow God's orders and take his only son, Isaac, to the land of Moriah and offer him as a burnt offering.

But Kierkegaard makes it clear that Abraham's faith here is not faith in a life to come, sustained by the prospect of some reward or revelation, but faith in life itself—affirmed in the thought of growing old in the country to which he belonged, of being honored among its people, blessed by posterity and remembered by his son.

The absurd is to be understood, therefore, as a commitment to speech that may fall upon deaf ears, to actions that may be misread, to an openness to the world that may be our undoing, to love that may not be requited and to life that harbors the imminent possibility of death.

Kierkegaard observes that everyone is "great in his own way, and everyone in proportion to the greatness of that which *he loved*."[29] But the greatest of all is not he who loves himself or he who loves others, but

---

28. Sören Kierkegaard, *Fear and Trembling*, trans. Howard V. Hong and Edna H. Hong (Princeton, N.J.: Princeton University Press, 1983), 17.

29. Ibid.

he who loves God. Not he who expects the possible, or he who expects the eternal, but he who expects the impossible. Not he who struggles with the world, or struggles with himself, but he who struggles with God.

Replace the word "God" with "life" and one comes close to the truth that Hans's Senya interpreter, Jonathan, was trying to convey to the woman whose son had been lost at sea, staking everything on the chance of a better life.

Metanoia

I was nearing the end of my book. For eighteen months I had carried its theme in my head, variations jotted down on scraps of paper as I trudged through snow on West Farm, shuffled through autumn leaves in the local woods, lay in summer grass watching the clouds, or walked back to my office after a long conversation over coffee with a Harvard colleague or old friend. What had at the outset seemed like a new departure was, I now realized, a topic to which I had been drawn for as long as I could remember, falling asleep when I was a child to the doleful whistle of a freight train in the hills that summoned images of a world beyond the small town in which I was confined, or loitering on the New Plymouth wharves where rusting tramp boats smelling of oil, splintered dunnage, and old rope offloaded their cargoes and put to sea again, disappearing over the horizon under a penciled hatching of smoke. There was always a frontier to cross, always an elsewhere calling me, another place where I would come into my own. Little wonder, then, that ethnography should become my passion and my profession, for it permitted the kind of controlled experimentation on oneself whose object is an enlarged understanding of what it means to be human. To place one's customary self in brackets, so to speak, is to invite a crisis that promotes critique—a way of seeing the world from another angle, seeing it anew.

Ethnography throws one into a world where one cannot be entirely oneself, where one is estranged from the ways of acting and thinking that sustain one's normal sense of identity. This emotional, intellectual, social, and sensory displacement can be so destabilizing that one has to fight the impulse to run for cover, to retrieve the sense of groundedness one has lost. But it can also be a window of opportunity, a way of understanding oneself from the standpoint of an-other, or from elsewhere.

This is not to imply that one can enter fully into the lifeworld of others, standing in their shoes, as we say. Nor does it imply the possibility of ever understanding the human, for that would require a comprehensive knowledge of how the world has appeared to everyone who lives and has ever lived. Ethnographic understanding simply means that one may glimpse oneself as one might be or might have been *under other circumstances*, and come to the realization that knowledge and identity are emergent properties of the unstable relationship between self and other, here and there, now and then, and not fixed and final truths that one has been privileged to possess by virtue of living in one particular society at one particular moment in history.

The justification and goal of ethnography is metanoia, "an on-going series of transformations each one of which alters the predicates of being."[30] However, few people are likely to ponder their own worldview as it appears from the standpoint of another unless circumstances compel them to. In reality, understanding is usually a result of *enforced* displacement, of crises that wrench a person out of his or her habitual routines of thought and behavior, rather than a product of philosophical choice or idle curiosity. Understanding others requires more than an intellectual movement from one's own position to theirs; it involves physical upheaval, psychological turmoil, and moral confusion. This is why suffering is an inescapable concomitant of understanding—the loss of the illusion that one's own particular worldview holds true for everyone, the pain of seeing in the face and gestures of a stranger the invalidation of oneself. And it is precisely because such hazards and symbolic deaths are the cost of going beyond the borders of the local world that we complacently regard as the measure of *the* world that most human beings resist seeking to know others as they know themselves. By this same token, we find the most compelling examples of how human beings suffer and struggle with the project of enlarging their understanding in those parts of the world where openness has become

30. Kenelm Burridge, "Other Peoples' Religions Are Absurd," in *Explorations in the Anthropology of Religion: Essays in Honour of Jan Van Baal*, ed. W. E. A. Beek and J. H. Scherer (The Hague: Martinus Nijhoff, 1975), 10.

the unavoidable condition of existence. It is here, in what Jaspers called border situations, rather than in European salons and seminars, that we may recognize and be reconciled to the sometimes painful truth that the human world constitutes our common ground, our shared heritage, *not as a place of comfortably consistent unity but as a site of contingency, difference, and struggle.*

What, then, is the value of exchanging comfort for hardship, of trying to see the world from the vantage point of others? Hermes, the patron of thieves, traders, travelers, and heralds, is also an obvious candidate for patron saint of ethnography, since he stands on the border or at the crossroads between quite different countries of the mind.[31]

But what message is born of his transgression and trickery? First: that oracular wisdom requires unsettling and questioning what we customarily take for granted or consider true. As a corollary, cultivating an ironic distance from our own conventional wisdom helps prevent the arrogance of seeing all contrary views as false, and all dissenters as threats. Second is the value of doubt, for it is through the loss of firm belief that one stands to gain a sense of belonging to a pluralistic world whose horizons are open—a world in which no one has the right to exercise power in the name of what he or she considers to be true and good; a world in which differences are no longer seen as obstacles to overcome but aporias to be accepted.

I worked in the Congo in 1964, in the midst of a bloody rebellion. The talk was all of change. Everyone had a recipe for the right course of action to ensure the Congo's future. The UN, with whom I worked in a voluntary capacity, was embarked upon the same kind of "civilizing mission" that had obsessed Conrad's doomed figure Kurtz in *Heart of Darkness*. By contrast, the rebel leader Christophe Gbenye wanted to erase colonial history from living memory, and he ordered the execution of everyone who was literate or had worked for the Belgians. "We must destroy what existed before, we must start again at zero with an ignorant mass." Like Pol Pot in Cambodia a generation later, for whom

---

31. "Hermes" is probably derived from the Greek for "stone-heap" and was represented as an ithyphallic block of stone. Norman O. Brown, *Hermes the Thief: The Evolution of a Myth* (Great Barrington, Mass.: Lindisfarne Press, 1990), 32. This symbolism is reminiscent of the phallic display whereby primate males mark and defend the edge of their home ranges.

French colonial rule and modernity had allegedly polluted Kymer culture; by purging "foreign" elements the Khmer Rouge sought to purify the social body—a foretaste of the ethnic cleansing that would sweep through Yugoslavia and Rwanda in the 1990s.

Nowadays I am less interested in inequality than in those moments of intimacy when the gap between oneself and another seems to close. As when a piece of music abolishes time.

Often the piece of music is banal, unworthy of the significance one attaches to the events it brings to mind.

In *Tristes Tropiques*, the French anthropologist Claude Lévi-Strauss recounts how, on the plateau of the Mato Grosso in Brazil in the late 1930s, he was haunted by a phrase from a Chopin étude.

For many weeks, the anthropologist has been plagued by questions he cannot answer. Why am I here? Why do I press on, enduring this heat and hardship, this unpalatable food, this loneliness? He thinks of his colleagues back in France, climbing the academic ladder, entering politics, while he treks "across desert wastes in pursuit of a few pathetic human remnants." He asks himself whether he is by temperament destined to be estranged from his own society. When he encounters a people as remote from his own kind as it is possible to imagine, he finds himself overcome by nostalgia for his own past.

> What came to me were fleeting visions of the French countryside I had cut myself off from, or snatches of music and poetry which were the most conventional expressions of a culture which I must convince myself I had renounced, if I were not to belie the direction I had given to my life. On the plateau of the western Mato Grosso, I had been haunted for weeks, not by the things that lay all around me and that I would never see again, but by a hackneyed melody, weakened still further by the deficiencies of my memory—the melody of Chopin's Étude no. 3, opus 10, which, by a bitterly ironical twist of which I was well aware, now seemed to epitomize all I had left behind.[32]

And yet, on those desolate savannas of central Brazil, Lévi-Strauss finds himself reliving some of the experiences of Montaigne, who, at Rouen in 1560, conversed with three Brazilian Indians and came to the

32. Claude Lévi-Strauss, *Tristes Tropiques*, trans. John and Doreen Weightman (London: Jonathan Cape, 1973), 376–77.

realization that our fear of the other is born of our blindness to ourselves. "Every man calls barbarous anything he is not accustomed to; it is indeed the case that we have no criterion of truth or right-reason than the example and form of the opinions and customs of our own country."[33] To dwell among others is not only to realize how much we share with them, despite appearances; it is to begin to understand "the basic psychological material from which all societies are constructed,"[34] and integrate within oneself the repudiated pieces one has passed, like counterfeit coin, onto others.

The Place Where We Live

That December, my family and I flew to Sydney to spend a few weeks with my eldest daughter, Heidi, her partner Pete, and my four-month-old grandson Nico, whom I had not yet held in my arms. Our flight landed shortly before nine in the morning, and after wearily negotiating Customs and Immigration we met Heidi, her arms outstretched and laughing with joy, at the exit to the concourse. After embracing with tears in our eyes, I asked Heidi if she had been waiting long. "Six months!" she said; at least the last few hours had seemed that long, her stomach in knots, her incredulity that we were finally there.

I felt the same, overwhelmed by this sudden sense of being where I truly wanted to be, together as a family again, breathing in the familiar brine-soaked, cindery, eucalypt-scented air of Sydney under blue skies. The wintriness of Boston was suddenly a world away, its timetables and agendas, its formalities and abstractions. For once I did not have to wear a mask, feign an identity, or monitor my speech.

That first night, I woke at 3:30 a.m. to the sound of my grandson at his mother's breast in the next room, each gulp drawing from him a soft cry of breathless satisfaction.

In the morning, I sat on the floor with him as he flexed and flailed his arms or jerked his chubby legs against my thighs, smiling in response to my infatuated smiles, then looking around, one moment lost in con-

33. Michel de Montaigne, "On the Cannibals," in *The Essays: A Selection*, trans. M. A. Screech (Harmondsworth: Penguin, 2004), 82.

34. Lévi-Strauss, *Tristes Tropiques*, 316.

templating the play of light on the window shade, the next startled by a sound from the street.

I felt that I was observing the basic building blocks of our humanity. The hands grasping. The legs and feet treading the air, as if preparing to walk. The oscillation of consciousness, one moment engaged with us, the next rapt in something far off or deep within. Active one moment, with gesture or sound; passive the next, and falling silent. And above all, the delight in play and in humor, as he responded to our teasing, our voices, our smiles, already consummately social.

After a week in Sydney we all traveled to the South Coast where Heidi and Pete had rented a house at Bendalong.

In my rambles along the beach, often alone, my observations seemed to reiterate my observations of Nico. Was it that the human world and the extrahuman world answered to the same description, or was it that one cannot see the natural world as it is for itself but only through our own human and cultural lens? What I did see, however, and tried to capture in writing, was the flow of antithetical forces in the transitional spaces between past and present, here and there—memories contending with present dreams, ideas giving way to images, my sense of myself dissolving in the presence of my grandson, as the sea poured itself ashore, its slick tongue licking the dry encrusted sand, its white-on-blue fretwork of foam resembling an afterimage in the mind.

A stretch of water
tautened by wind,
myself nearing this turning point
as the waves roll in.

The eucalypts solid
in the distance,
and as green,
the deep sea's indigo . . .
is, will be, has been.

Leaving Australia was not easy. At the airport, waves of pain and heartache washed over me as I remembered holding my grandson for the last time that morning, his warm head against my cheek, baptized with my tears.

Three hours out from Sydney we entered the region of the oncoming night—the last streaks of red fading from the sky, snow banks of cloud graying under the sickly hues of the upper atmosphere, and one star showing.

The penumbra is where light fades into darkness—the most elementary metaphor we possess for the threshold that separates the familiar realms in which we live and those impinging realms that we subject to endless speculation, but that ultimately elude our grasp.

Before I had written these lines in my journal, night's gloved hand had taken hold of us, and the day was merely a memory. So one's life slips through the fingers of the mind like grain. So the sea eats away at the sand under one's naked feet. So one waits for the new day and the wide-eyed gaze of a child whose attention is momentarily held by the play of light in the eucalypts outside the window, or the susurrus of the incoming tide . . .

Cambridge, Mass., October 2005–April 2007

ACKNOWLEDGMENTS

Michael Puett was one of the first people to contact me when I came to Harvard in the fall of 2005, and in the course of many conversations over coffee or lunch since then Michael has responded generously and incisively to my evolving ideas. To other colleagues I am similarly indebted: David Carrasco, Sutopa Dasgupta, Mark Edwards, Ghassan Hage, Michael Herzfeld, Arthur Kleinman, Robert Orsi, Patrick Provost-Smith, Lucien G. Taylor, and Don Swearer. I owe special thanks to Francine Lorimer and Hans Lucht who made their fieldnotes available to me (respectively, on Peter Fisher and on Senya migration to Italy), and so allowing me to amplify my limited memory of certain events. Friends and family in London, Copenhagen, Wellington, Auckland, and Sydney also gave unstintingly of their time, supporting my research in ways that probably, in some cases, seemed totally unrelated to it: Jennifer Shennan, Allan Thomas, Heidi Jackson, Peter Oxley, Kathy Golski, Woycieck Dabrowski, Michael Whyte, Susan Reynolds Whyte, Brian Moeran, Bronwen Nicolson, Brian Boyd, Vincent O'Sullivan, Khalil and Isata Jah, Sewa Magba Koroma, Ade Koroma, Rebecca Williams, Abu Marah, Chelmansah Marah, Kaima Marah, and Baromie Marah.

Travel and fieldwork expenses were covered by small research grants from the Harvard Divinity School and the Center for the Study of World Religions. Without this financial assistance, my research would have been impossible.

MICHAEL JACKSON
is Distinguished Visiting Professor in World Religions
at Harvard Divinity School. Some of his recent books include
Excursions (2007); *Dead Reckoning* (Auckland, 2006); *In Sierra Leone*
(2004); and *Existential Anthropology: Events, Exigencies,*
and Effects (2004).

Library of Congress Cataloging-in-Publication Data
Jackson, Michael
The palm at the end of the mind : relatedness, religiosity, and the real /
Michael Jackson.
p. cm.
Includes bibliographical references and index.
ISBN 978-0-8223-4359-2 (cloth : alk. paper)
ISBN 978-0-8223-4381-3 (pbk. : alk. paper)
1. Jackson, Michael, 1940—Travel. 2. Existentialism. 3. Philosophical
anthropology. I. Title.
PR9639.3.J3Z46 2009
828'.91409—dc22
2008041779